LOKI
AGENT OF ASGARD

LOKI: AGENT OF ASGARD VOL. 1 — TRUST ME. Contains material originally published in magazine form as LOKI: AGENT OF ASGARD #1-5 and ALL-NEW MARVEL NOW! POINT ONE #1. First printing 2014. ISBN# 978-0-7851-8931-2. Published by MARVEL WORLDWIDE, INC., a subsidiary of MARVEL ENTERTAINMENT, LLC. OFFICE OF PUBLICATION: 135 West 50th Street, New York, NY 10020. Copyright © 2014 Marvel Characters, Inc. All rights reserved. All characters featured in this issue and the distinctive names and likenesses thereof, and all related indicia are trademarks of Marvel Characters, Inc. No similarity between any of the names, characters, persons, and/or institutions in this magazine with those of any living or dead person or institution is intended, and any such similarity which may exist is purely coincidental. **Printed in Canada.** ALAN FINE, EVP - Office of the President, Marvel Worldwide, Inc. and EVP & CMO Marvel Characters B.V.; DAN BUCKLEY, Publisher & President - Print, Animation & Digital Divisions; JOE QUESADA, Chief Creative Officer; TOM BREVOORT, SVP of Publishing; DAVID BOGART, SVP of Operations & Procurement, Publishing; C.B. CEBULSKI, SVP of Creator & Content Development; DAVID GABRIEL, SVP Print, Sales & Marketing; JIM O'KEEFE, VP of Operations & Logistics; DAN CARR, Executive Director of Publishing Technology; SUSAN CRESPI, Editorial Operations Manager; ALEX MORALES, Publishing Operations Manager; STAN LEE, Chairman Emeritus. For information regarding advertising in Marvel Comics or on Marvel.com, please contact Niza Disla, Director of Marvel Partnerships, at ndisla@marvel.com. For Marvel subscription inquiries, please call 800-217-9158. Manufactured between 6/27/2014 and 8/4/2014 by SOLISCO PRINTERS, SCOTT, QC, CANADA.

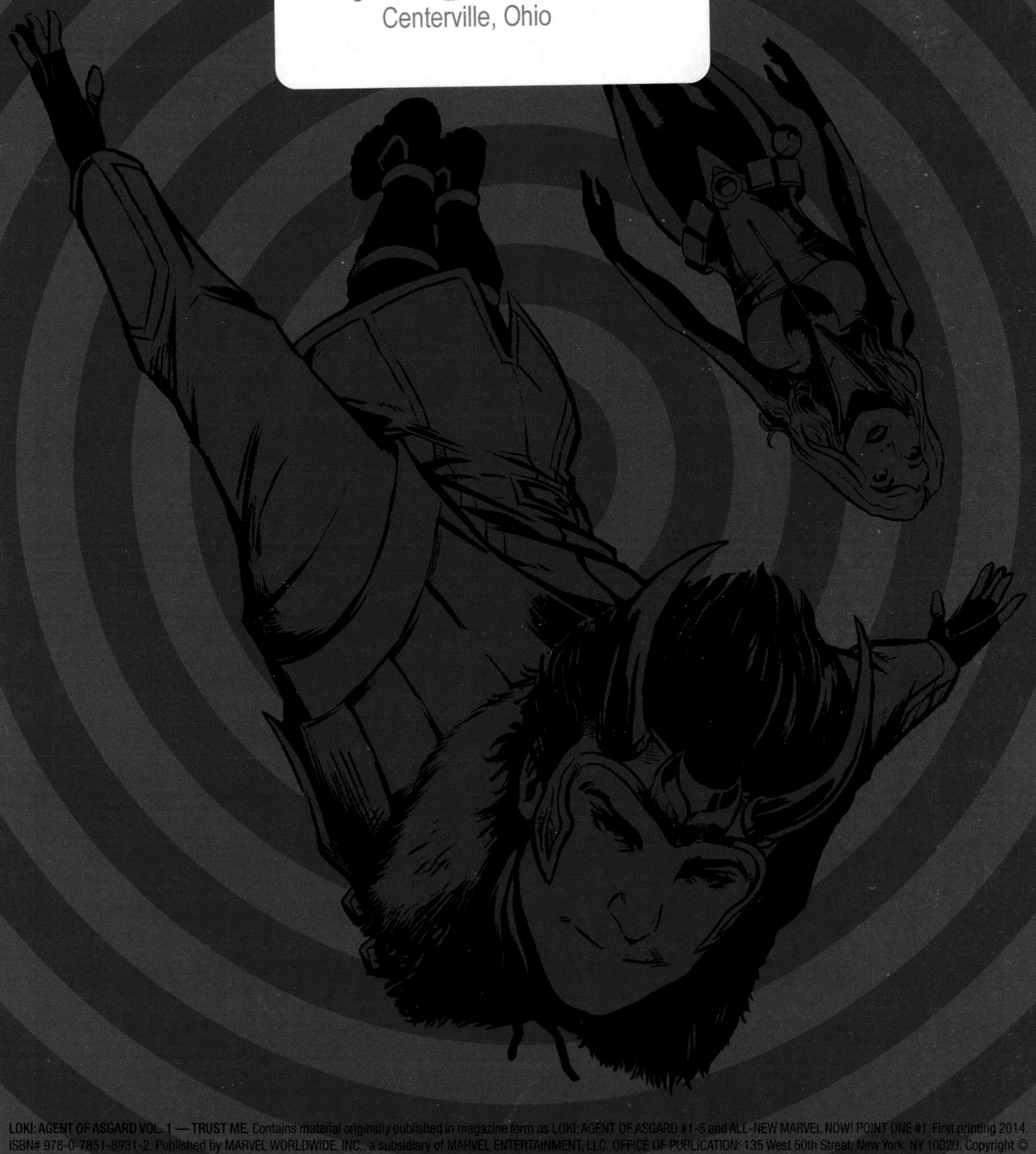

10 9 8 7 6 5 4 3 2 1

TRUST ME

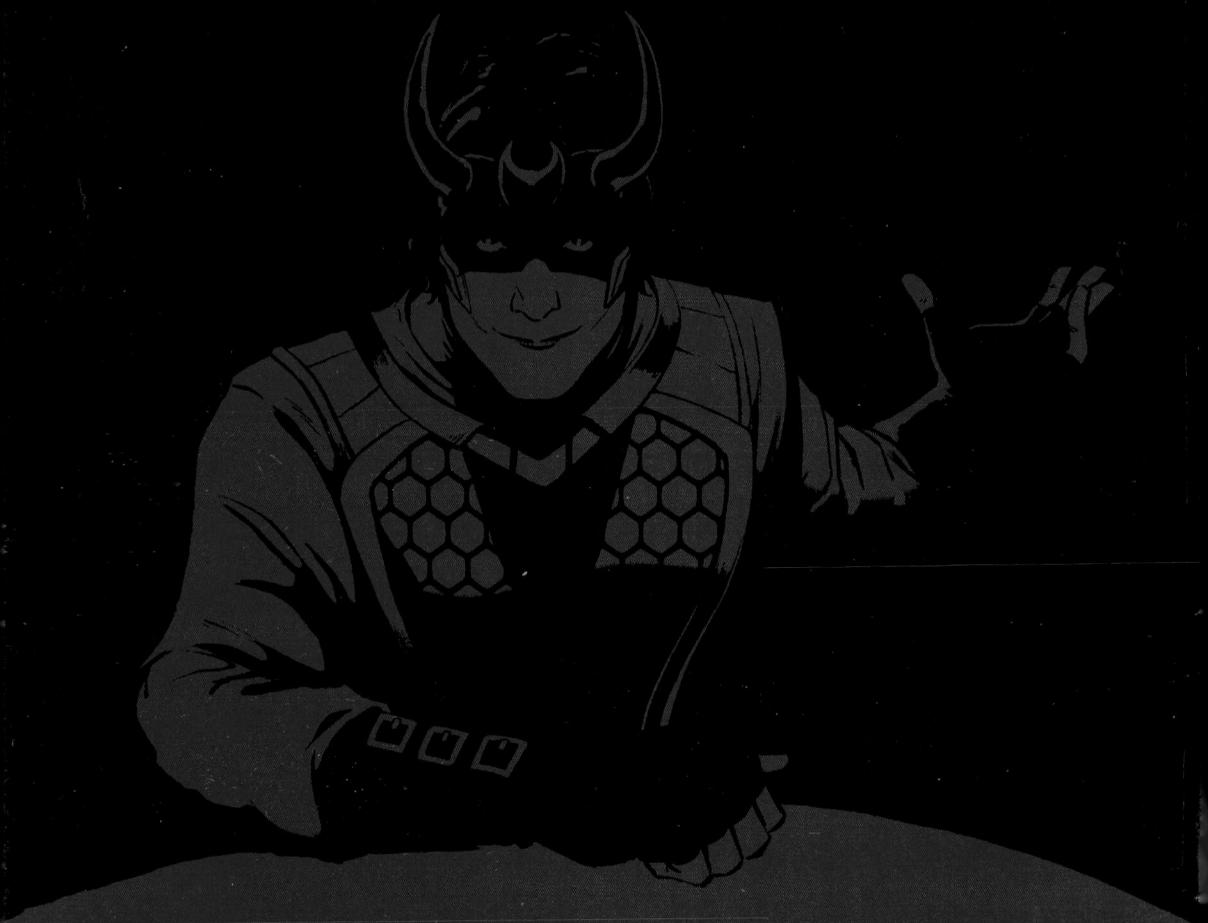

WRITER AL EWING
ARTIST LEE GARBETT
COLOR ARTIST NOLAN WOODARD
LETTERER VC'S CLAYTON COWLES
COVER ARTIST JENNY FRISON
ASSISTANT EDITOR JON MOISAN
EDITORS WIL MOSS & LAUREN SANKOVITCH

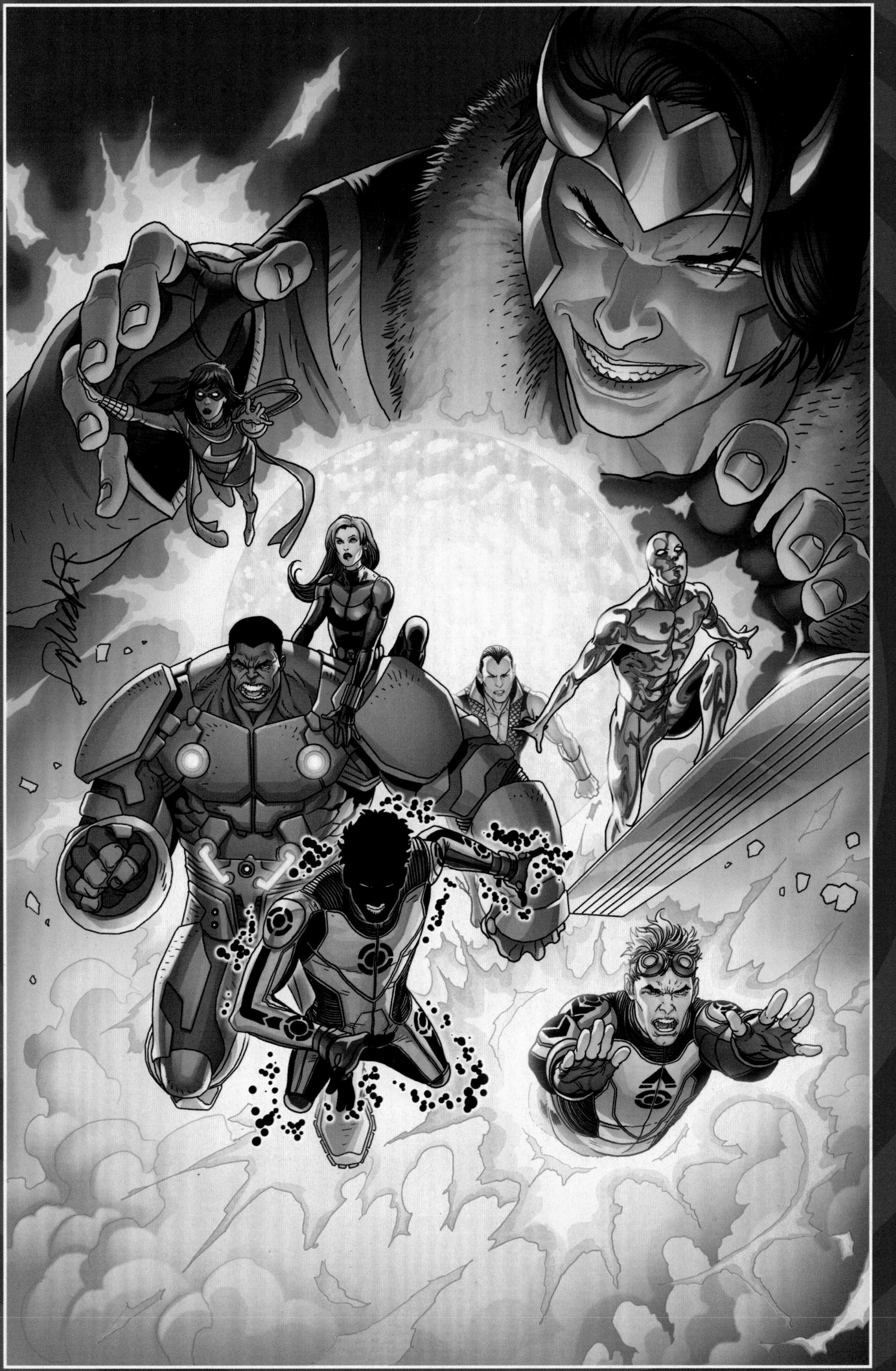

ALL-NEW MARVEL NOW! POINT ONE #1
BY SALVADOR LARROCA & LAURA MARTIN

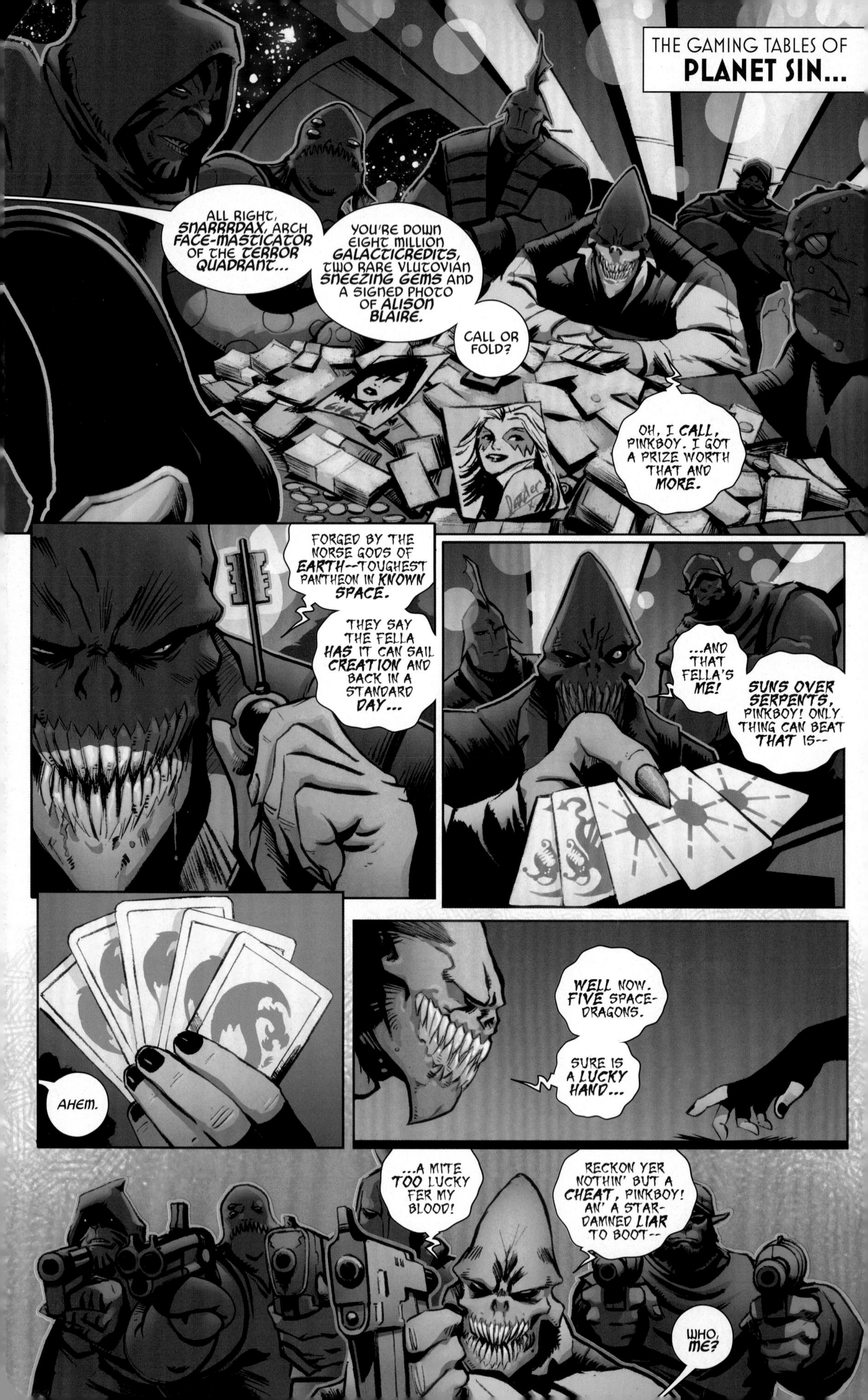
THE GAMING TABLES OF PLANET SIN...
ALL RIGHT, SNARRRDAX, ARCH FACE-MASTICATOR OF THE TERROR QUADRANT...
YOU'RE DOWN EIGHT MILLION GALACTICREDITS, TWO RARE VLUTOVIAN SNEEZING GEMS AND A SIGNED PHOTO OF ALISON BLAIRE.
CALL OR FOLD?
OH, I CALL, PINKBOY. I GOT A PRIZE WORTH THAT AND MORE.
FORGED BY THE NORSE GODS OF EARTH--TOUGHEST PANTHEON IN KNOWN SPACE.
THEY SAY THE FELLA HAS IT CAN SAIL CREATION AND BACK IN A STANDARD DAY...
...AND THAT FELLA'S ME!
SUNS OVER SERPENTS, PINKBOY! ONLY THING CAN BEAT THAT IS--
AHEM.
WELL NOW. FIVE SPACE-DRAGONS.
SURE IS A LUCKY HAND...
...A MITE TOO LUCKY FER MY BLOOD!
RECKON YER NOTHIN' BUT A CHEAT, PINKBOY! AN' A STAR-DAMNED LIAR TO BOOT--
WHO, ME?

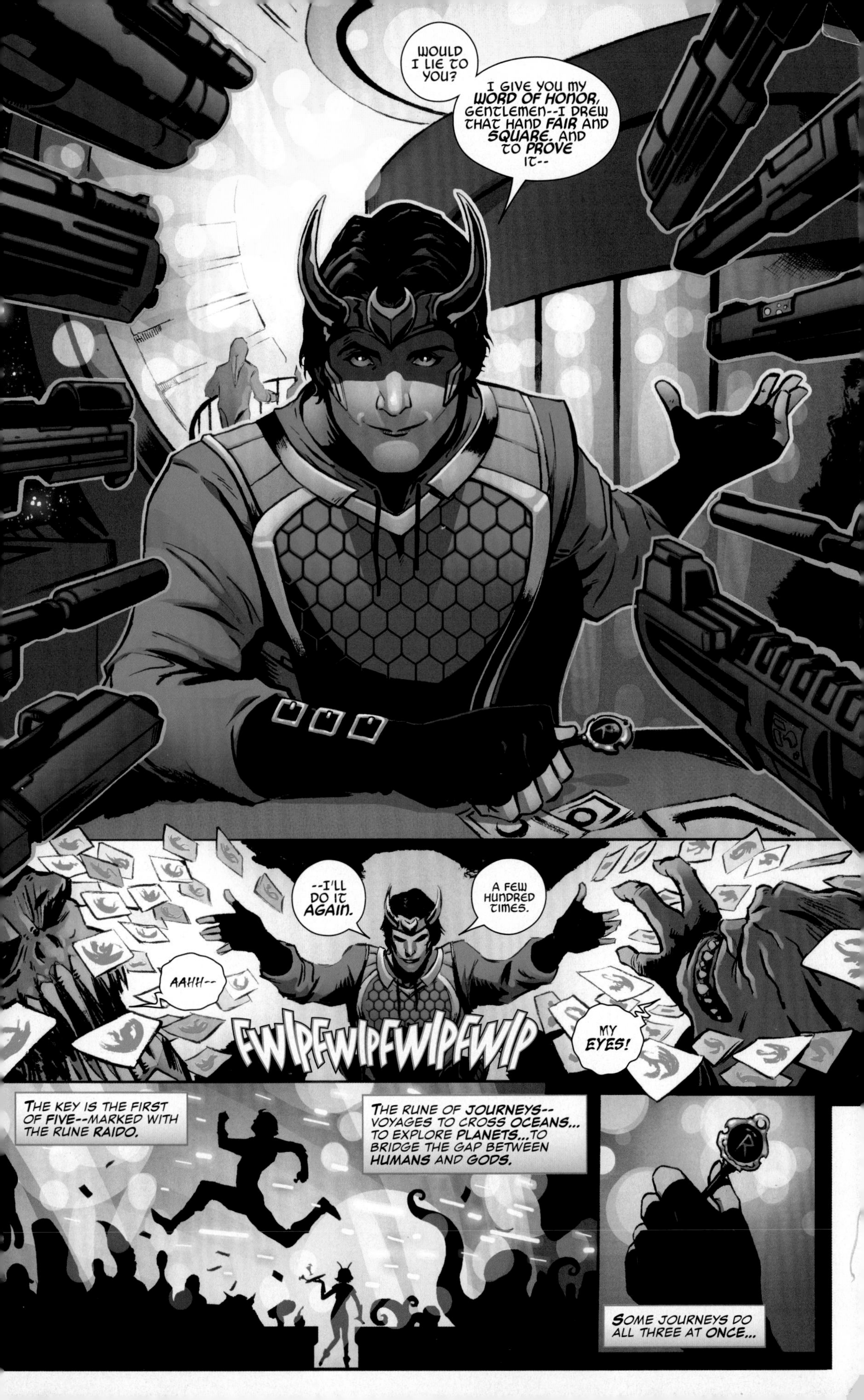
WOULD I LIE TO YOU?
I GIVE YOU MY WORD OF HONOR, GENTLEMEN--I DREW THAT HAND FAIR AND SQUARE. AND TO PROVE IT--
--I'LL DO IT AGAIN.
A FEW HUNDRED TIMES.
AAHH--
FWIPFWIPFWIPFWIP
MY EYES!
THE KEY IS THE FIRST OF FIVE--MARKED WITH THE RUNE RAIDO.
THE RUNE OF JOURNEYS--VOYAGES TO CROSS OCEANS...TO EXPLORE PLANETS...TO BRIDGE THE GAP BETWEEN HUMANS AND GODS.
SOME JOURNEYS DO ALL THREE AT ONCE...

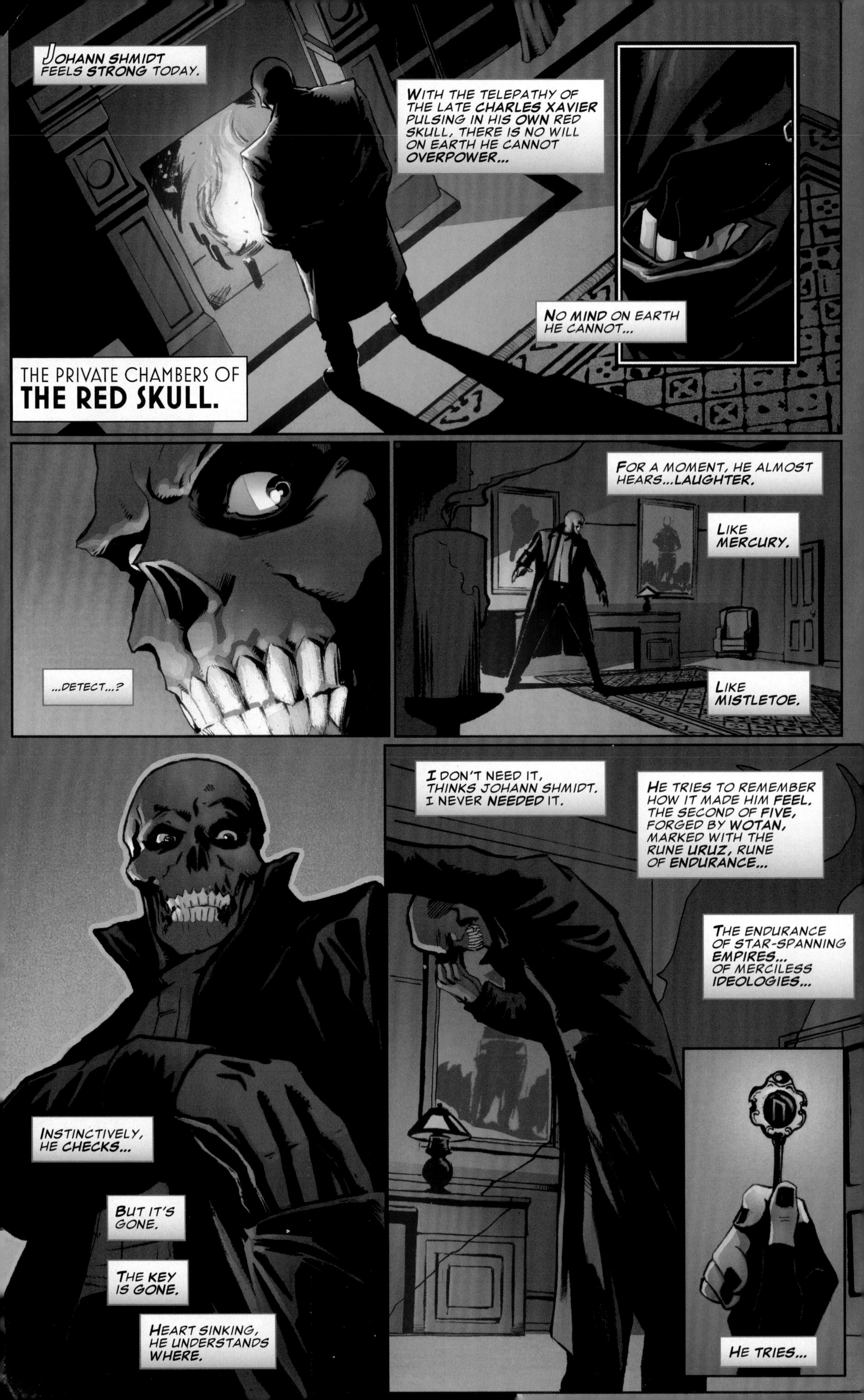
JOHANN SHMIDT FEELS STRONG TODAY.
WITH THE TELEPATHY OF THE LATE CHARLES XAVIER PULSING IN HIS OWN RED SKULL, THERE IS NO WILL ON EARTH HE CANNOT OVERPOWER...
NO MIND ON EARTH HE CANNOT...
THE PRIVATE CHAMBERS OF THE RED SKULL.
...DETECT...?
FOR A MOMENT, HE ALMOST HEARS...LAUGHTER.
LIKE MERCURY.
LIKE MISTLETOE.
INSTINCTIVELY, HE CHECKS...
BUT IT'S GONE.
THE KEY IS GONE.
HEART SINKING, HE UNDERSTANDS WHERE.
I DON'T NEED IT, THINKS JOHANN SHMIDT. I NEVER NEEDED IT.
HE TRIES TO REMEMBER HOW IT MADE HIM FEEL. THE SECOND OF FIVE, FORGED BY WOTAN, MARKED WITH THE RUNE URUZ, RUNE OF ENDURANCE...
THE ENDURANCE OF STAR-SPANNING EMPIRES... OF MERCILESS IDEOLOGIES...
HE TRIES...

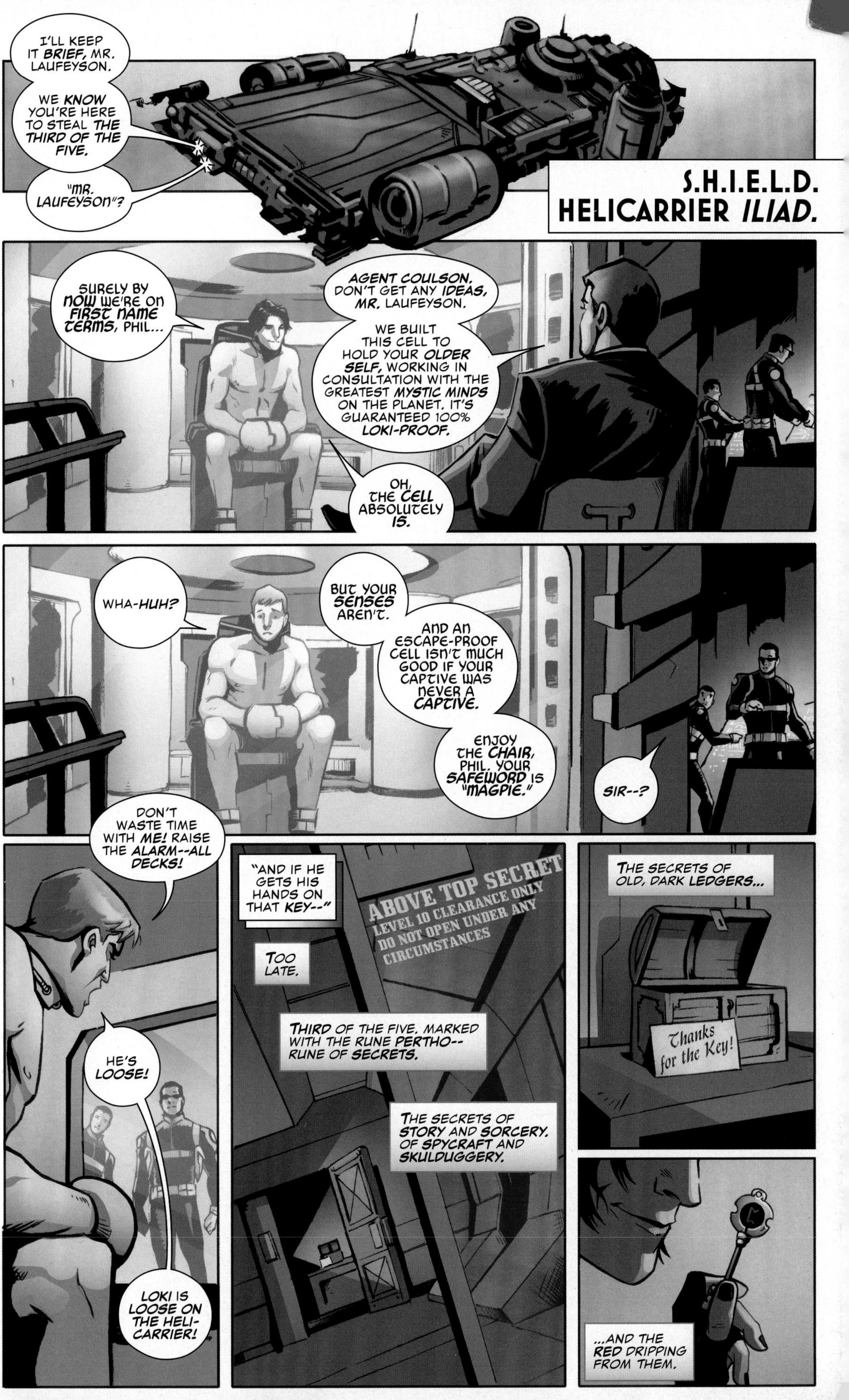

I'LL KEEP IT BRIEF, MR. LAUFEYSON.
WE KNOW YOU'RE HERE TO STEAL THE THIRD OF THE FIVE.
"MR. LAUFEYSON"?
S.H.I.E.L.D. HELICARRIER ILIAD.
SURELY BY NOW WE'RE ON FIRST NAME TERMS, PHIL...
AGENT COULSON. DON'T GET ANY IDEAS, MR. LAUFEYSON.
WE BUILT THIS CELL TO HOLD YOUR OLDER SELF, WORKING IN CONSULTATION WITH THE GREATEST MYSTIC MINDS ON THE PLANET. IT'S GUARANTEED 100% LOKI-PROOF.
OH, THE CELL ABSOLUTELY IS.
WHA-HUH?
BUT YOUR SENSES AREN'T.
AND AN ESCAPE-PROOF CELL ISN'T MUCH GOOD IF YOUR CAPTIVE WAS NEVER A CAPTIVE.
ENJOY THE CHAIR, PHIL. YOUR SAFEWORD IS "MAGPIE."
SIR--?
DON'T WASTE TIME WITH ME! RAISE THE ALARM--ALL DECKS!
HE'S LOOSE!
LOKI IS LOOSE ON THE HELI-CARRIER!
"AND IF HE GETS HIS HANDS ON THAT KEY--"
ABOVE TOP SECRET
LEVEL 10 CLEARANCE ONLY
DO NOT OPEN UNDER ANY CIRCUMSTANCES
TOO LATE.
THIRD OF THE FIVE. MARKED WITH THE RUNE PERTHO-- RUNE OF SECRETS.
THE SECRETS OF STORY AND SORCERY. OF SPYCRAFT AND SKULDUGGERY.
THE SECRETS OF OLD, DARK LEDGERS...
Thanks for the Key!
...AND THE RED DRIPPING FROM THEM.

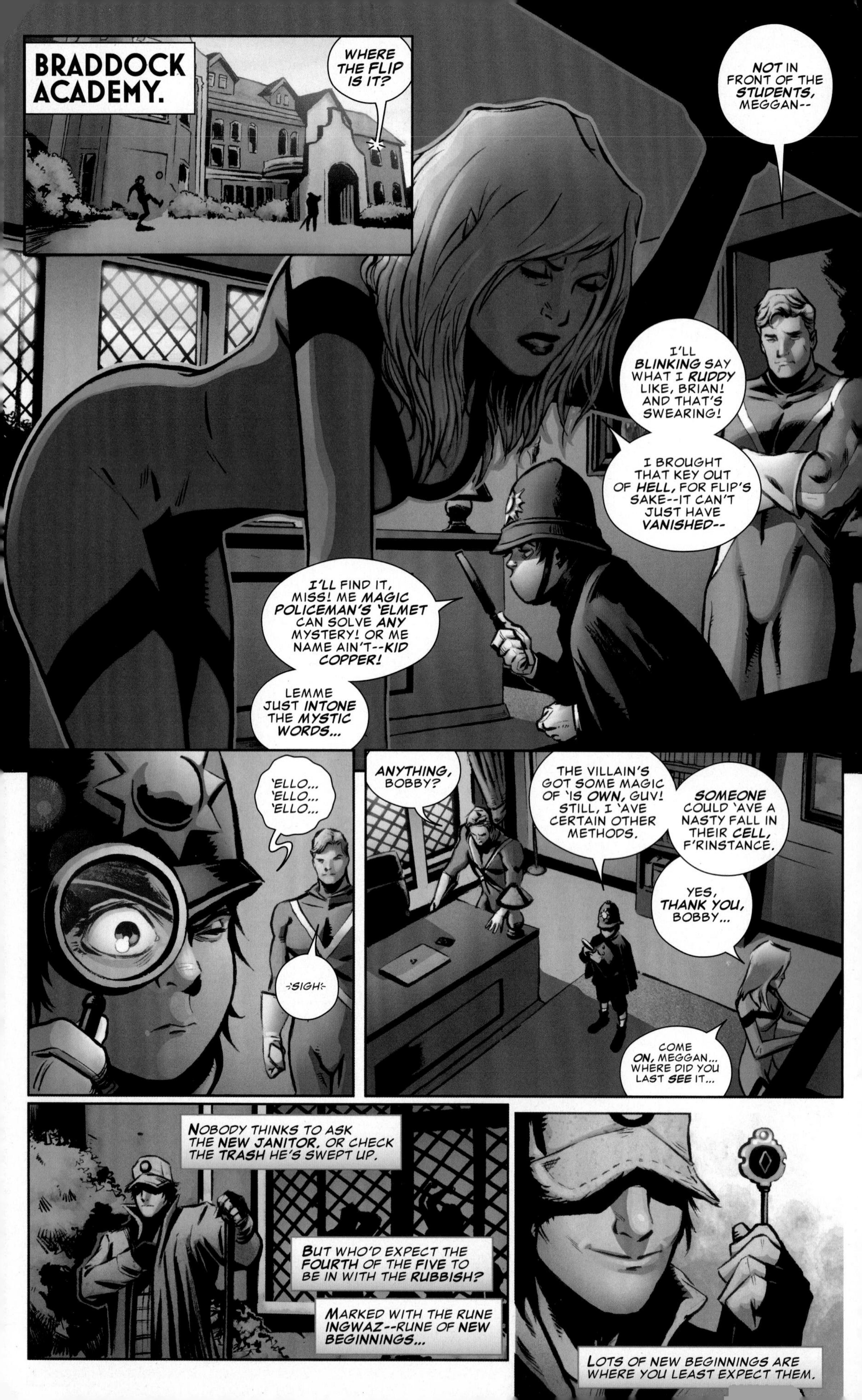
BRADDOCK ACADEMY.
WHERE THE FLIP IS IT?
NOT IN FRONT OF THE STUDENTS, MEGGAN--
I'LL BLINKING SAY WHAT I RUDDY LIKE, BRIAN! AND THAT'S SWEARING!
I BROUGHT THAT KEY OUT OF HELL, FOR FLIP'S SAKE--IT CAN'T JUST HAVE VANISHED--
I'LL FIND IT, MISS! ME MAGIC POLICEMAN'S 'ELMET CAN SOLVE ANY MYSTERY! OR ME NAME AIN'T--KID COPPER!
LEMME JUST INTONE THE MYSTIC WORDS...
'ELLO... 'ELLO... 'ELLO...
SIGH
ANYTHING, BOBBY?
THE VILLAIN'S GOT SOME MAGIC OF 'IS OWN, GUV! STILL, I 'AVE CERTAIN OTHER METHODS.
SOMEONE COULD 'AVE A NASTY FALL IN THEIR CELL, F'RINSTANCE.
YES, THANK YOU, BOBBY...
COME ON, MEGGAN... WHERE DID YOU LAST SEE IT...
NOBODY THINKS TO ASK THE NEW JANITOR, OR CHECK THE TRASH HE'S SWEPT UP.
BUT WHO'D EXPECT THE FOURTH OF THE FIVE TO BE IN WITH THE RUBBISH?
MARKED WITH THE RUNE INGWAZ--RUNE OF NEW BEGINNINGS...
LOTS OF NEW BEGINNINGS ARE WHERE YOU LEAST EXPECT THEM.

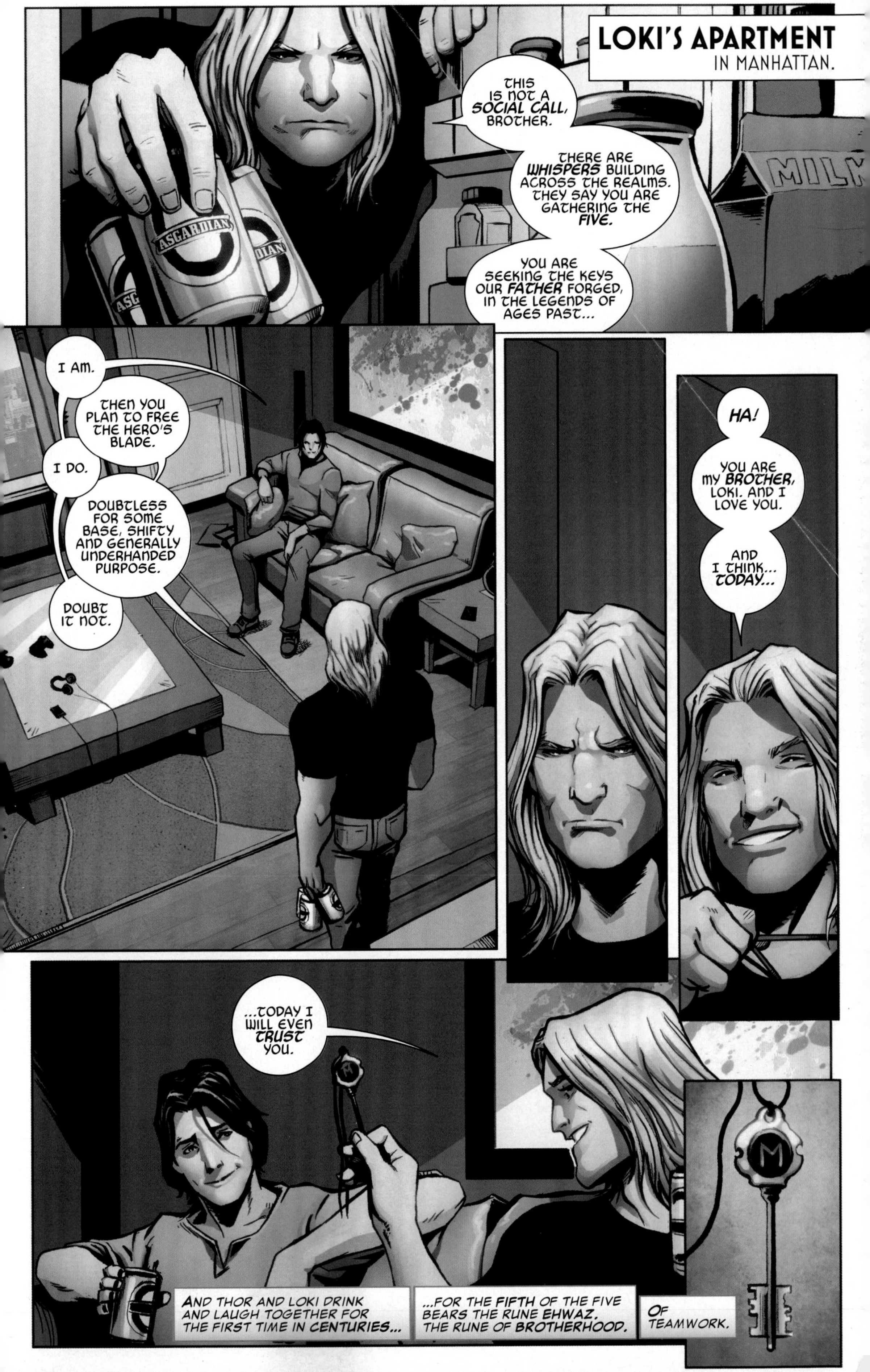
LOKI'S APARTMENT IN MANHATTAN.
THIS IS NOT A SOCIAL CALL, BROTHER.
THERE ARE WHISPERS BUILDING ACROSS THE REALMS. THEY SAY YOU ARE GATHERING THE FIVE.
YOU ARE SEEKING THE KEYS OUR FATHER FORGED, IN THE LEGENDS OF AGES PAST...
ASGARDIAN
I AM.
THEN YOU PLAN TO FREE THE HERO'S BLADE.
I DO.
DOUBTLESS FOR SOME BASE, SHIFTY AND GENERALLY UNDERHANDED PURPOSE.
DOUBT IT NOT.
HA!
YOU ARE MY BROTHER, LOKI. AND I LOVE YOU.
AND I THINK... TODAY...
...TODAY I WILL EVEN TRUST YOU.
AND THOR AND LOKI DRINK AND LAUGH TOGETHER FOR THE FIRST TIME IN CENTURIES...
...FOR THE FIFTH OF THE FIVE BEARS THE RUNE EHWAZ. THE RUNE OF BROTHERHOOD.
OF TEAMWORK.

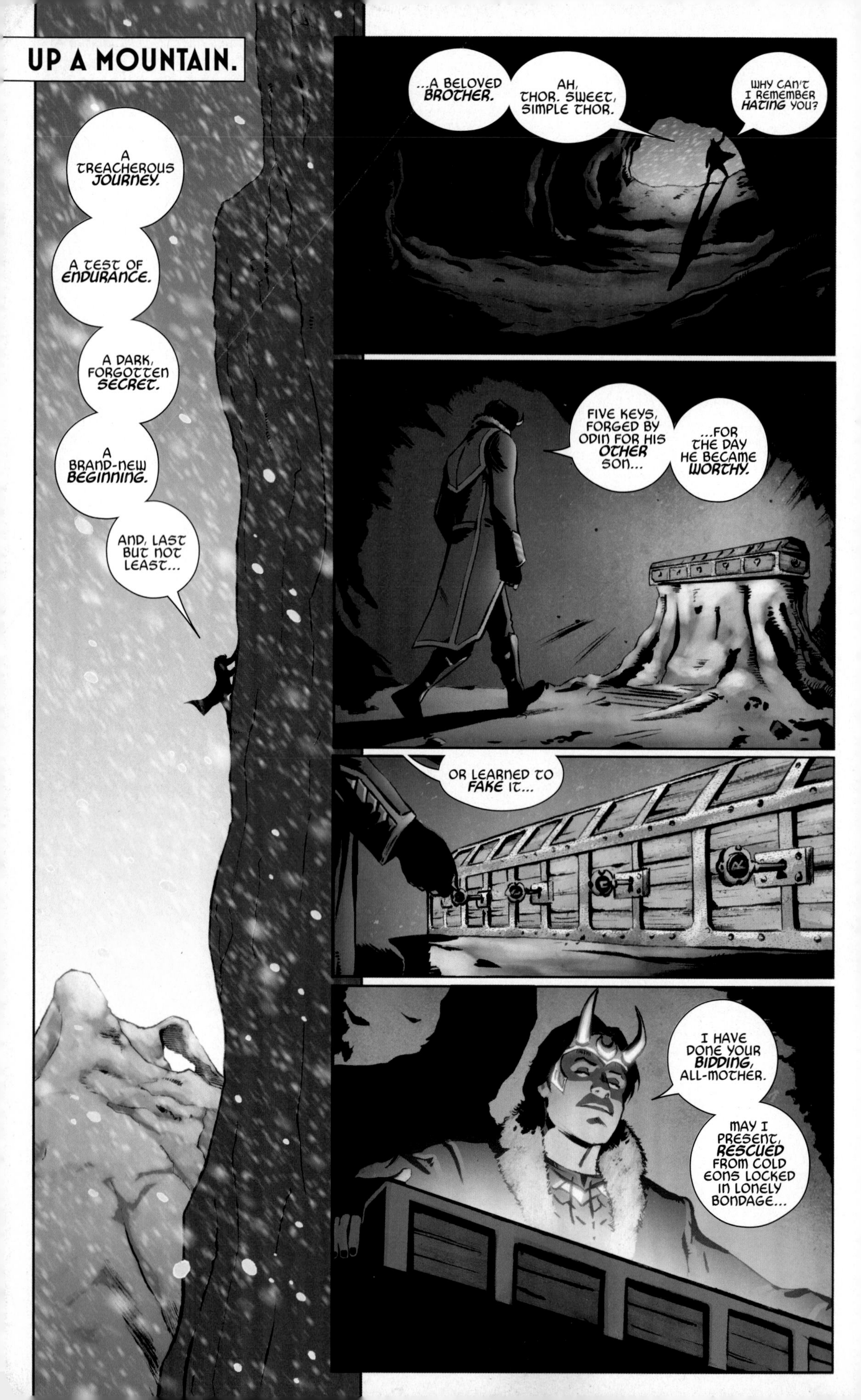
UP A MOUNTAIN.
A TREACHEROUS JOURNEY.
A TEST OF ENDURANCE.
A DARK, FORGOTTEN SECRET.
A BRAND-NEW BEGINNING.
AND, LAST BUT NOT LEAST...
...A BELOVED BROTHER.
AH, THOR. SWEET, SIMPLE THOR.
WHY CAN'T I REMEMBER HATING YOU?
FIVE KEYS, FORGED BY ODIN FOR HIS OTHER SON...
...FOR THE DAY HE BECAME WORTHY.
OR LEARNED TO FAKE IT...
I HAVE DONE YOUR BIDDING, ALL-MOTHER.
MAY I PRESENT, RESCUED FROM COLD EONS LOCKED IN LONELY BONDAGE...

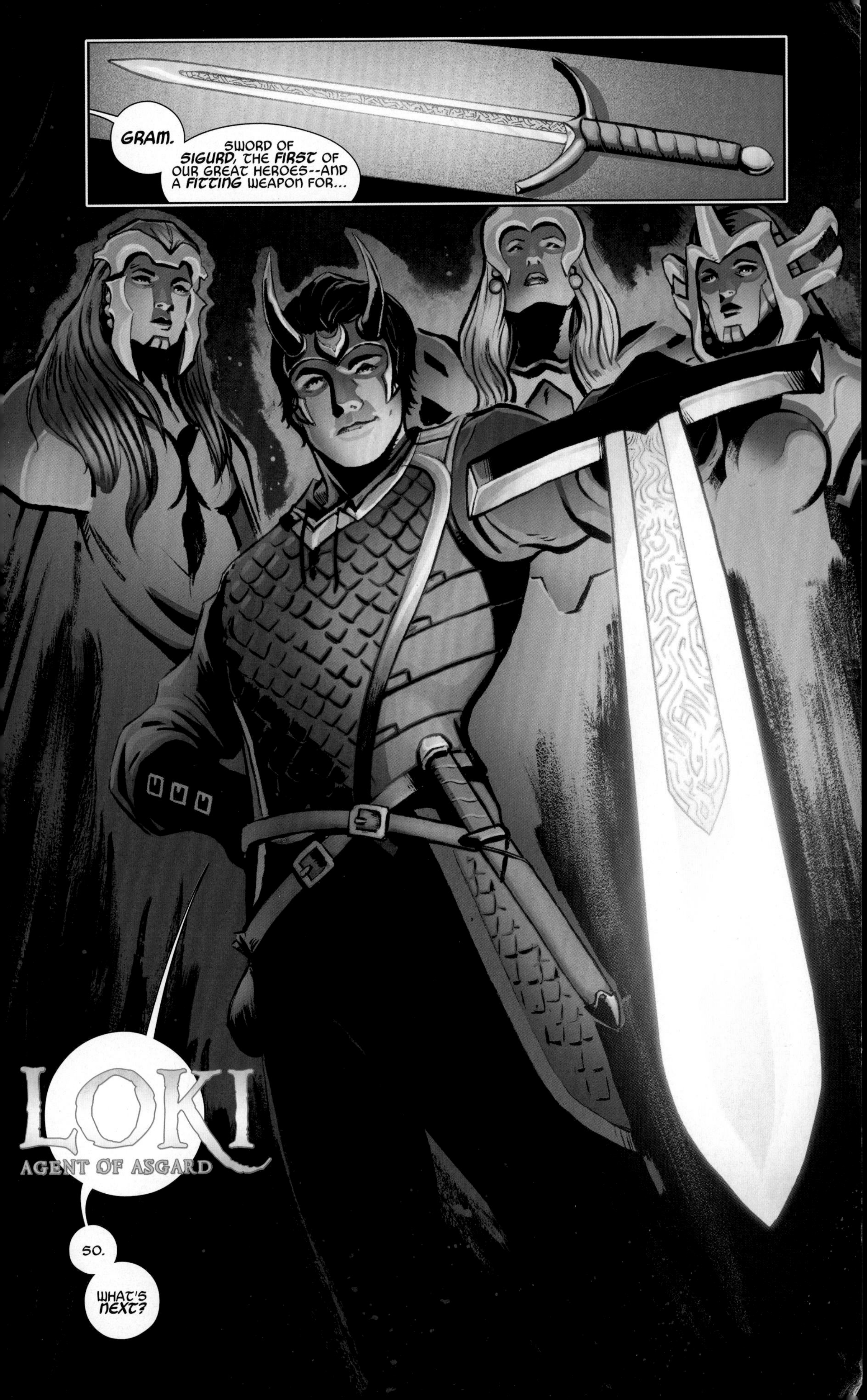
GRAM.
SWORD OF SIGURD, THE FIRST OF OUR GREAT HEROES--AND A FITTING WEAPON FOR...
LOKI
AGENT OF ASGARD
SO.
WHAT'S NEXT?

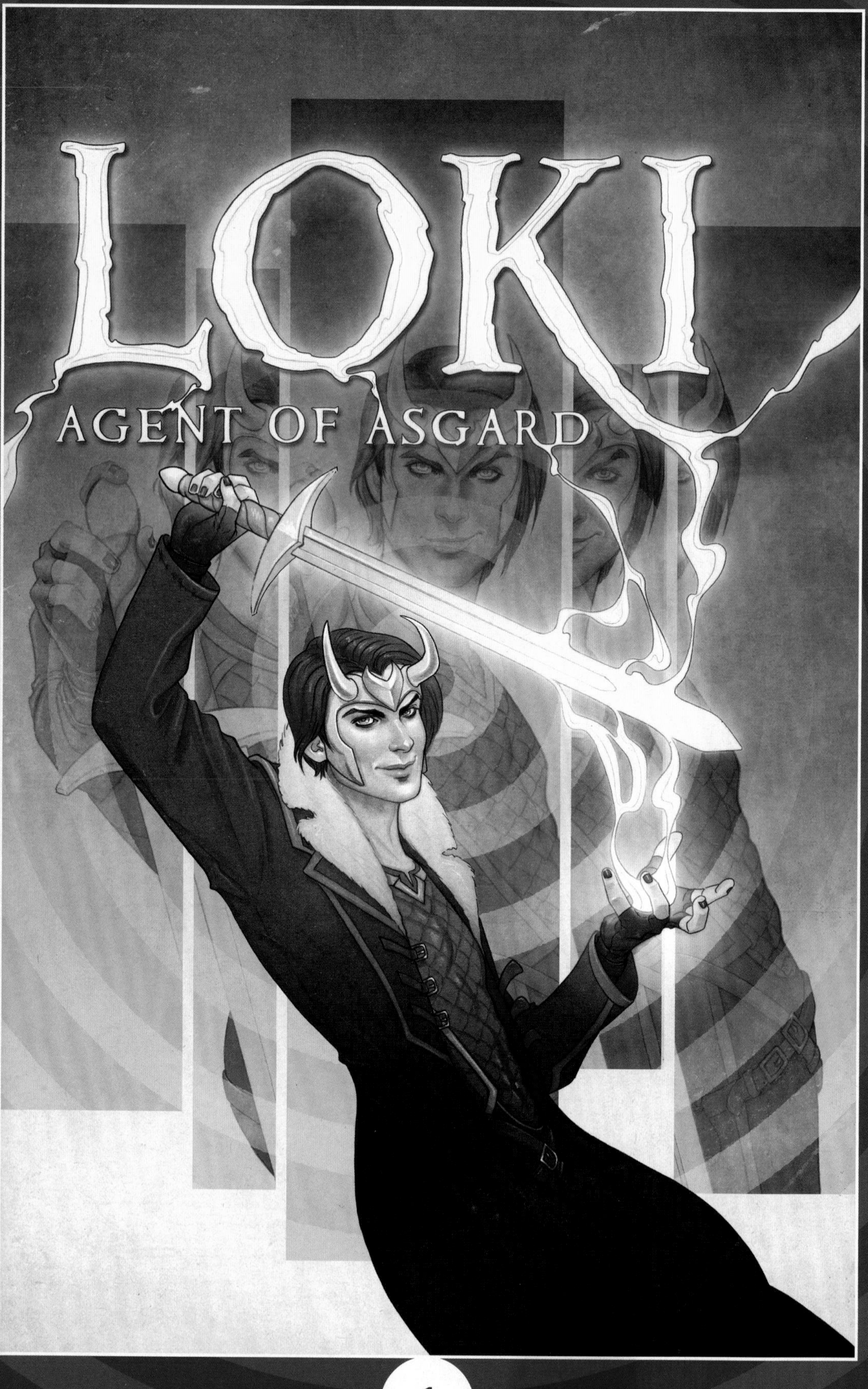
LOKI
AGENT OF ASGARD

1

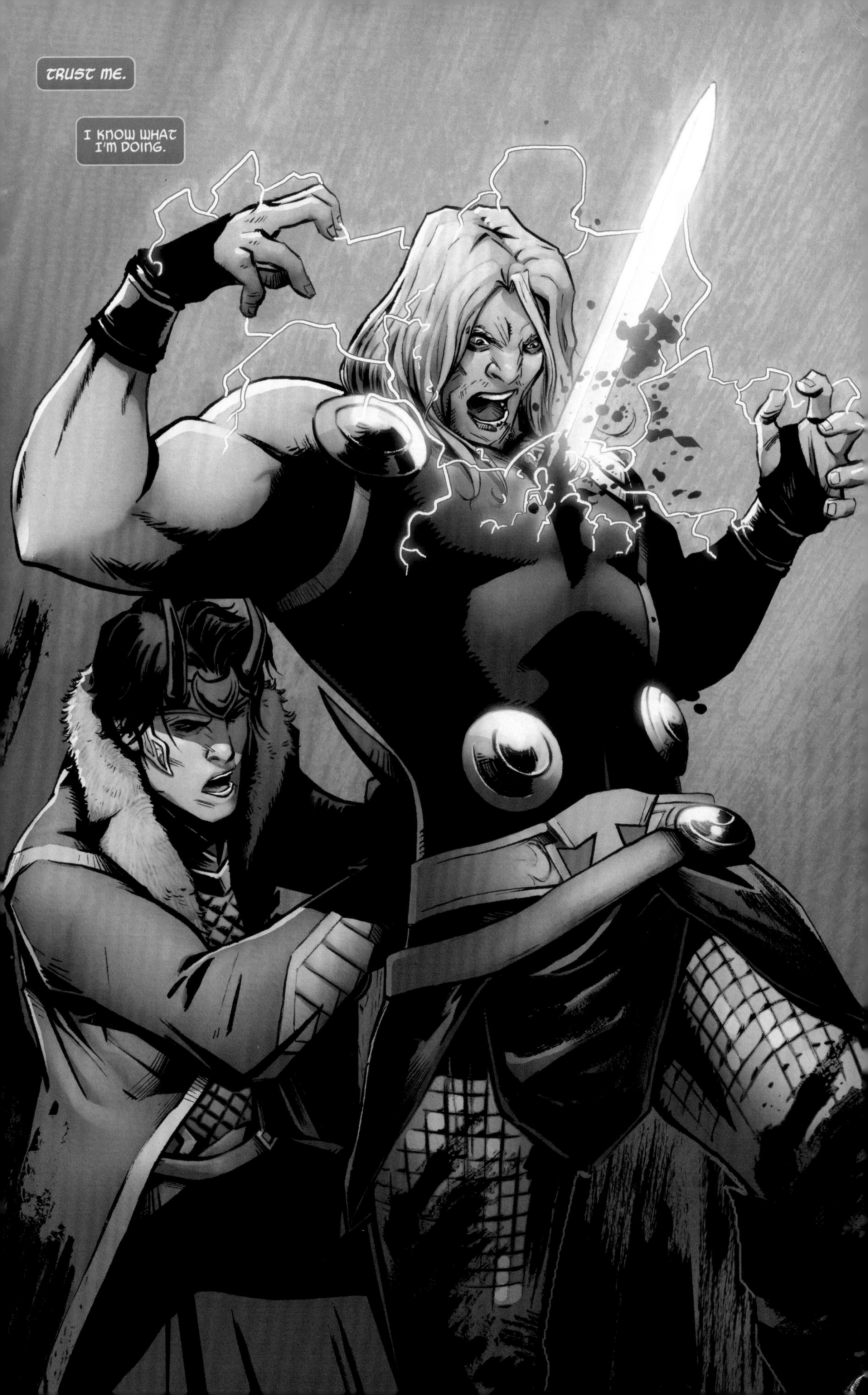
TRUST ME.
I KNOW WHAT I'M DOING.

THIS IS THE STORY OF LOKI.

ADOPTED ON THE BATTLEFIELD BY ODIN, KING OF ASGARD, LOKI WAS THE FOSTER BROTHER OF THOR. THEY DIDN'T ALWAYS GET ALONG.

ADMITTEDLY, THAT WAS BECAUSE LOKI BECAME INVOLVED IN INCREASINGLY WICKED SCHEMES OVER THE LONG CENTURIES, UNTIL EVENTUALLY, HE WAS KNOWN BY ALL AS THE GOD OF EVIL.

AND HE WAS TRAPPED BY THAT DEFINITION – SPIRALING DEEPER INTO INFAMY WITH EACH NEW MISDEED, UNABLE TO ESCAPE HIS ROLE, UNABLE TO ESCAPE HIMSELF. DOOMED TO NEVER BE ANYTHING BUT LOKI – LOKI THE BAD SON, LOKI THE VILLAIN – UNTIL THE DAY HE DIED.

SO...HE DIED.

WHICH WAS, OF COURSE, HIS GREATEST SCHEME OF ALL.

FOR SOON HE WAS REBORN INTO A NEW, YOUTHFUL BODY, FREE TO CHOOSE HIS OWN FATE. WITH THE SWORD OF ASGARD'S EARLIEST HERO IN HIS HAND AND MISSIONS FROM THE ALL-MOTHER, RULING TRIUMVIRATE OF ASGARDIA, TO HELP POLISH HIS SPARKLING NEW REPUTATION.

SO OBVIOUSLY, AFTER ALL THAT, HE WOULDN'T JUST STAB HIS BROTHER RIGHT IN THE BACK.

SURELY.

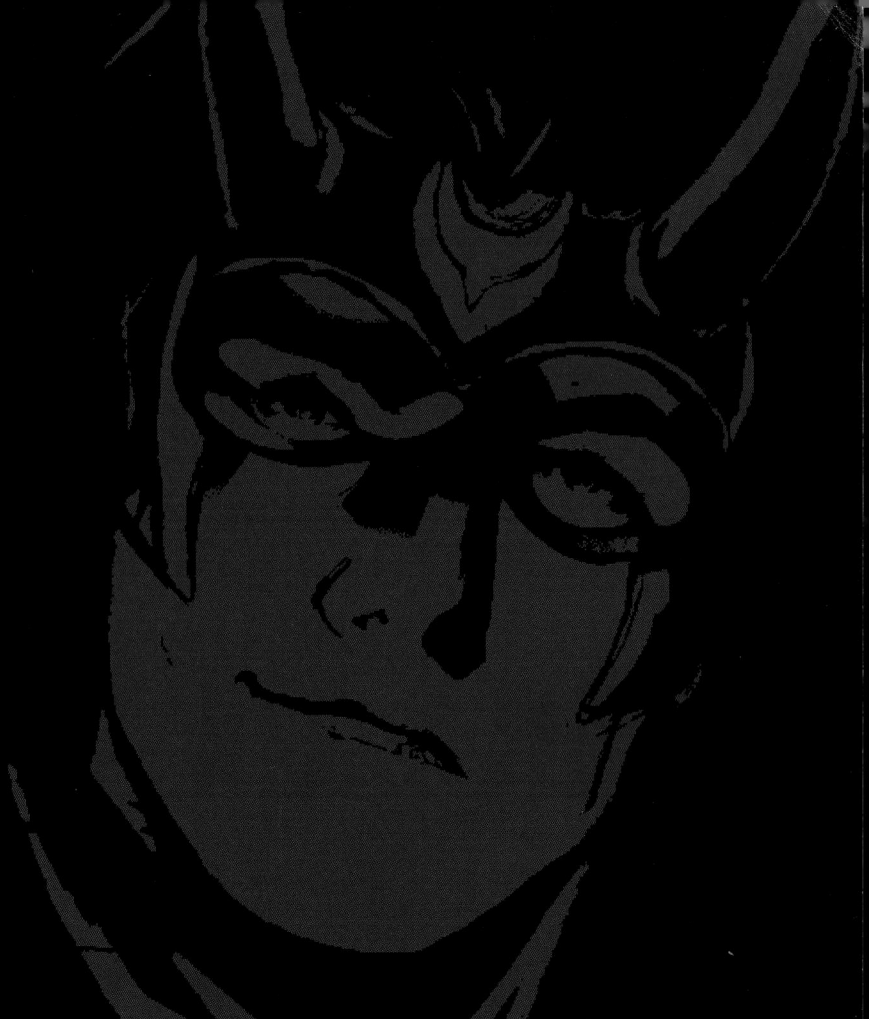

LOKI: AGENT OF ASGARD IN

TRUST ME

WRITER	**AL EWING**
ARTIST	**LEE GARBETT**
COLOR ARTIST	**NOLAN WOODARD**
LETTERER & PRODUCTION	**VC'S CLAYTON COWLES**
COVER ARTIST	**JENNY FRISON**

VARIANT COVER ARTISTS	**FRANK CHO & JASON KEITH; MIKE DEL MUNDO**
ASSISTANT EDITOR	**JON MOISAN**
EDITORS	**LAUREN SANKOVITCH & WIL MOSS**
EXECUTIVE EDITOR	**TOM BREVOORT**
EDITOR IN CHIEF	**AXEL ALONSO**
CHIEF CREATIVE OFFICER	**JOE QUESADA**
PUBLISHER	**DAN BUCKLEY**
EXECUTIVE PRODUCER	**ALAN FINE**

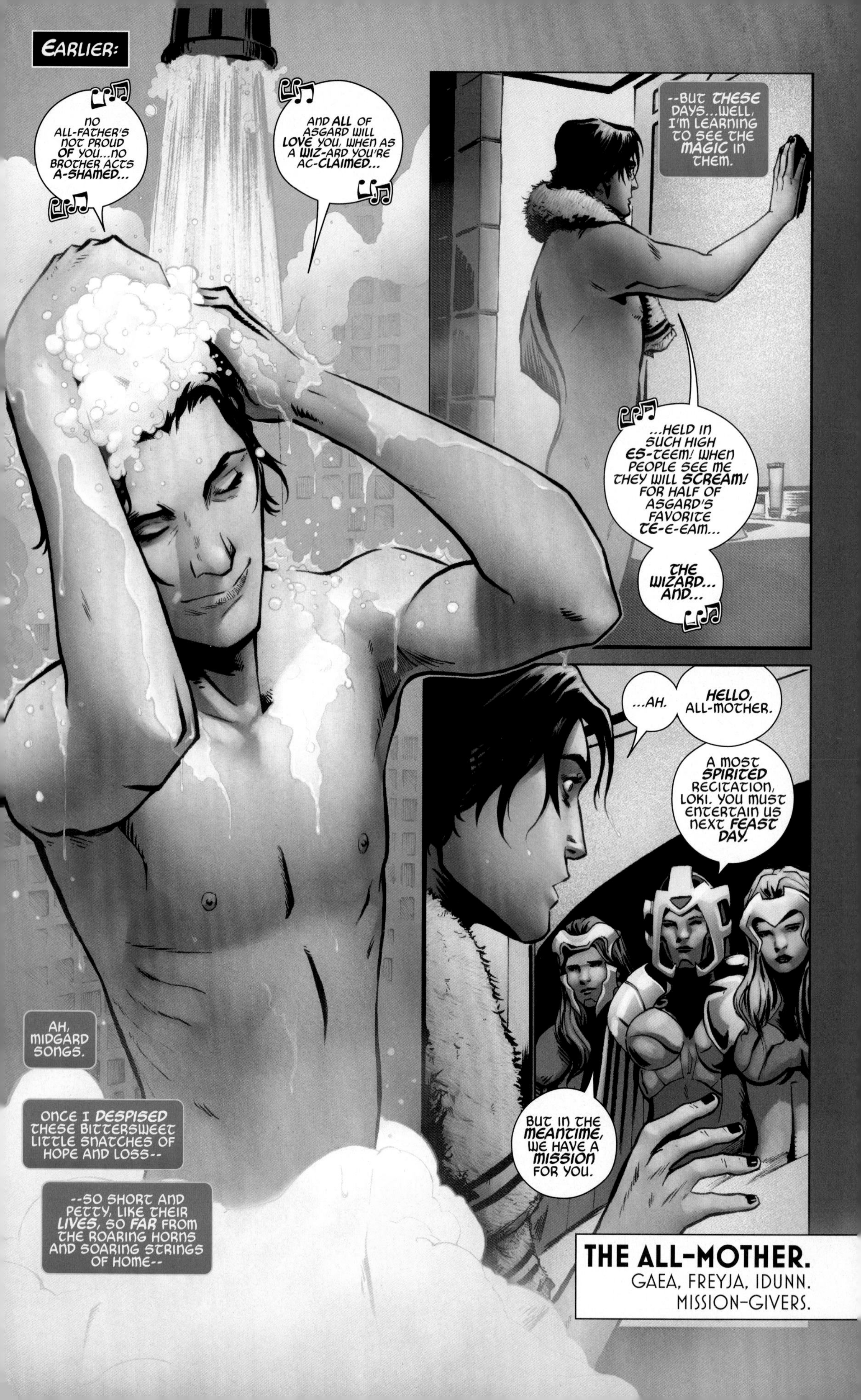
EARLIER:
NO ALL-FATHER'S NOT PROUD OF YOU...NO BROTHER ACTS A-SHAMED...
AND ALL OF ASGARD WILL LOVE YOU, WHEN AS A WIZ-ARD YOU'RE AC-CLAIMED...
AH, MIDGARD SONGS.
ONCE I DESPISED THESE BITTERSWEET LITTLE SNATCHES OF HOPE AND LOSS--
--SO SHORT AND PETTY, LIKE THEIR LIVES, SO FAR FROM THE ROARING HORNS AND SOARING STRINGS OF HOME--
--BUT THESE DAYS...WELL, I'M LEARNING TO SEE THE MAGIC IN THEM.
...HELD IN SUCH HIGH ES-TEEM! WHEN PEOPLE SEE ME THEY WILL SCREAM! FOR HALF OF ASGARD'S FAVORITE TE-E-EAM...
THE WIZARD... AND...
...AH.
HELLO, ALL-MOTHER.
A MOST SPIRITED RECITATION, LOKI. YOU MUST ENTERTAIN US NEXT FEAST DAY.
BUT IN THE MEANTIME, WE HAVE A MISSION FOR YOU.
THE ALL-MOTHER.
GAEA, FREYJA, IDUNN.
MISSION-GIVERS.

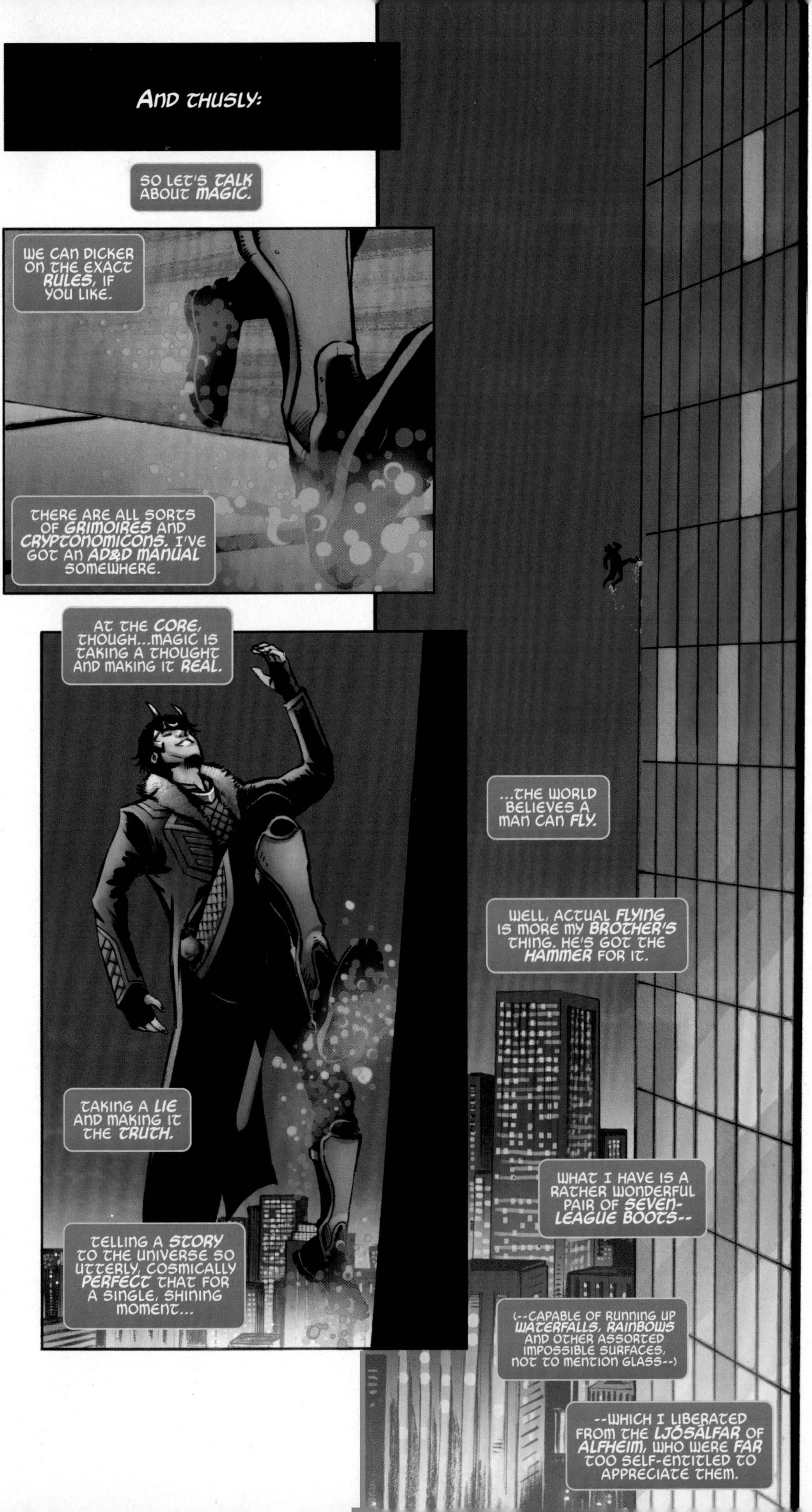
AND THUSLY:
SO LET'S TALK ABOUT MAGIC.
WE CAN DICKER ON THE EXACT RULES, IF YOU LIKE.
THERE ARE ALL SORTS OF GRIMOIRES AND CRYPTONOMICONS. I'VE GOT AN AD&D MANUAL SOMEWHERE.
AT THE CORE, THOUGH...MAGIC IS TAKING A THOUGHT AND MAKING IT REAL.
TAKING A LIE AND MAKING IT THE TRUTH.
TELLING A STORY TO THE UNIVERSE SO UTTERLY, COSMICALLY PERFECT THAT FOR A SINGLE, SHINING MOMENT...
...THE WORLD BELIEVES A MAN CAN FLY.
WELL, ACTUAL FLYING IS MORE MY BROTHER'S THING. HE'S GOT THE HAMMER FOR IT.
WHAT I HAVE IS A RATHER WONDERFUL PAIR OF SEVEN-LEAGUE BOOTS--
(--CAPABLE OF RUNNING UP WATERFALLS, RAINBOWS AND OTHER ASSORTED IMPOSSIBLE SURFACES, NOT TO MENTION GLASS--)
--WHICH I LIBERATED FROM THE LJÓSALFAR OF ALFHEIM, WHO WERE FAR TOO SELF-ENTITLED TO APPRECIATE THEM.

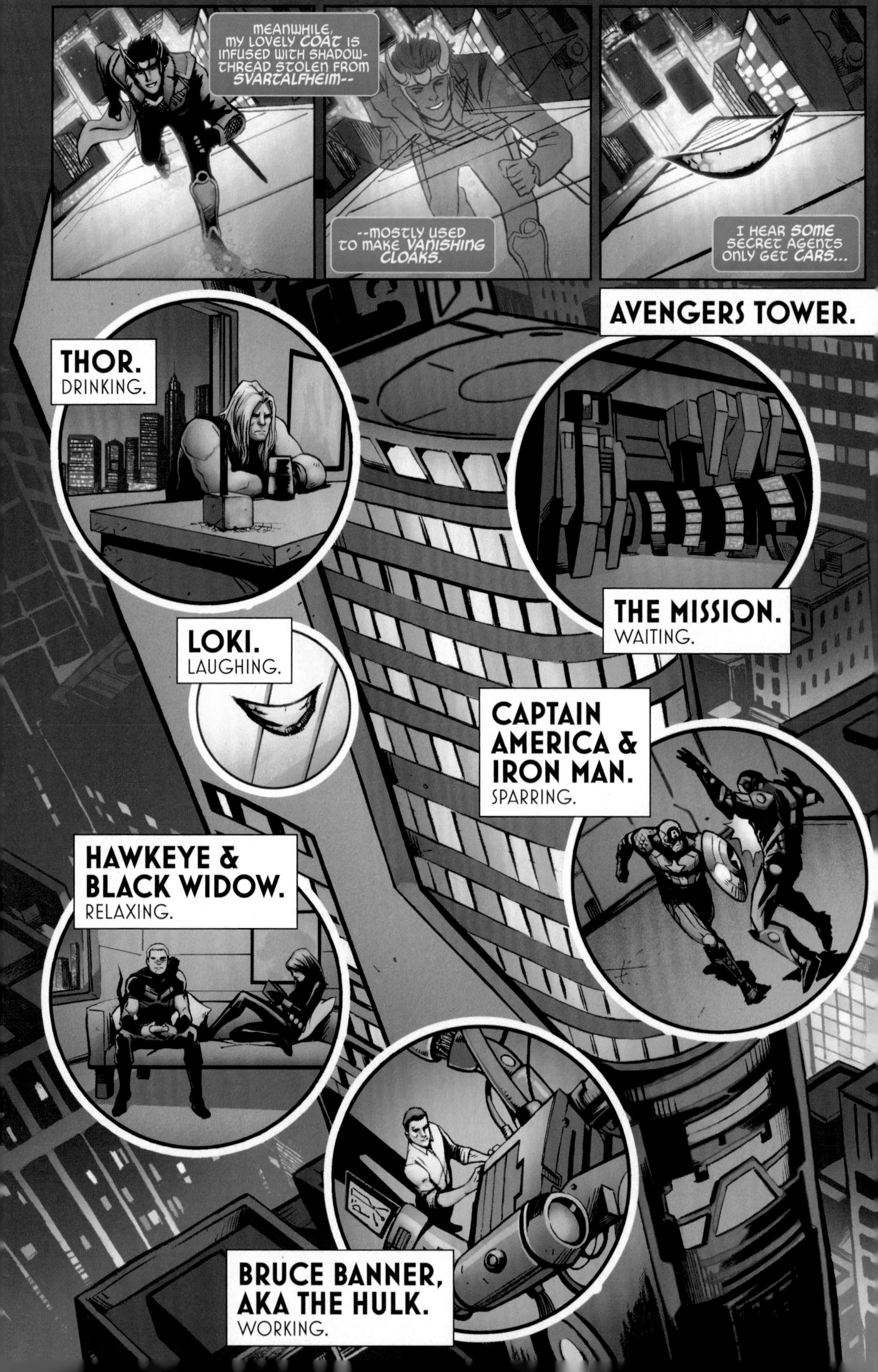
MEANWHILE, MY LOVELY COAT IS INFUSED WITH SHADOW-THREAD STOLEN FROM SVARTALFHEIM--
--MOSTLY USED TO MAKE VANISHING CLOAKS.
I HEAR SOME SECRET AGENTS ONLY GET CARS...
AVENGERS TOWER.
THOR. DRINKING.
THE MISSION. WAITING.
LOKI. LAUGHING.
CAPTAIN AMERICA & IRON MAN. SPARRING.
HAWKEYE & BLACK WIDOW. RELAXING.
BRUCE BANNER, AKA THE HULK. WORKING.

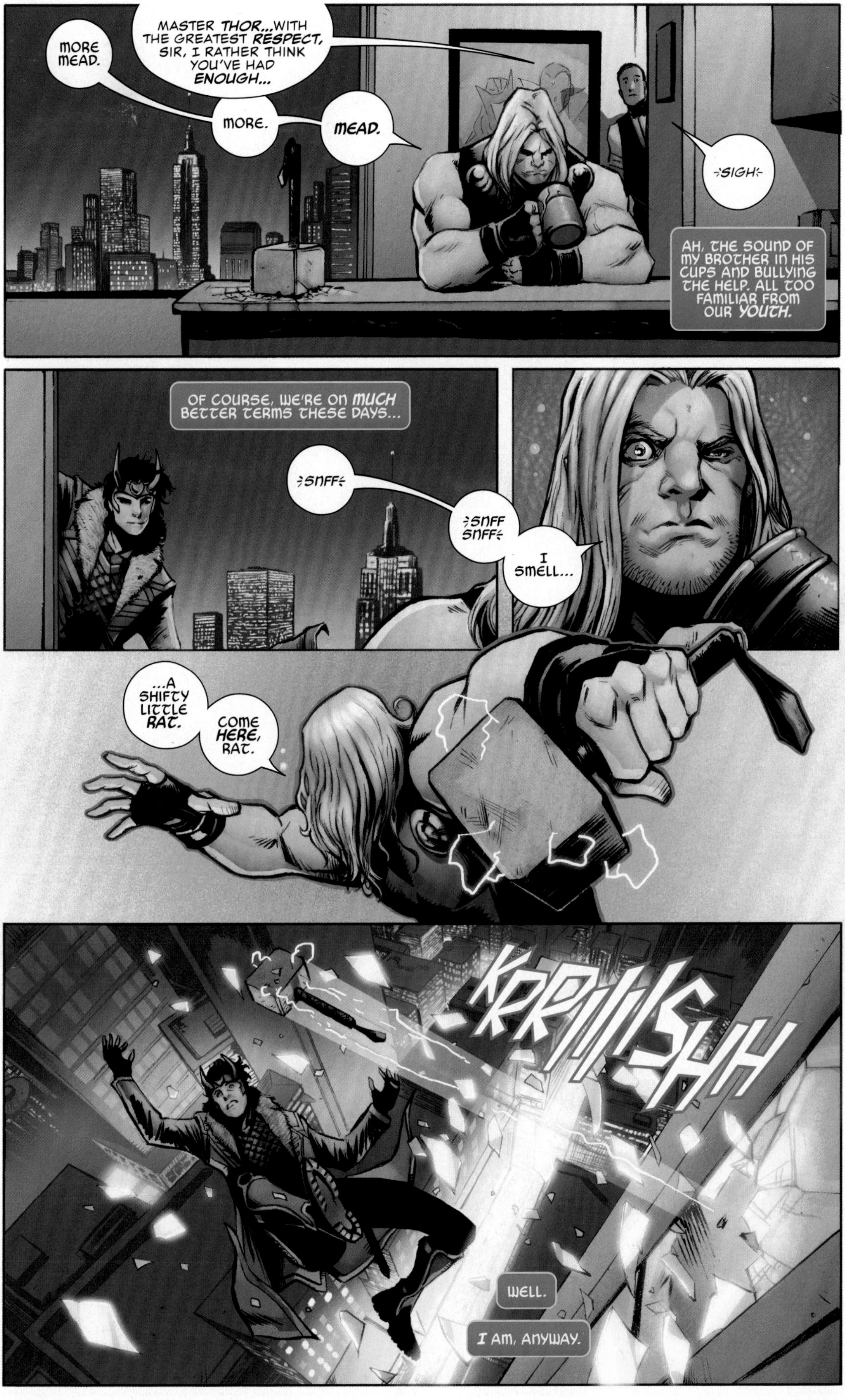
MORE MEAD.
MASTER THOR...WITH THE GREATEST RESPECT, SIR, I RATHER THINK YOU'VE HAD ENOUGH...
MORE.
MEAD.
SIGH
AH, THE SOUND OF MY BROTHER IN HIS CUPS AND BULLYING THE HELP. ALL TOO FAMILIAR FROM OUR YOUTH.
OF COURSE, WE'RE ON MUCH BETTER TERMS THESE DAYS...
SNFF
SNFF SNFF
I SMELL...
...A SHIFTY LITTLE RAT.
COME HERE, RAT.
KRRIIIISHH
WELL.
I AM, ANYWAY.

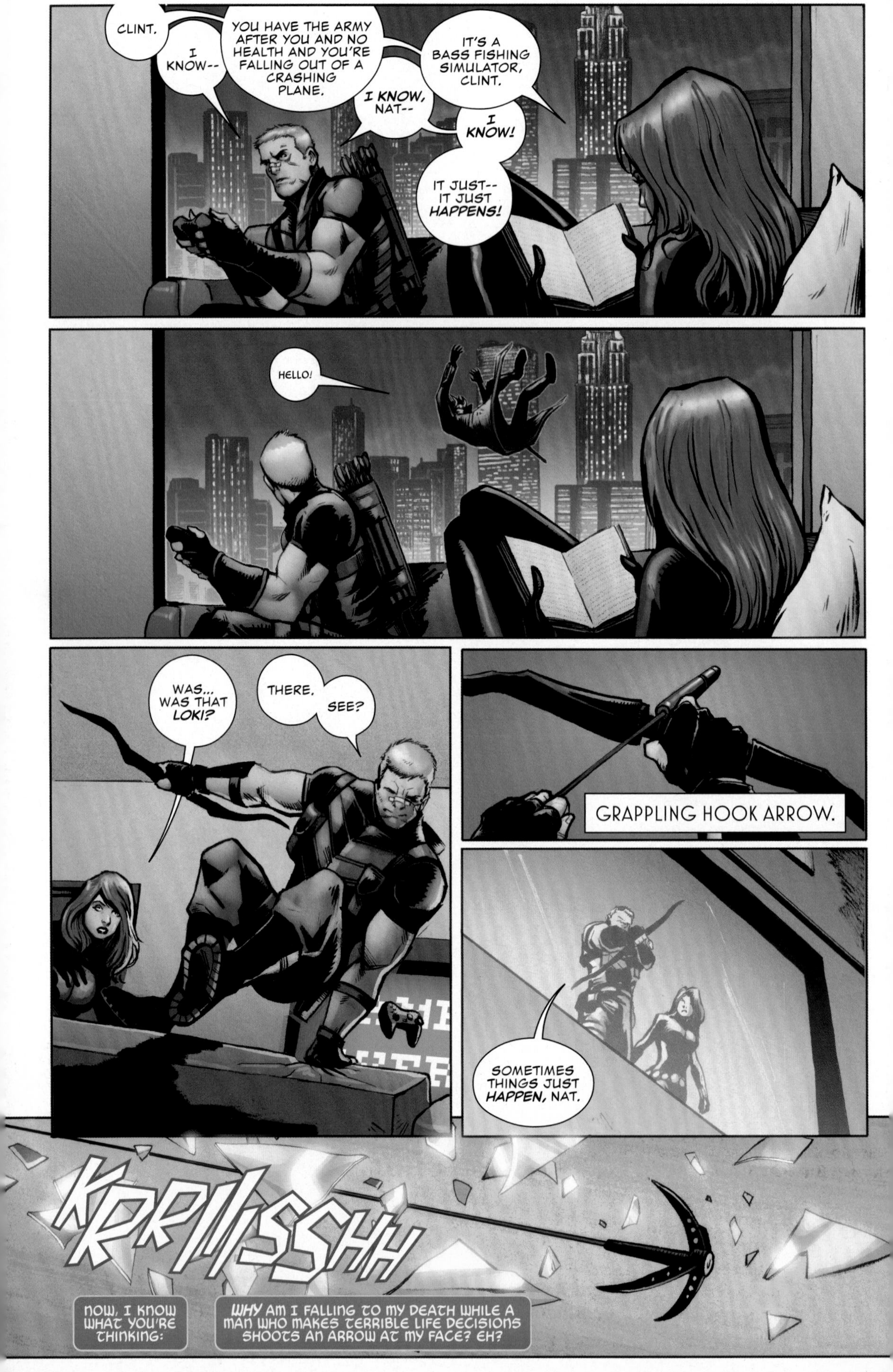
CLINT.
I KNOW--
YOU HAVE THE ARMY AFTER YOU AND NO HEALTH AND YOU'RE FALLING OUT OF A CRASHING PLANE.
I KNOW, NAT--
IT'S A BASS FISHING SIMULATOR, CLINT.
I KNOW!
IT JUST-- IT JUST HAPPENS!
HELLO!
WAS... WAS THAT LOKI?
THERE.
SEE?
GRAPPLING HOOK ARROW.
SOMETIMES THINGS JUST HAPPEN, NAT.
KRRSSHH
NOW, I KNOW WHAT YOU'RE THINKING:
WHY AM I FALLING TO MY DEATH WHILE A MAN WHO MAKES TERRIBLE LIFE DECISIONS SHOOTS AN ARROW AT MY FACE? EH?

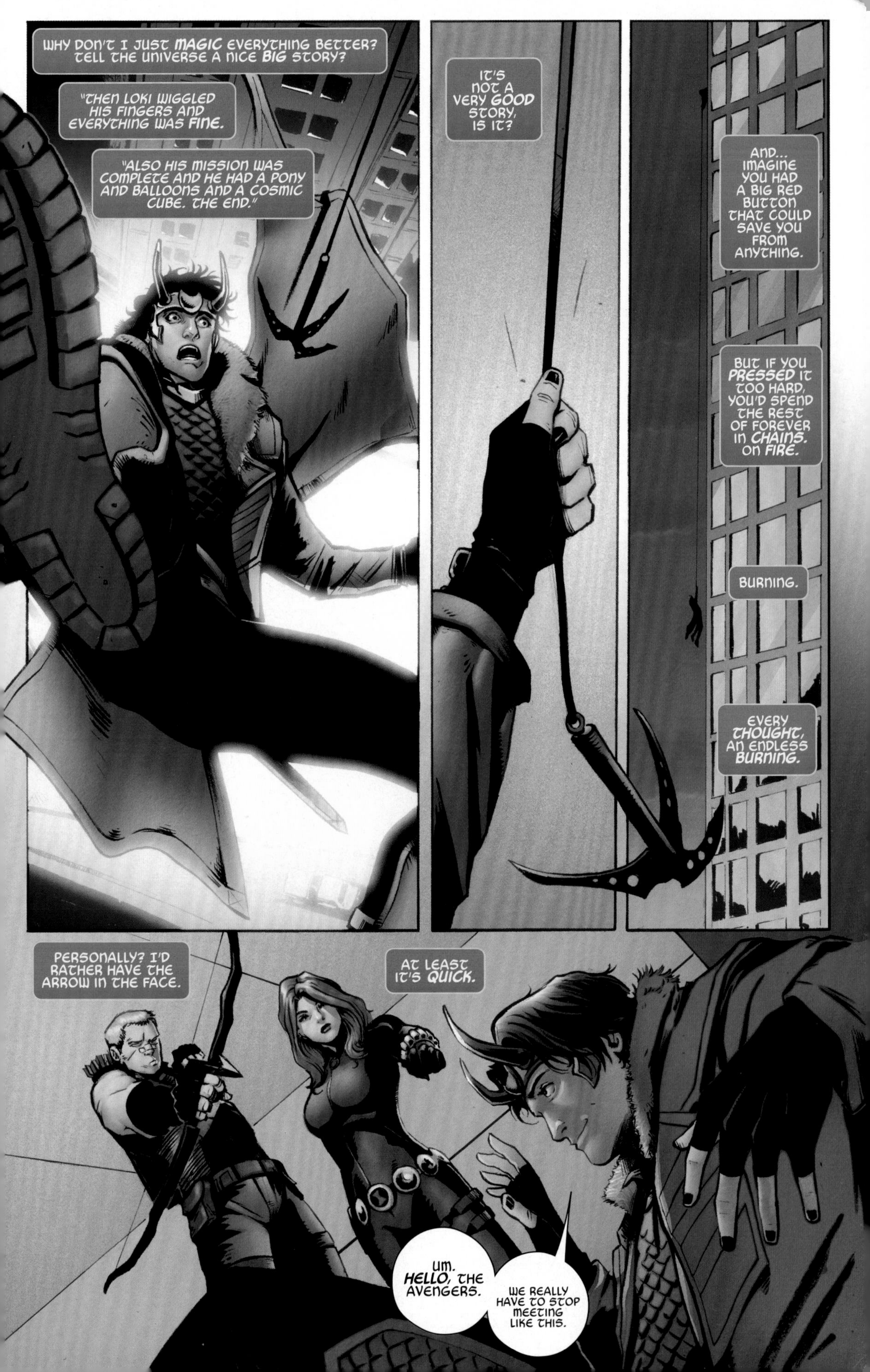
WHY DON'T I JUST MAGIC EVERYTHING BETTER? TELL THE UNIVERSE A NICE BIG STORY?
"THEN LOKI WIGGLED HIS FINGERS AND EVERYTHING WAS FINE.
"ALSO HIS MISSION WAS COMPLETE AND HE HAD A PONY AND BALLOONS AND A COSMIC CUBE. THE END."
IT'S NOT A VERY GOOD STORY, IS IT?
AND... IMAGINE YOU HAD A BIG RED BUTTON THAT COULD SAVE YOU FROM ANYTHING.
BUT IF YOU PRESSED IT TOO HARD, YOU'D SPEND THE REST OF FOREVER IN CHAINS. ON FIRE.
BURNING.
EVERY THOUGHT, AN ENDLESS BURNING.
PERSONALLY? I'D RATHER HAVE THE ARROW IN THE FACE.
AT LEAST IT'S QUICK.
UM. HELLO, THE AVENGERS.
WE REALLY HAVE TO STOP MEETING LIKE THIS.

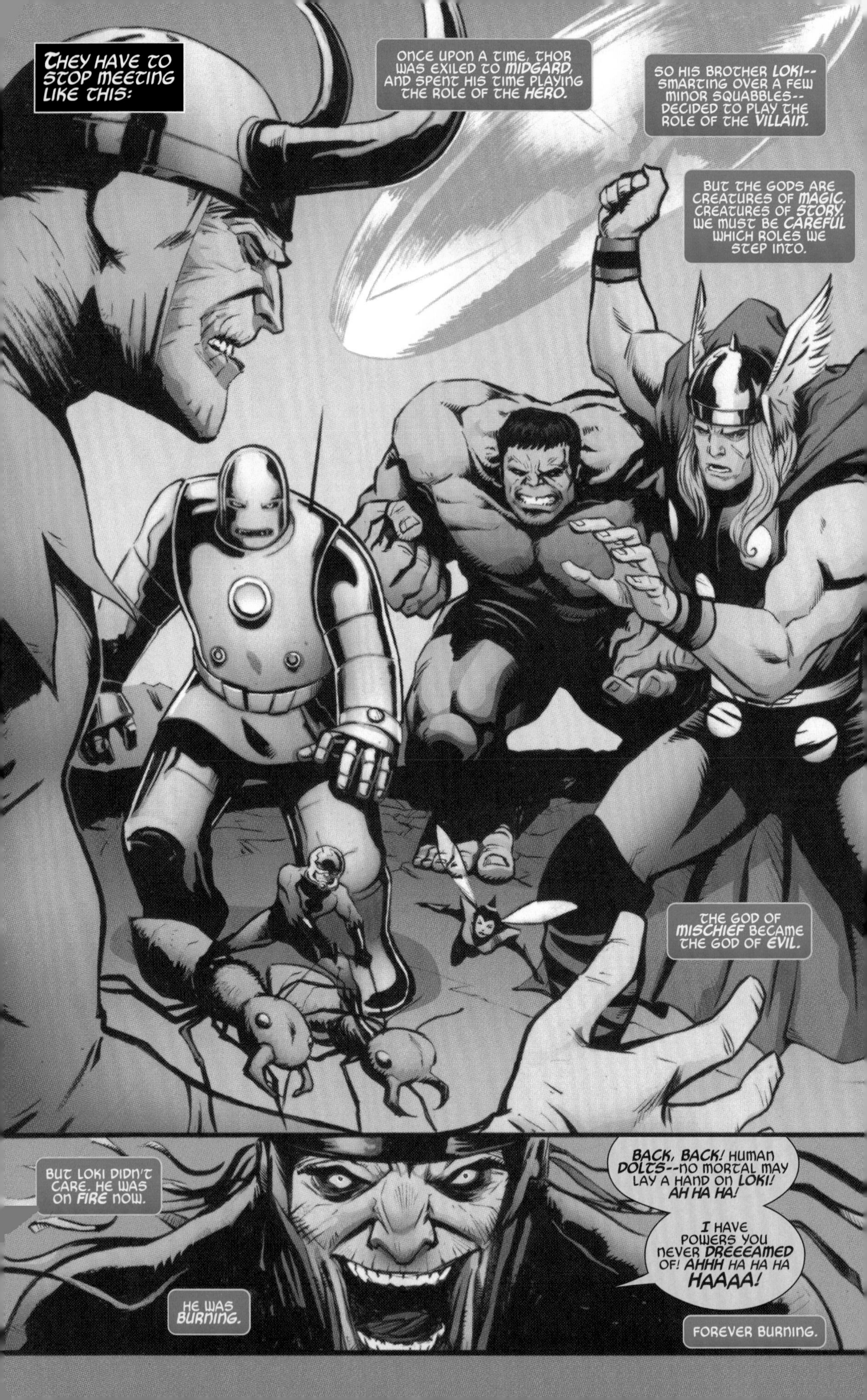
THEY HAVE TO STOP MEETING LIKE THIS:
ONCE UPON A TIME, THOR WAS EXILED TO MIDGARD, AND SPENT HIS TIME PLAYING THE ROLE OF THE HERO.
SO HIS BROTHER LOKI--SMARTING OVER A FEW MINOR SQUABBLES--DECIDED TO PLAY THE ROLE OF THE VILLAIN.
BUT THE GODS ARE CREATURES OF MAGIC. CREATURES OF STORY. WE MUST BE CAREFUL WHICH ROLES WE STEP INTO.
THE GOD OF MISCHIEF BECAME THE GOD OF EVIL.
BUT LOKI DIDN'T CARE. HE WAS ON FIRE NOW.
BACK, BACK! HUMAN DOLTS--NO MORTAL MAY LAY A HAND ON LOKI! AH HA HA!
I HAVE POWERS YOU NEVER DREEEAMED OF! AHHH HA HA HA HAAAA!
HE WAS BURNING.
FOREVER BURNING.

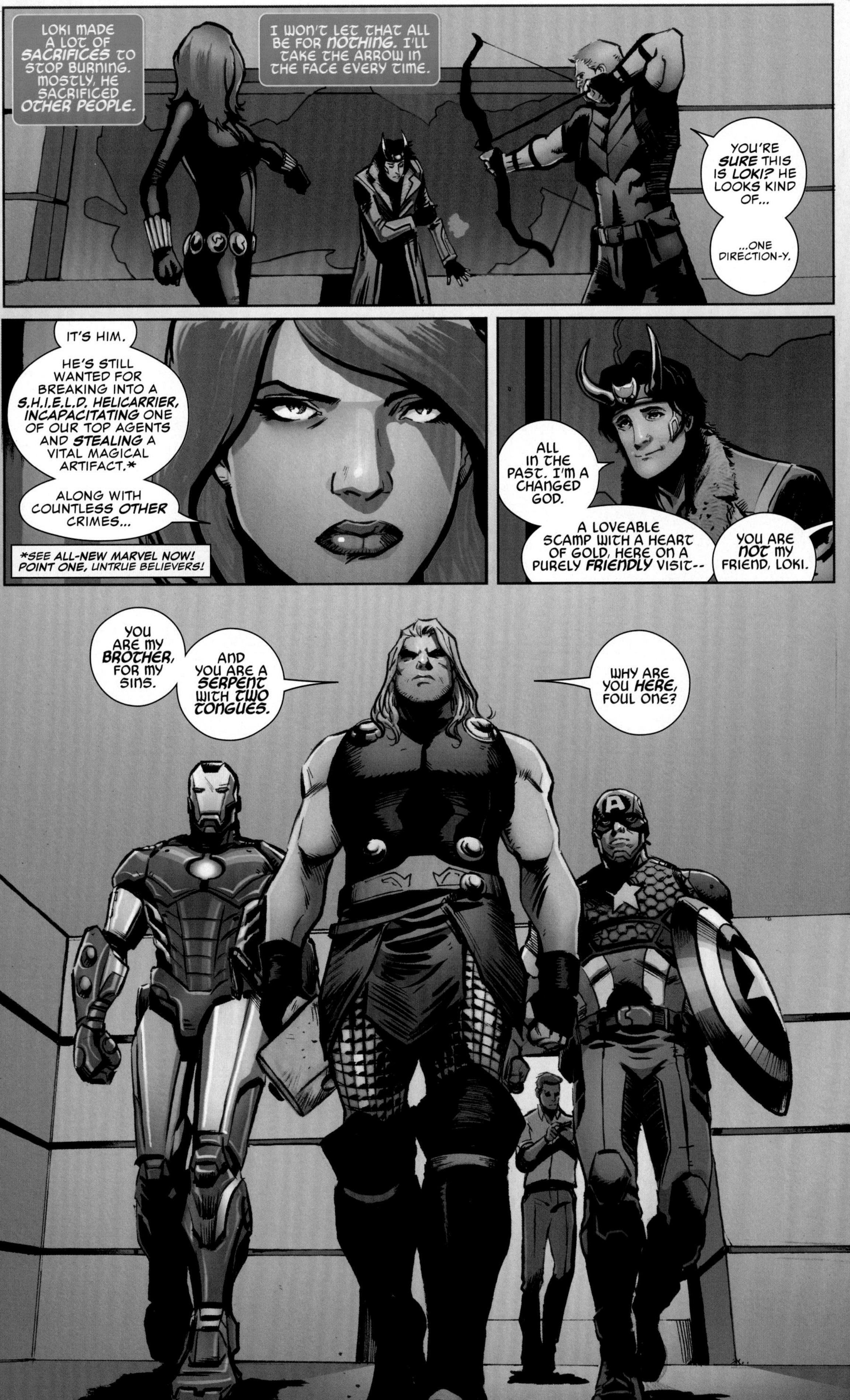
LOKI MADE A LOT OF SACRIFICES TO STOP BURNING. MOSTLY, HE SACRIFICED OTHER PEOPLE.
I WON'T LET THAT ALL BE FOR NOTHING. I'LL TAKE THE ARROW IN THE FACE EVERY TIME.
YOU'RE SURE THIS IS LOKI? HE LOOKS KIND OF...
...ONE DIRECTION-Y.
IT'S HIM.
HE'S STILL WANTED FOR BREAKING INTO A S.H.I.E.L.D. HELICARRIER, INCAPACITATING ONE OF OUR TOP AGENTS AND STEALING A VITAL MAGICAL ARTIFACT.*
ALONG WITH COUNTLESS OTHER CRIMES...
*SEE ALL-NEW MARVEL NOW! POINT ONE, UNTRUE BELIEVERS!
ALL IN THE PAST. I'M A CHANGED GOD.
A LOVEABLE SCAMP WITH A HEART OF GOLD, HERE ON A PURELY FRIENDLY VISIT--
YOU ARE NOT MY FRIEND, LOKI.
YOU ARE MY BROTHER, FOR MY SINS.
AND YOU ARE A SERPENT WITH TWO TONGUES.
WHY ARE YOU HERE, FOUL ONE?

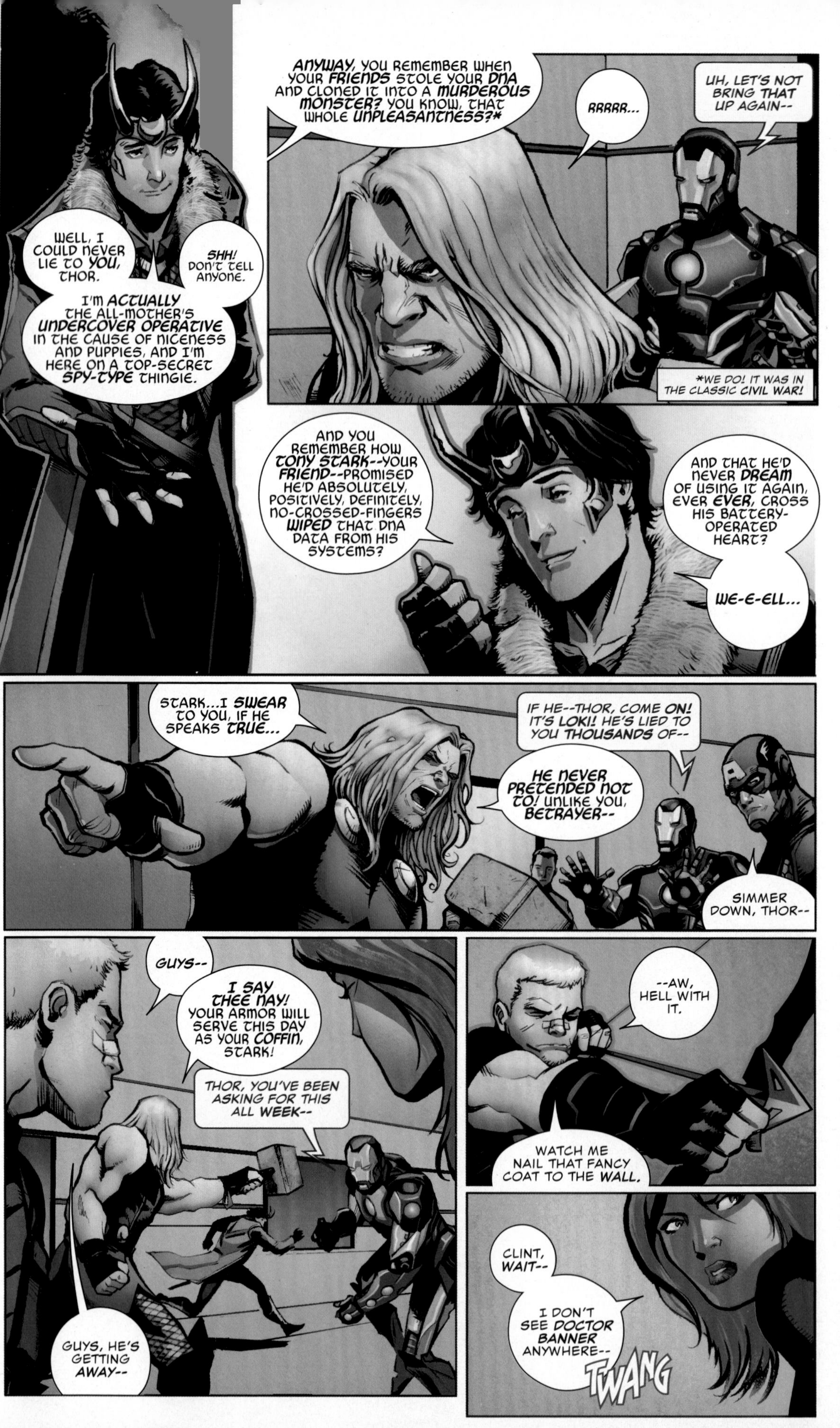

WELL, I COULD NEVER LIE TO YOU, THOR.
SHH! DON'T TELL ANYONE.
I'M ACTUALLY THE ALL-MOTHER'S UNDERCOVER OPERATIVE IN THE CAUSE OF NICENESS AND PUPPIES, AND I'M HERE ON A TOP-SECRET SPY-TYPE THINGIE.
ANYWAY, YOU REMEMBER WHEN YOUR FRIENDS STOLE YOUR DNA AND CLONED IT INTO A MURDEROUS MONSTER? YOU KNOW, THAT WHOLE UNPLEASANTNESS?*
RRRRR...
UH, LET'S NOT BRING THAT UP AGAIN--
*WE DO! IT WAS IN THE CLASSIC CIVIL WAR!
AND YOU REMEMBER HOW TONY STARK--YOUR FRIEND--PROMISED HE'D ABSOLUTELY, POSITIVELY, DEFINITELY, NO-CROSSED-FINGERS WIPED THAT DNA DATA FROM HIS SYSTEMS?
AND THAT HE'D NEVER DREAM OF USING IT AGAIN, EVER EVER, CROSS HIS BATTERY-OPERATED HEART?
WE-E-ELL...
STARK...I SWEAR TO YOU, IF HE SPEAKS TRUE...
IF HE--THOR, COME ON! IT'S LOKI! HE'S LIED TO YOU THOUSANDS OF--
HE NEVER PRETENDED NOT TO! UNLIKE YOU, BETRAYER--
SIMMER DOWN, THOR--
GUYS--
I SAY THEE NAY! YOUR ARMOR WILL SERVE THIS DAY AS YOUR COFFIN, STARK!
THOR, YOU'VE BEEN ASKING FOR THIS ALL WEEK--
GUYS, HE'S GETTING AWAY--
--AW, HELL WITH IT.
WATCH ME NAIL THAT FANCY COAT TO THE WALL.
CLINT, WAIT--
I DON'T SEE DOCTOR BANNER ANYWHERE--
TWANG

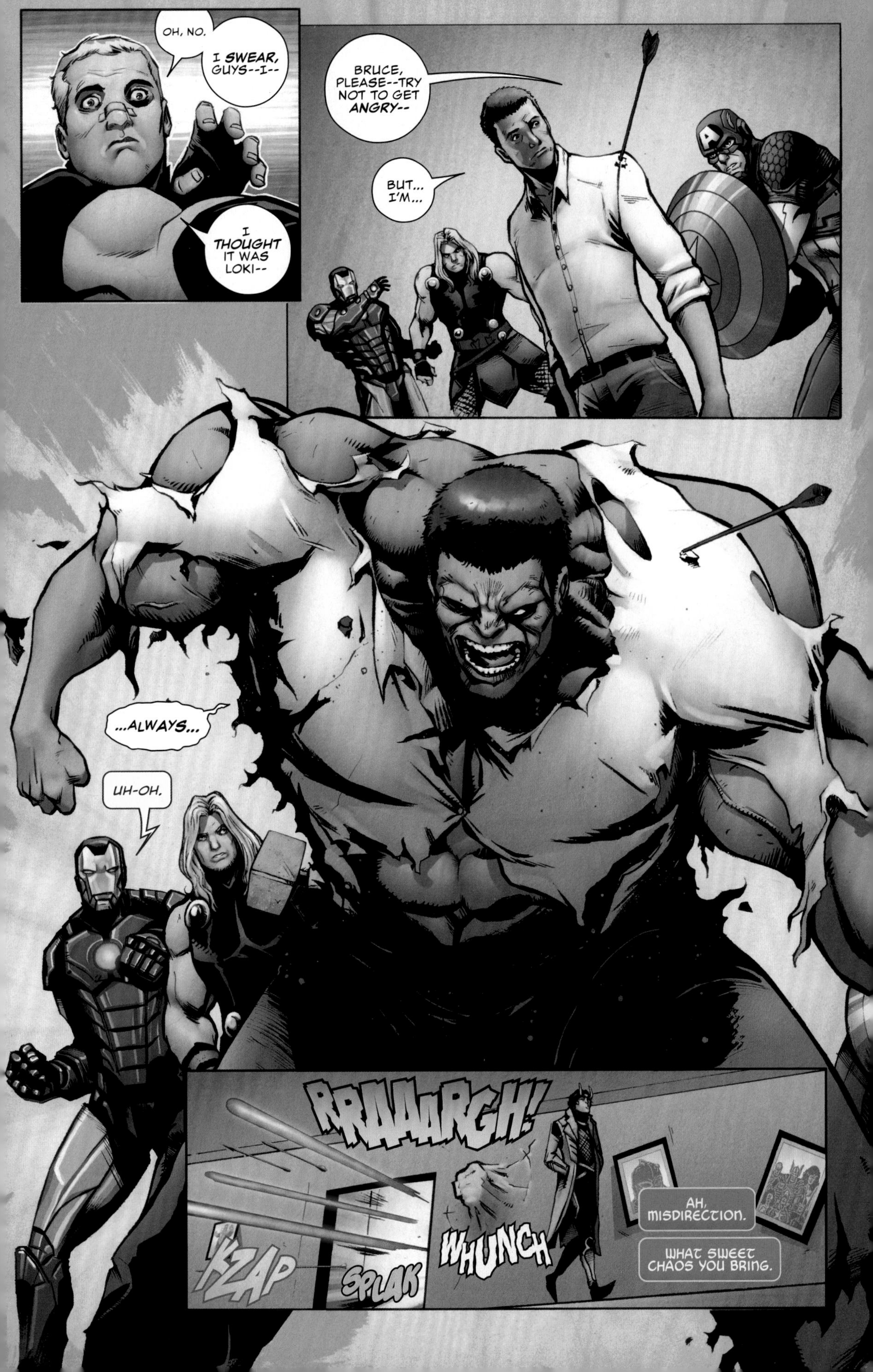

OH, NO.
I SWEAR, GUYS--I--
I THOUGHT IT WAS LOKI--
BRUCE, PLEASE--TRY NOT TO GET ANGRY--
BUT... I'M...
...ALWAYS...
UH-OH.
RRAAARGH!
KZAP
SPLAK
WHUNCH
AH, MISDIRECTION.
WHAT SWEET CHAOS YOU BRING.

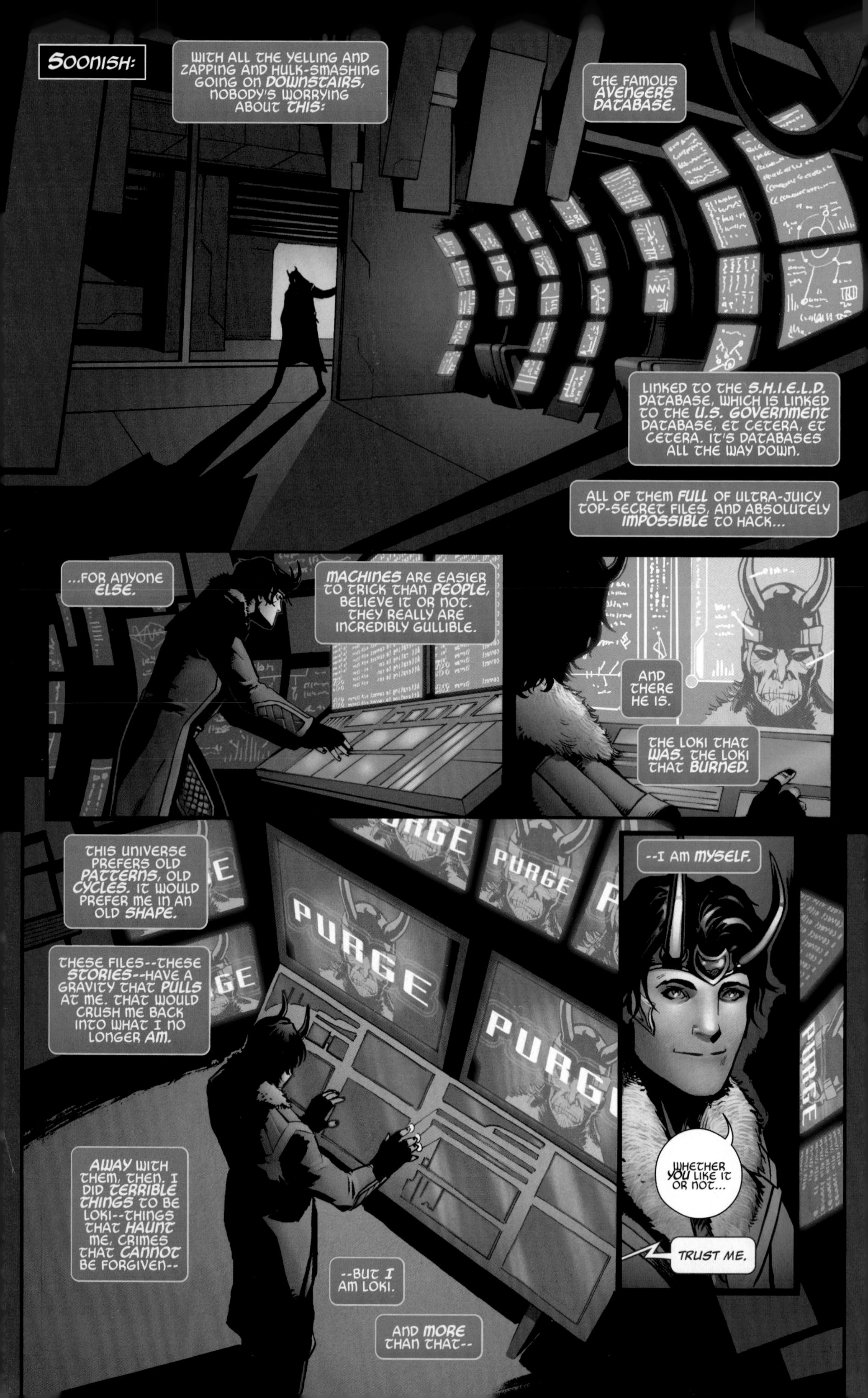
SOONISH:
WITH ALL THE YELLING AND ZAPPING AND HULK-SMASHING GOING ON DOWNSTAIRS, NOBODY'S WORRYING ABOUT THIS:
THE FAMOUS AVENGERS DATABASE.
LINKED TO THE S.H.I.E.L.D. DATABASE, WHICH IS LINKED TO THE U.S. GOVERNMENT DATABASE, ET CETERA, ET CETERA. IT'S DATABASES ALL THE WAY DOWN.
ALL OF THEM FULL OF ULTRA-JUICY TOP-SECRET FILES, AND ABSOLUTELY IMPOSSIBLE TO HACK...
...FOR ANYONE ELSE.
MACHINES ARE EASIER TO TRICK THAN PEOPLE, BELIEVE IT OR NOT. THEY REALLY ARE INCREDIBLY GULLIBLE.
AND THERE HE IS.
THE LOKI THAT WAS. THE LOKI THAT BURNED.
THIS UNIVERSE PREFERS OLD PATTERNS, OLD CYCLES. IT WOULD PREFER ME IN AN OLD SHAPE.
THESE FILES--THESE STORIES--HAVE A GRAVITY THAT PULLS AT ME. THAT WOULD CRUSH ME BACK INTO WHAT I NO LONGER AM.
AWAY WITH THEM, THEN. I DID TERRIBLE THINGS TO BE LOKI--THINGS THAT HAUNT ME, CRIMES THAT CANNOT BE FORGIVEN--
--BUT I AM LOKI.
AND MORE THAN THAT--
--I AM MYSELF.
WHETHER YOU LIKE IT OR NOT...
TRUST ME.
PURGE

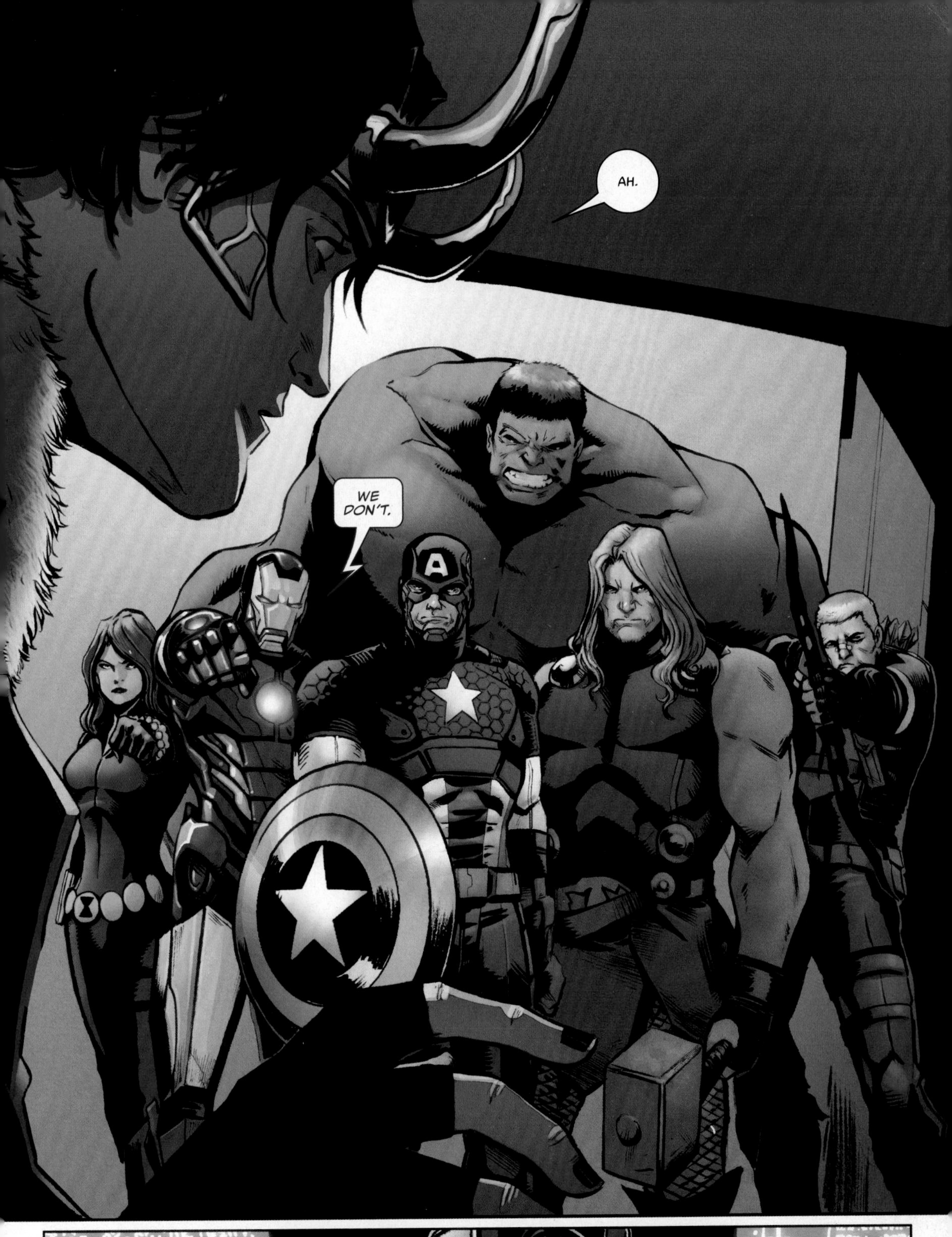
AH.
WE DON'T.

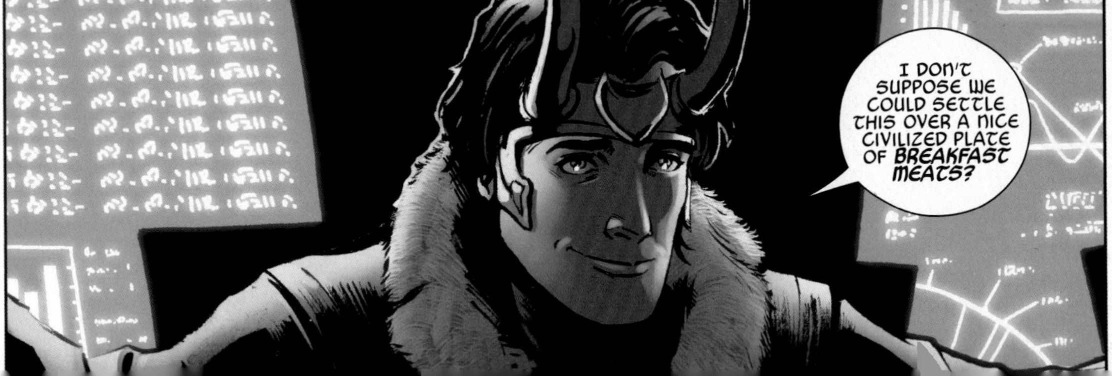
I DON'T SUPPOSE WE COULD SETTLE THIS OVER A NICE CIVILIZED PLATE OF *BREAKFAST MEATS?*

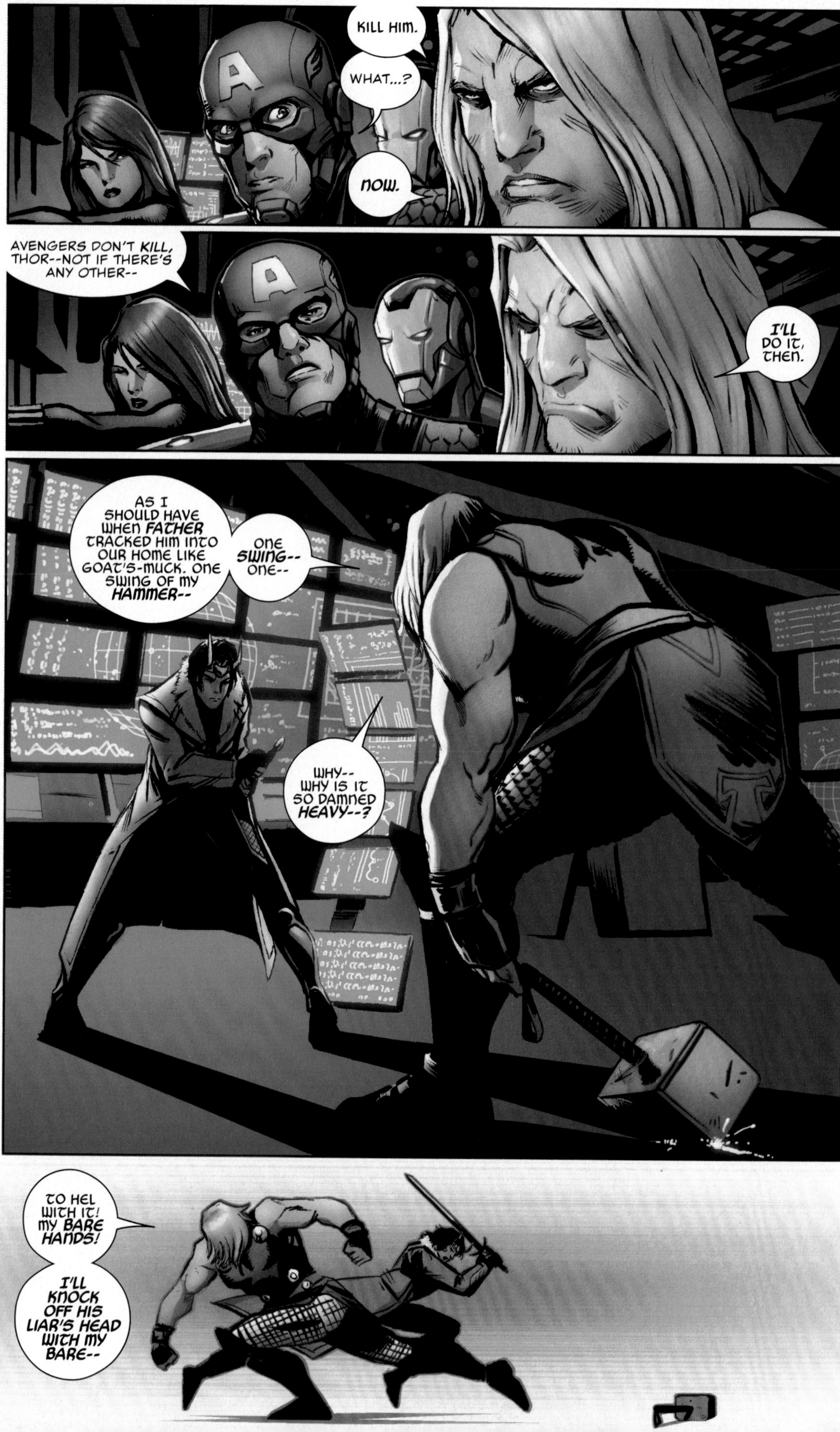
KILL HIM.
WHAT...?
NOW.
AVENGERS DON'T KILL, THOR--NOT IF THERE'S ANY OTHER--
I'LL DO IT, THEN.
AS I SHOULD HAVE WHEN FATHER TRACKED HIM INTO OUR HOME LIKE GOAT'S-MUCK. ONE SWING OF MY HAMMER--
ONE SWING-- ONE--
WHY-- WHY IS IT SO DAMNED HEAVY--?
TO HEL WITH IT! MY BARE HANDS!
I'LL KNOCK OFF HIS LIAR'S HEAD WITH MY BARE--

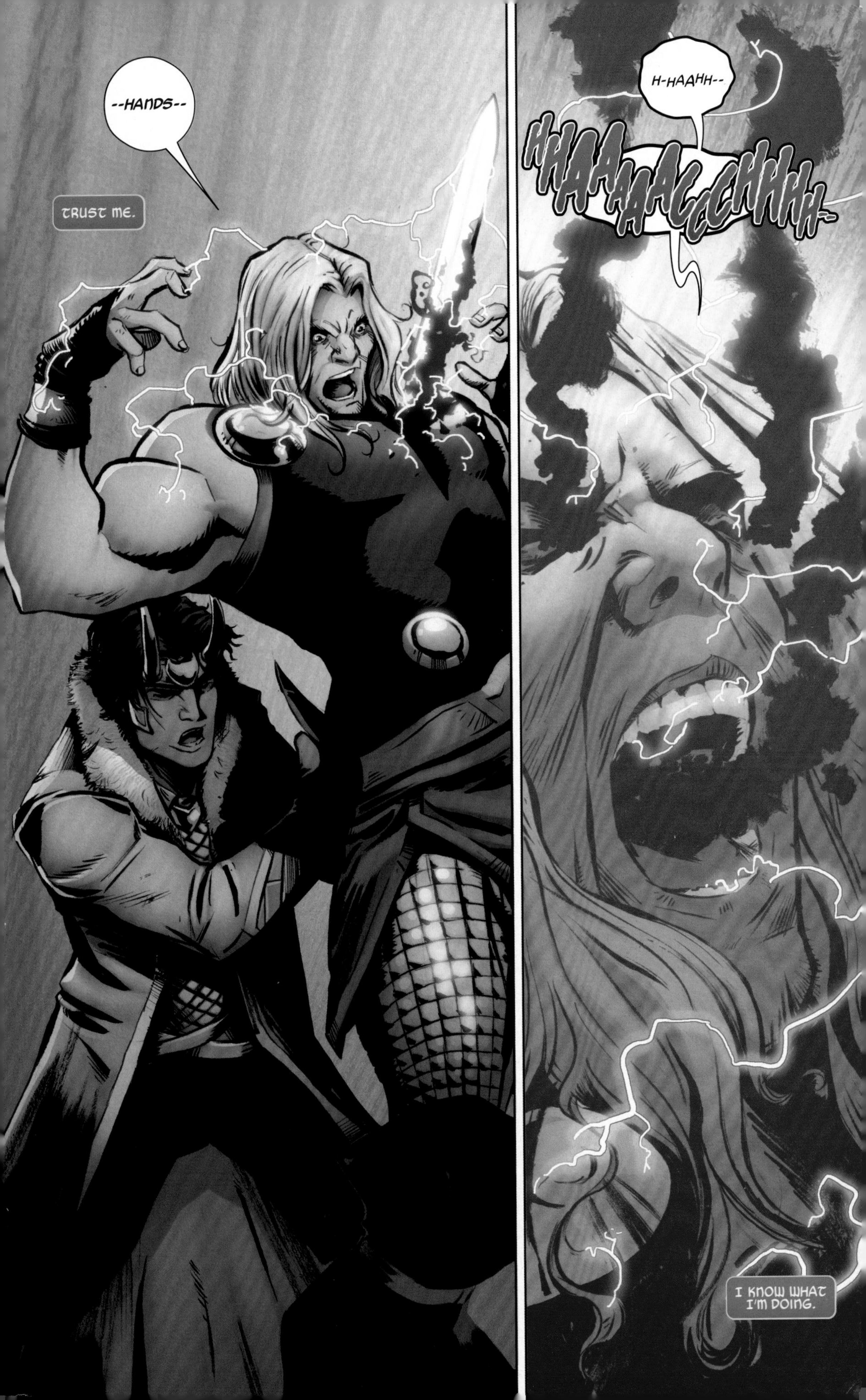

--HANDS--
TRUST ME.
H-HAAHH--
HHAAAAAACCCHHHH-
I KNOW WHAT I'M DOING.

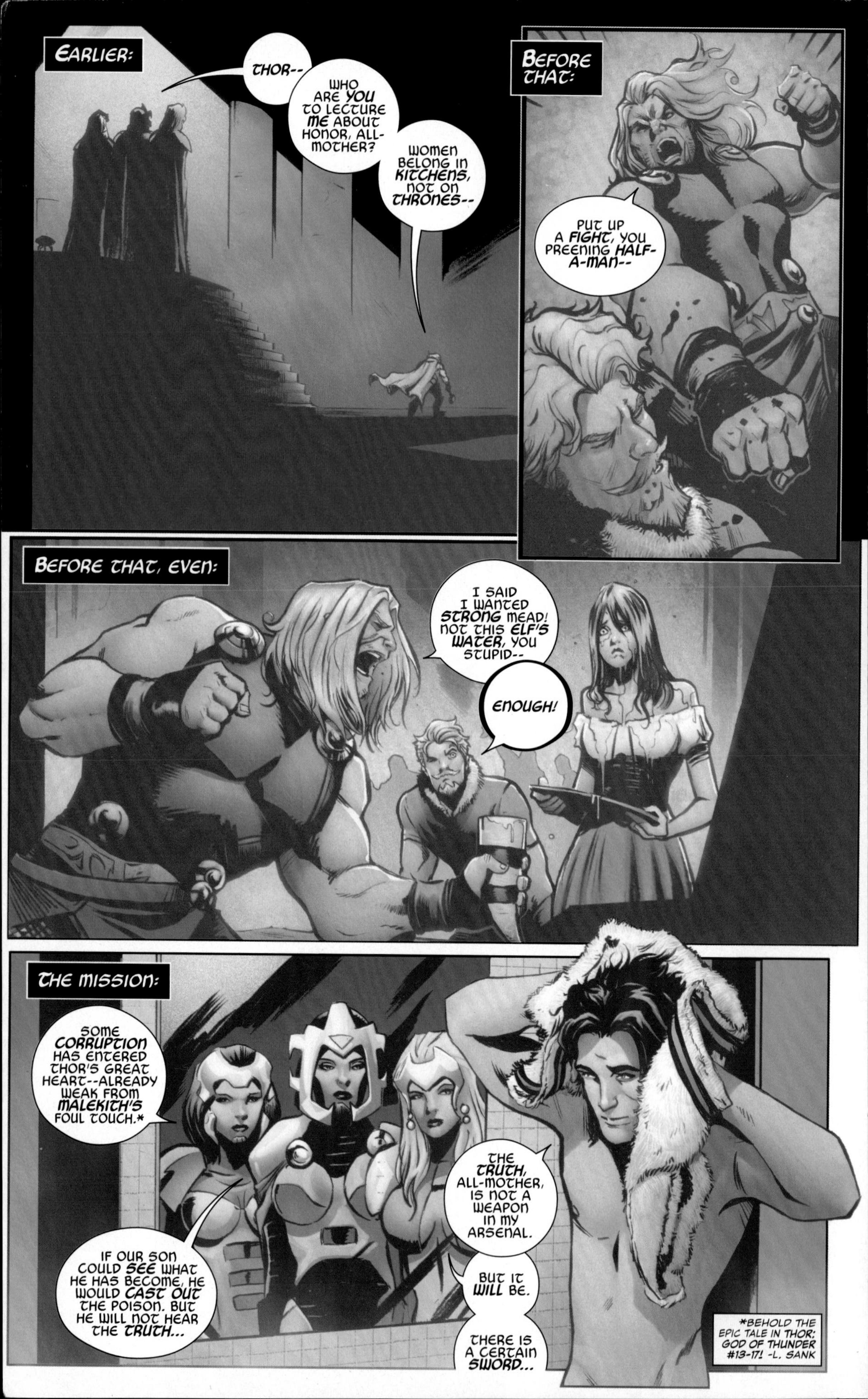
EARLIER:
THOR--
WHO ARE YOU TO LECTURE ME ABOUT HONOR, ALL-MOTHER?
WOMEN BELONG IN KITCHENS, NOT ON THRONES--
BEFORE THAT:
PUT UP A FIGHT, YOU PREENING HALF-A-MAN--
BEFORE THAT, EVEN:
I SAID I WANTED STRONG MEAD! NOT THIS ELF'S WATER, YOU STUPID--
ENOUGH!
THE MISSION:
SOME CORRUPTION HAS ENTERED THOR'S GREAT HEART--ALREADY WEAK FROM MALEKITH'S FOUL TOUCH.*
IF OUR SON COULD SEE WHAT HE HAS BECOME, HE WOULD CAST OUT THE POISON. BUT HE WILL NOT HEAR THE TRUTH...
THE TRUTH, ALL-MOTHER, IS NOT A WEAPON IN MY ARSENAL.
BUT IT WILL BE.
THERE IS A CERTAIN SWORD...
*BEHOLD THE EPIC TALE IN THOR: GOD OF THUNDER #13-17! -L. SANK

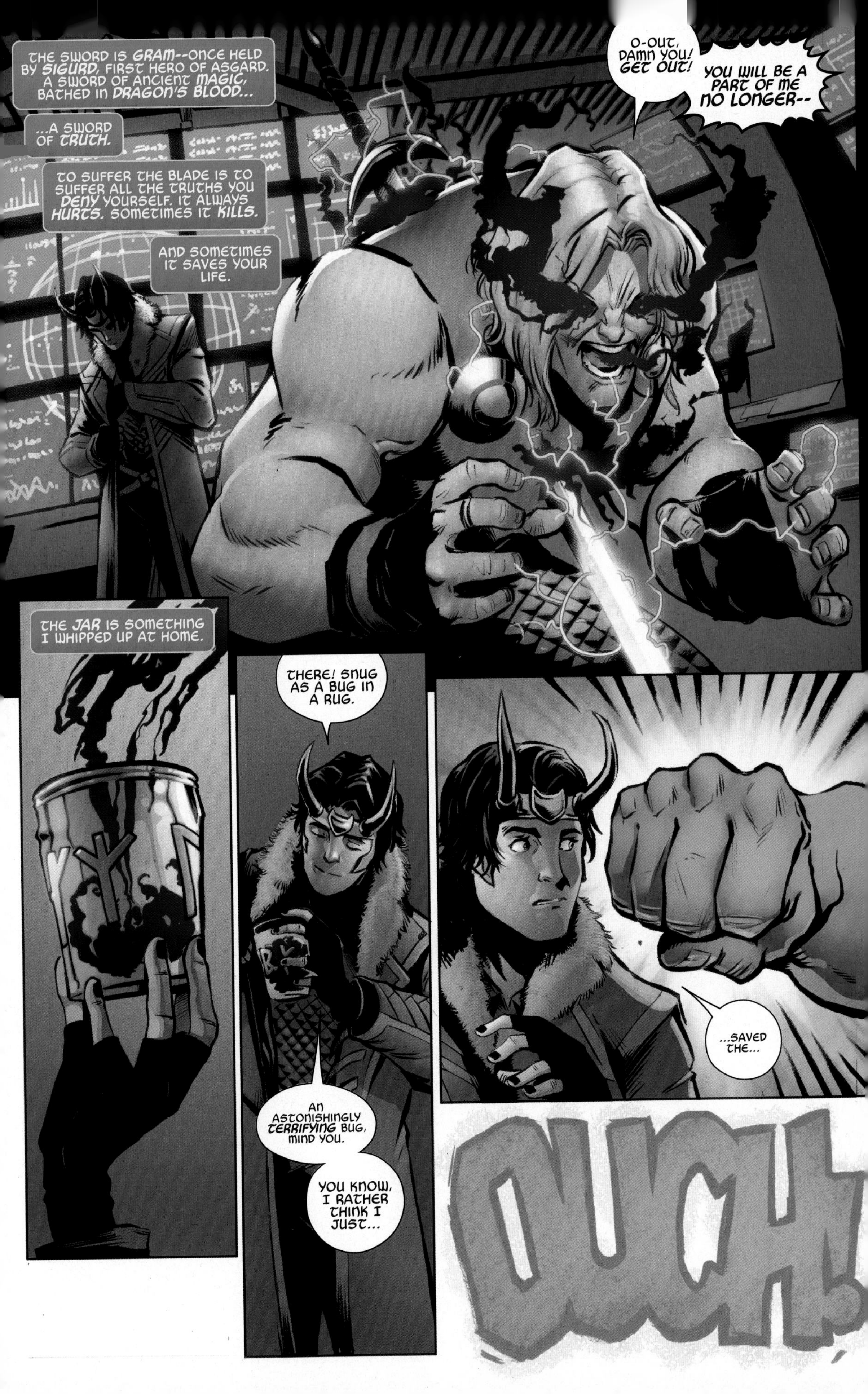
THE SWORD IS GRAM--ONCE HELD BY SIGURD, FIRST HERO OF ASGARD. A SWORD OF ANCIENT MAGIC, BATHED IN DRAGON'S BLOOD...
...A SWORD OF TRUTH.
TO SUFFER THE BLADE IS TO SUFFER ALL THE TRUTHS YOU DENY YOURSELF. IT ALWAYS HURTS. SOMETIMES IT KILLS.
AND SOMETIMES IT SAVES YOUR LIFE.
O-OUT, DAMN YOU! GET OUT!
YOU WILL BE A PART OF ME NO LONGER--
THE JAR IS SOMETHING I WHIPPED UP AT HOME.
THERE! SNUG AS A BUG IN A RUG.
AN ASTONISHINGLY TERRIFYING BUG, MIND YOU.
YOU KNOW, I RATHER THINK I JUST...
...SAVED THE...
OUCH!

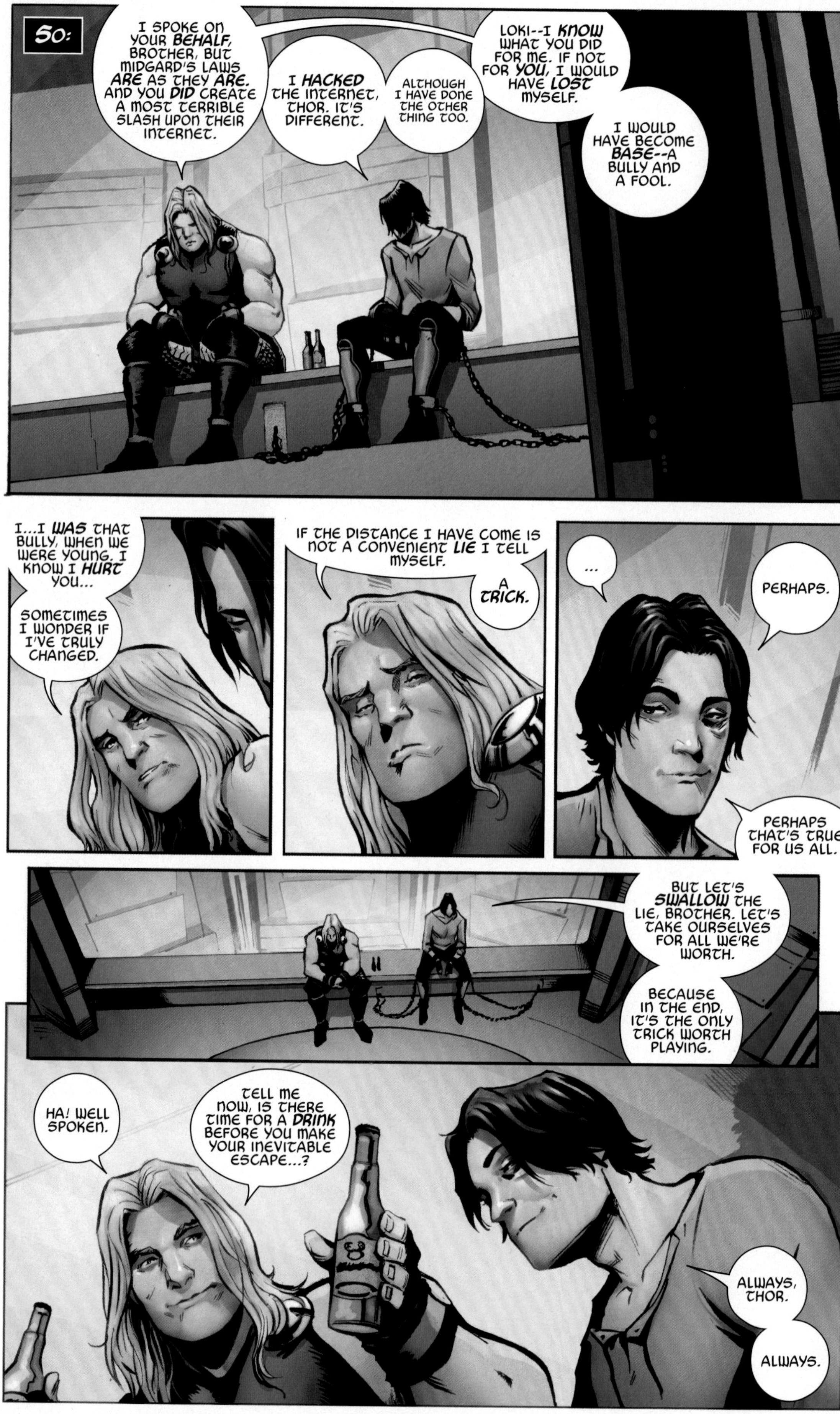
50:
I SPOKE ON YOUR BEHALF, BROTHER, BUT MIDGARD'S LAWS ARE AS THEY ARE. AND YOU DID CREATE A MOST TERRIBLE SLASH UPON THEIR INTERNET.
I HACKED THE INTERNET, THOR. IT'S DIFFERENT.
ALTHOUGH I HAVE DONE THE OTHER THING TOO.
LOKI--I KNOW WHAT YOU DID FOR ME. IF NOT FOR YOU, I WOULD HAVE LOST MYSELF.
I WOULD HAVE BECOME BASE--A BULLY AND A FOOL.
I...I WAS THAT BULLY, WHEN WE WERE YOUNG. I KNOW I HURT YOU...
SOMETIMES I WONDER IF I'VE TRULY CHANGED.
IF THE DISTANCE I HAVE COME IS NOT A CONVENIENT LIE I TELL MYSELF.
A TRICK.
...
PERHAPS.
PERHAPS THAT'S TRUE FOR US ALL.
BUT LET'S SWALLOW THE LIE, BROTHER. LET'S TAKE OURSELVES FOR ALL WE'RE WORTH.
BECAUSE IN THE END, IT'S THE ONLY TRICK WORTH PLAYING.
HA! WELL SPOKEN.
TELL ME NOW, IS THERE TIME FOR A DRINK BEFORE YOU MAKE YOUR INEVITABLE ESCAPE...?
ALWAYS, THOR.
ALWAYS.

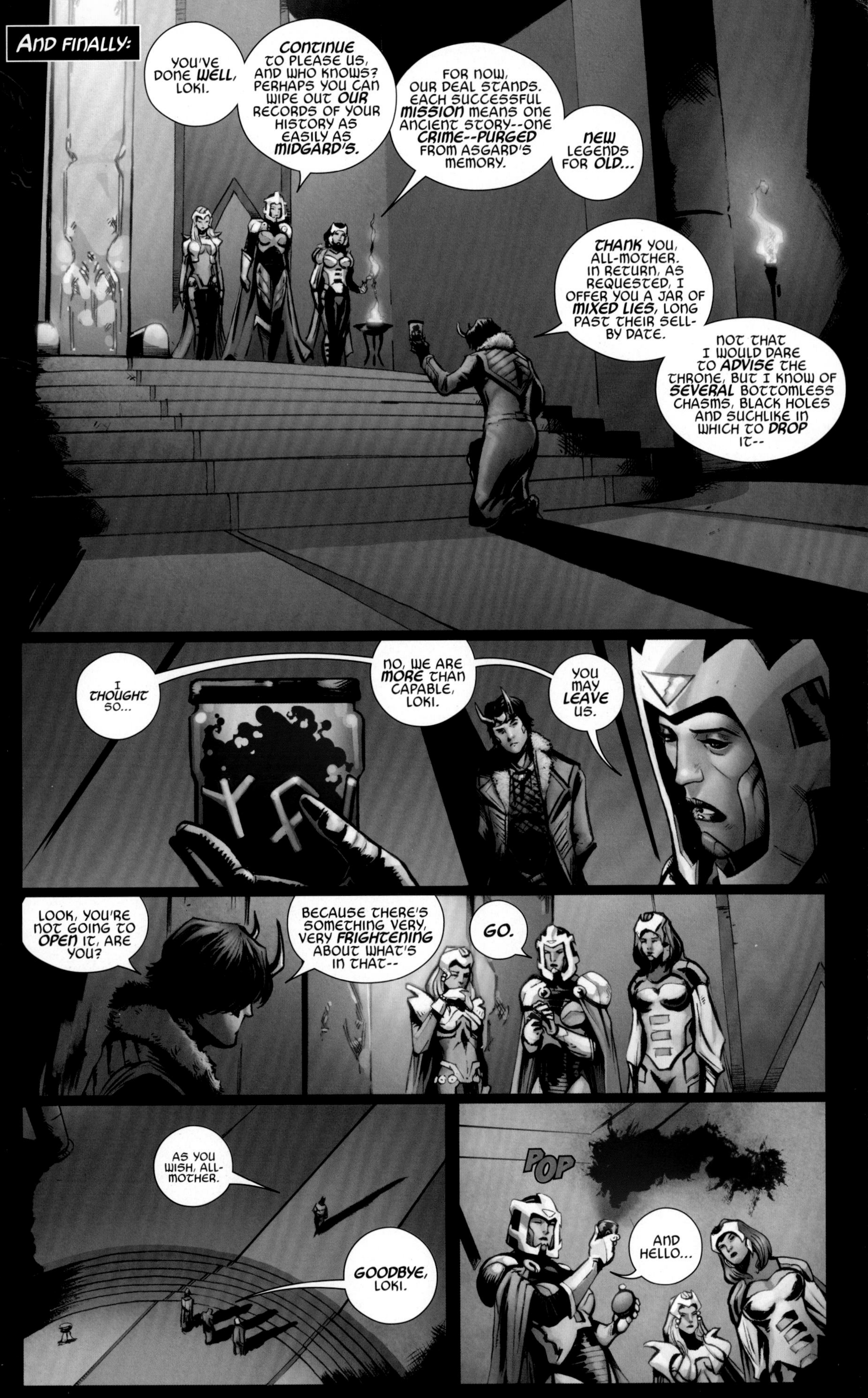
AND FINALLY:
YOU'VE DONE WELL, LOKI.
CONTINUE TO PLEASE US, AND WHO KNOWS? PERHAPS YOU CAN WIPE OUT OUR RECORDS OF YOUR HISTORY AS EASILY AS MIDGARD'S.
FOR NOW, OUR DEAL STANDS. EACH SUCCESSFUL MISSION MEANS ONE ANCIENT STORY--ONE CRIME--PURGED FROM ASGARD'S MEMORY.
NEW LEGENDS FOR OLD...
THANK YOU, ALL-MOTHER. IN RETURN, AS REQUESTED, I OFFER YOU A JAR OF MIXED LIES, LONG PAST THEIR SELL-BY DATE.
NOT THAT I WOULD DARE TO ADVISE THE THRONE, BUT I KNOW OF SEVERAL BOTTOMLESS CHASMS, BLACK HOLES AND SUCHLIKE IN WHICH TO DROP IT--
NO, WE ARE MORE THAN CAPABLE, LOKI.
I THOUGHT SO...
YOU MAY LEAVE US.
LOOK, YOU'RE NOT GOING TO OPEN IT, ARE YOU?
BECAUSE THERE'S SOMETHING VERY, VERY FRIGHTENING ABOUT WHAT'S IN THAT--
GO.
AS YOU WISH, ALL-MOTHER.
GOODBYE, LOKI.
POP
AND HELLO...

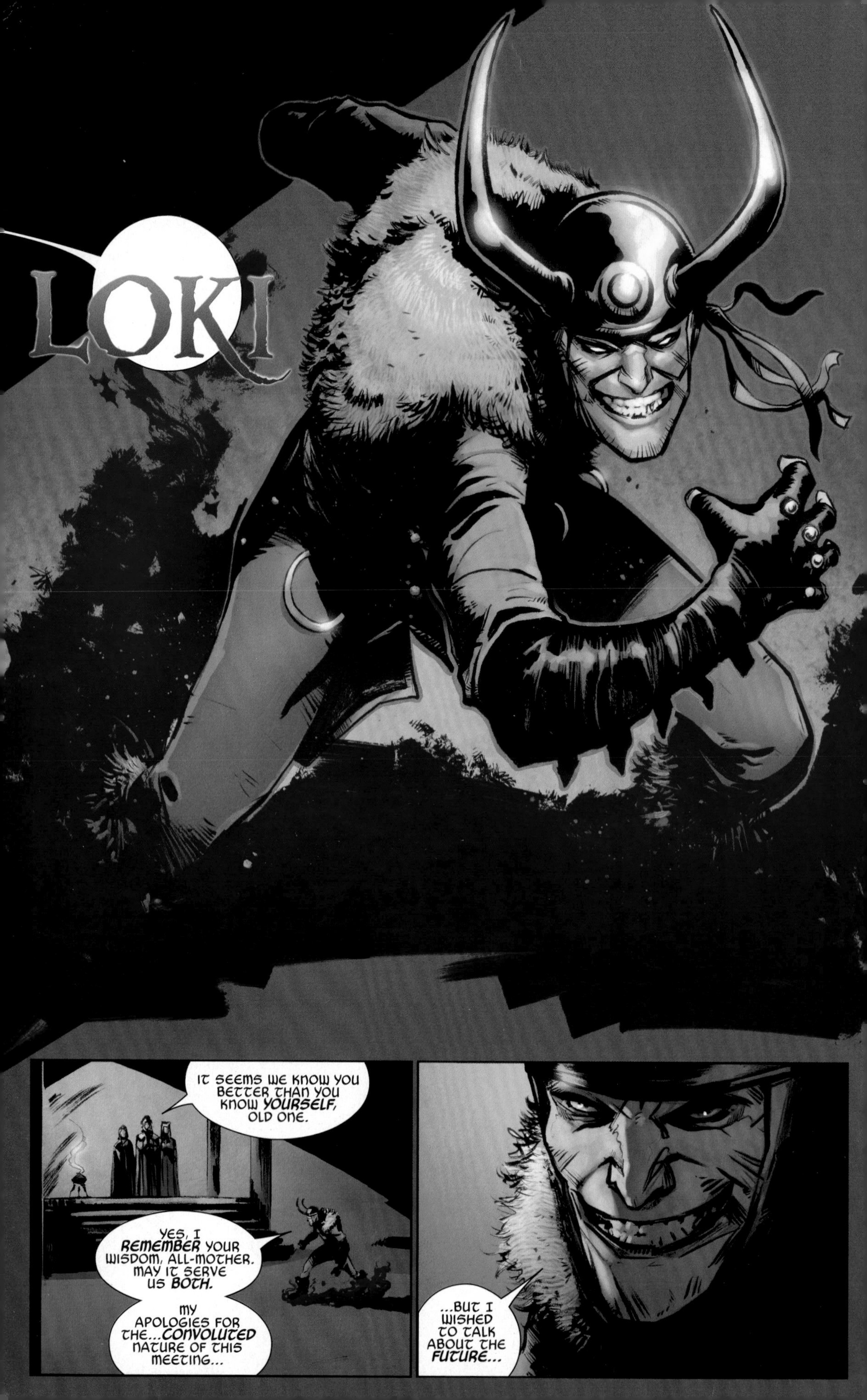
LOKI
IT SEEMS WE KNOW YOU BETTER THAN YOU KNOW YOURSELF, OLD ONE.
YES, I REMEMBER YOUR WISDOM, ALL-MOTHER. MAY IT SERVE US BOTH.
MY APOLOGIES FOR THE...CONVOLUTED NATURE OF THIS MEETING...
...BUT I WISHED TO TALK ABOUT THE FUTURE...

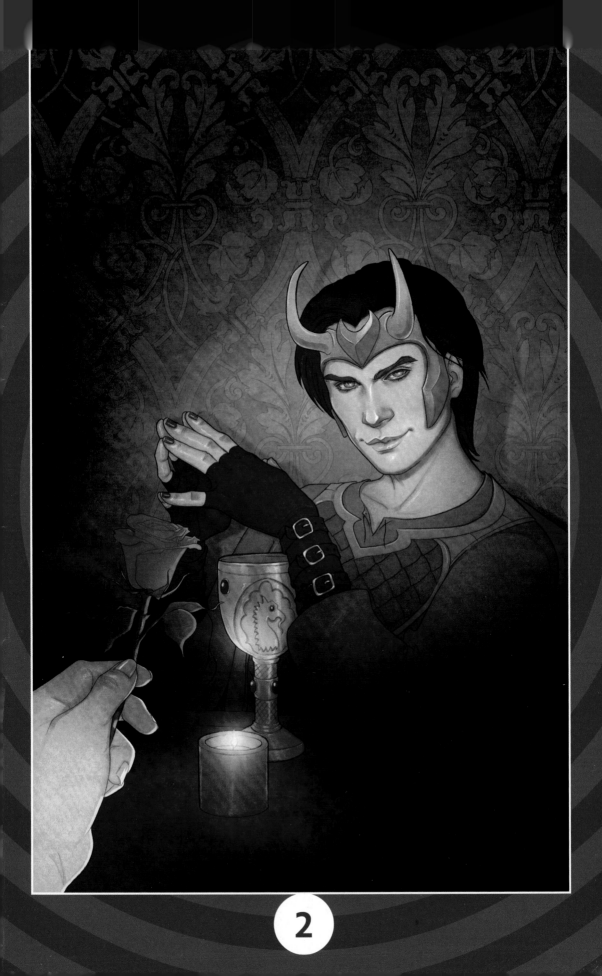

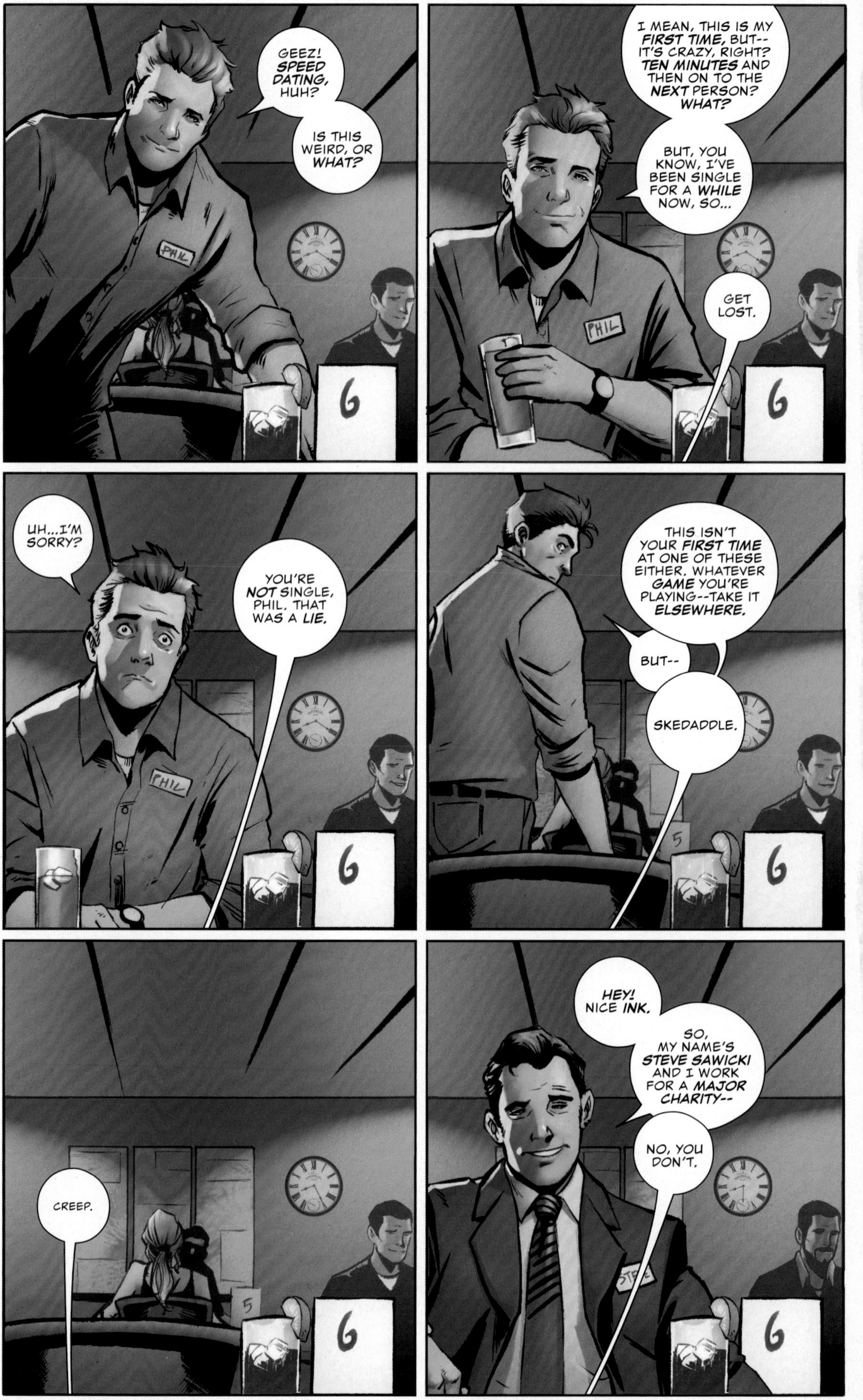
GEEZ! SPEED DATING, HUH?
IS THIS WEIRD, OR WHAT?
I MEAN, THIS IS MY FIRST TIME, BUT-- IT'S CRAZY, RIGHT? TEN MINUTES AND THEN ON TO THE NEXT PERSON? WHAT?
BUT, YOU KNOW, I'VE BEEN SINGLE FOR A WHILE NOW, SO...
GET LOST.
PHIL
UH...I'M SORRY?
YOU'RE NOT SINGLE, PHIL. THAT WAS A LIE.
THIS ISN'T YOUR FIRST TIME AT ONE OF THESE EITHER. WHATEVER GAME YOU'RE PLAYING--TAKE IT ELSEWHERE.
BUT--
SKEDADDLE.
CREEP.
HEY! NICE INK.
SO, MY NAME'S STEVE SAWICKI AND I WORK FOR A MAJOR CHARITY--
NO, YOU DON'T.
6

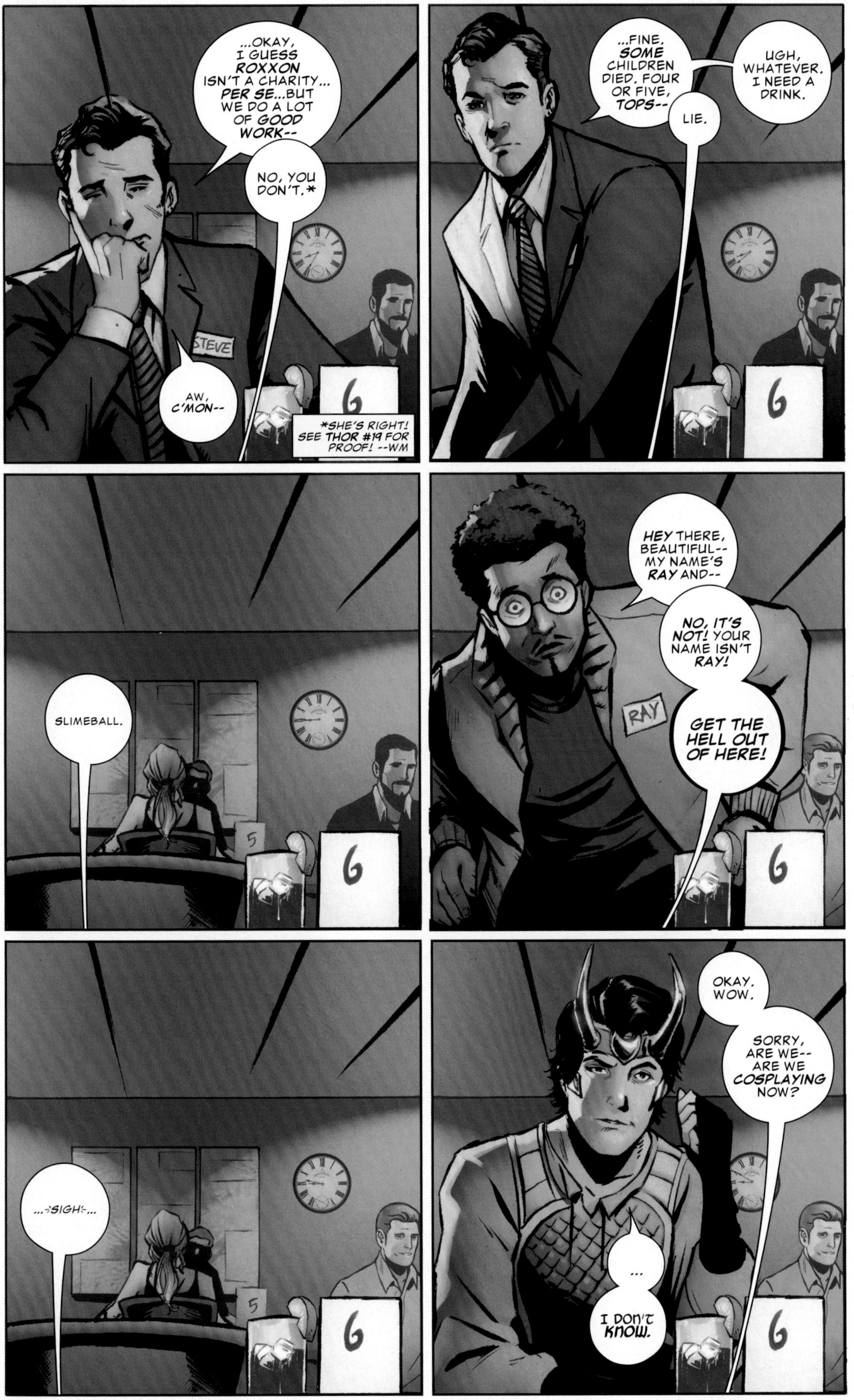

...OKAY, I GUESS ROXXON ISN'T A CHARITY... PER SE...BUT WE DO A LOT OF GOOD WORK--
NO, YOU DON'T.*
AW, C'MON--
*SHE'S RIGHT! SEE THOR #19 FOR PROOF! --WM
...FINE. SOME CHILDREN DIED. FOUR OR FIVE, TOPS--
LIE.
UGH, WHATEVER. I NEED A DRINK.
STEVE
6
SLIMEBALL.
5
HEY THERE, BEAUTIFUL-- MY NAME'S RAY AND--
NO, IT'S NOT! YOUR NAME ISN'T RAY!
GET THE HELL OUT OF HERE!
RAY
...⊰SIGH⊱...
OKAY. WOW.
SORRY, ARE WE-- ARE WE COSPLAYING NOW?
...
I DON'T KNOW.

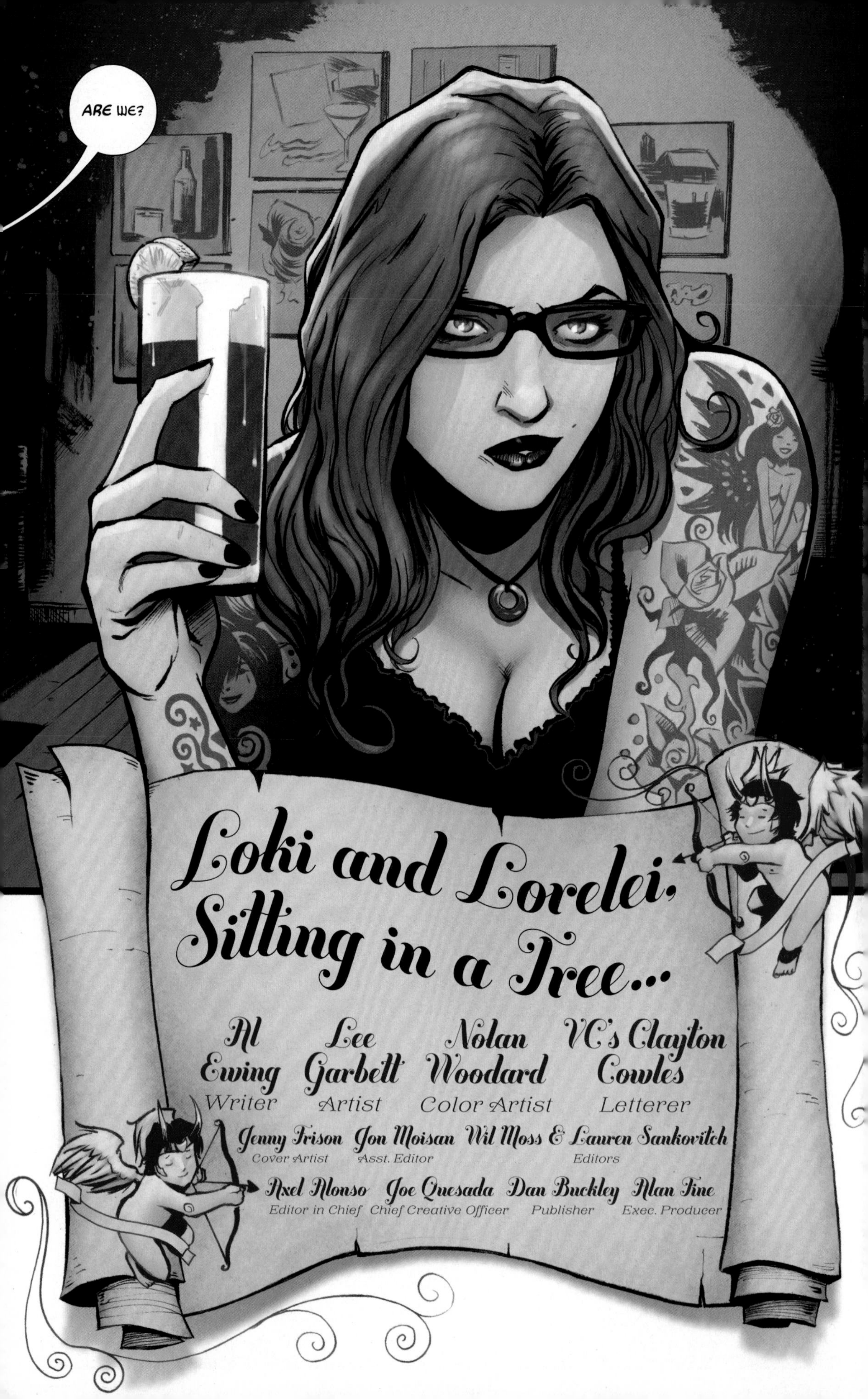
ARE WE?
Loki and Lorelei, Sitting in a Tree...
Al Ewing Writer
Lee Garbett Artist
Nolan Woodard Color Artist
VC's Clayton Cowles Letterer
Jenny Frison Cover Artist
Jon Moisan Asst. Editor
Wil Moss & Lauren Sankovitch Editors
Axel Alonso Editor in Chief
Joe Quesada Chief Creative Officer
Dan Buckley Publisher
Alan Fine Exec. Producer

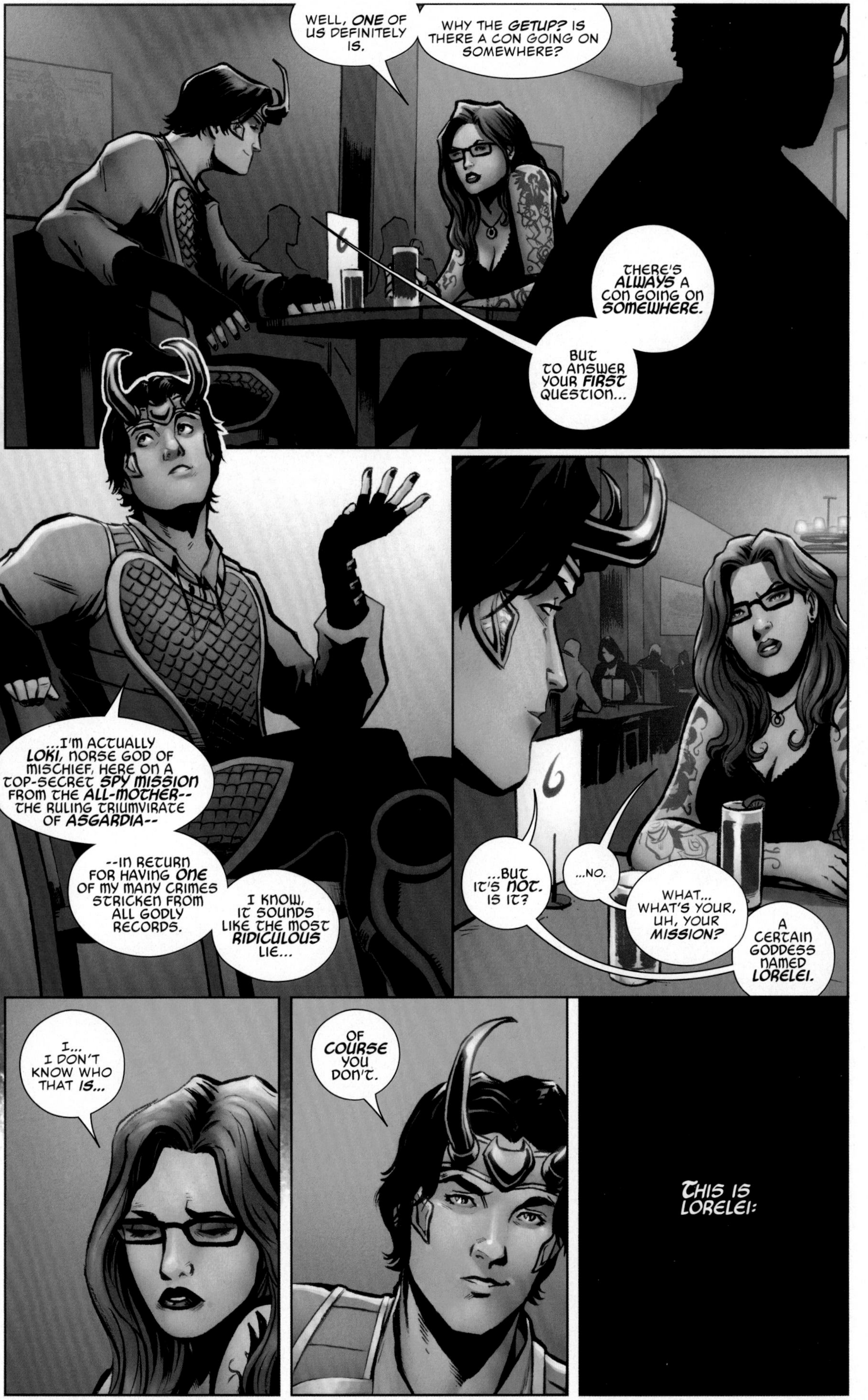
WELL, ONE OF US DEFINITELY IS.
WHY THE GETUP? IS THERE A CON GOING ON SOMEWHERE?
THERE'S ALWAYS A CON GOING ON SOMEWHERE.
BUT TO ANSWER YOUR FIRST QUESTION...
...I'M ACTUALLY LOKI, NORSE GOD OF MISCHIEF, HERE ON A TOP-SECRET SPY MISSION FROM THE ALL-MOTHER-- THE RULING TRIUMVIRATE OF ASGARDIA--
--IN RETURN FOR HAVING ONE OF MY MANY CRIMES STRICKEN FROM ALL GODLY RECORDS.
I KNOW, IT SOUNDS LIKE THE MOST RIDICULOUS LIE...
...BUT IT'S NOT. IS IT?
...NO.
WHAT... WHAT'S YOUR, UH, YOUR MISSION?
A CERTAIN GODDESS NAMED LORELEI.
I... I DON'T KNOW WHO THAT IS...
OF COURSE YOU DON'T.
THIS IS LORELEI:

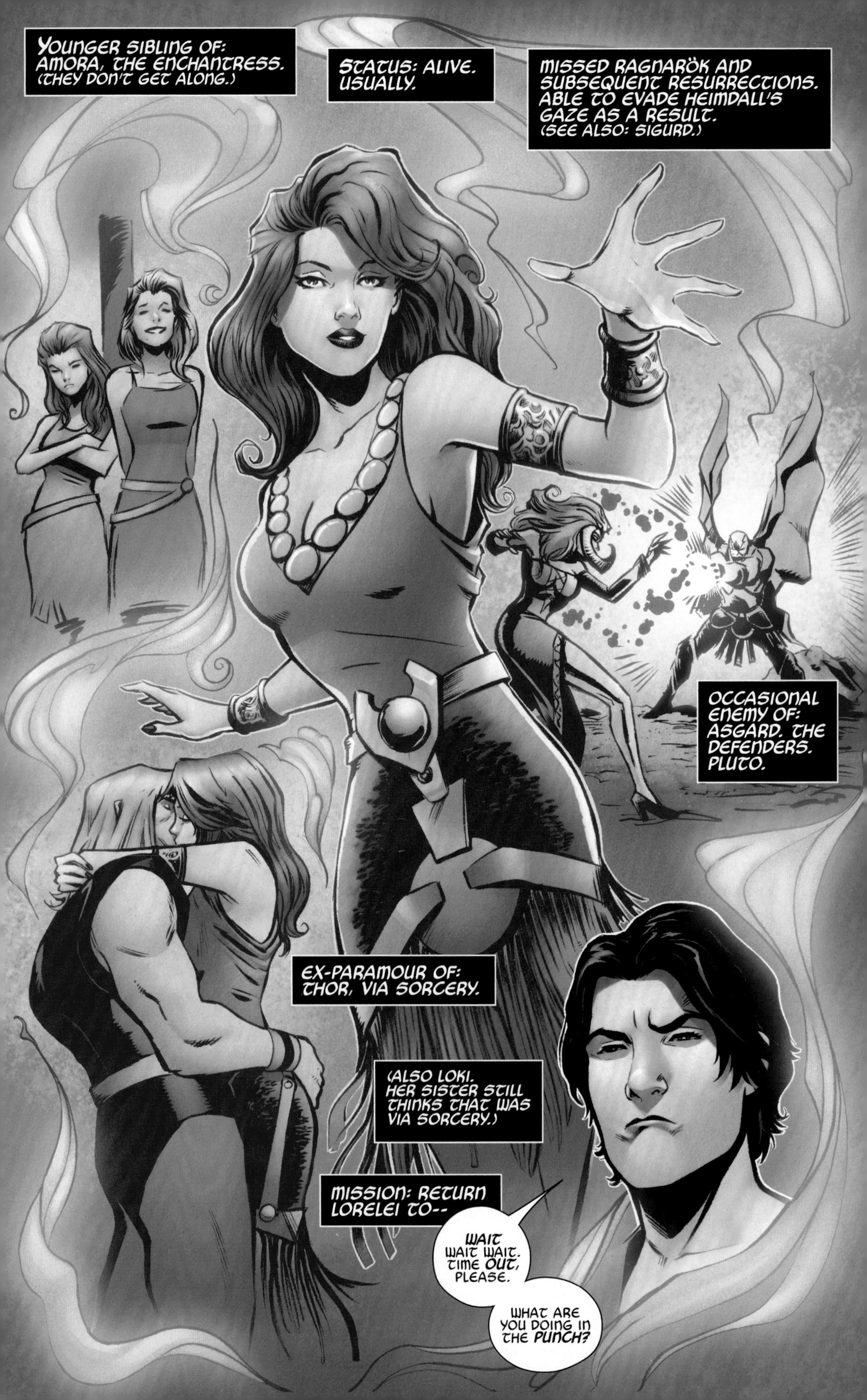
YOUNGER SIBLING OF: AMORA, THE ENCHANTRESS. (THEY DON'T GET ALONG.)
STATUS: ALIVE. USUALLY.
MISSED RAGNARÖK AND SUBSEQUENT RESURRECTIONS. ABLE TO EVADE HEIMDALL'S GAZE AS A RESULT. (SEE ALSO: SIGURD.)
OCCASIONAL ENEMY OF: ASGARD. THE DEFENDERS. PLUTO.
EX-PARAMOUR OF: THOR, VIA SORCERY.
(ALSO LOKI. HER SISTER STILL THINKS THAT WAS VIA SORCERY.)
MISSION: RETURN LORELEI TO--
WAIT WAIT WAIT. TIME OUT, PLEASE.
WHAT ARE YOU DOING IN THE PUNCH?

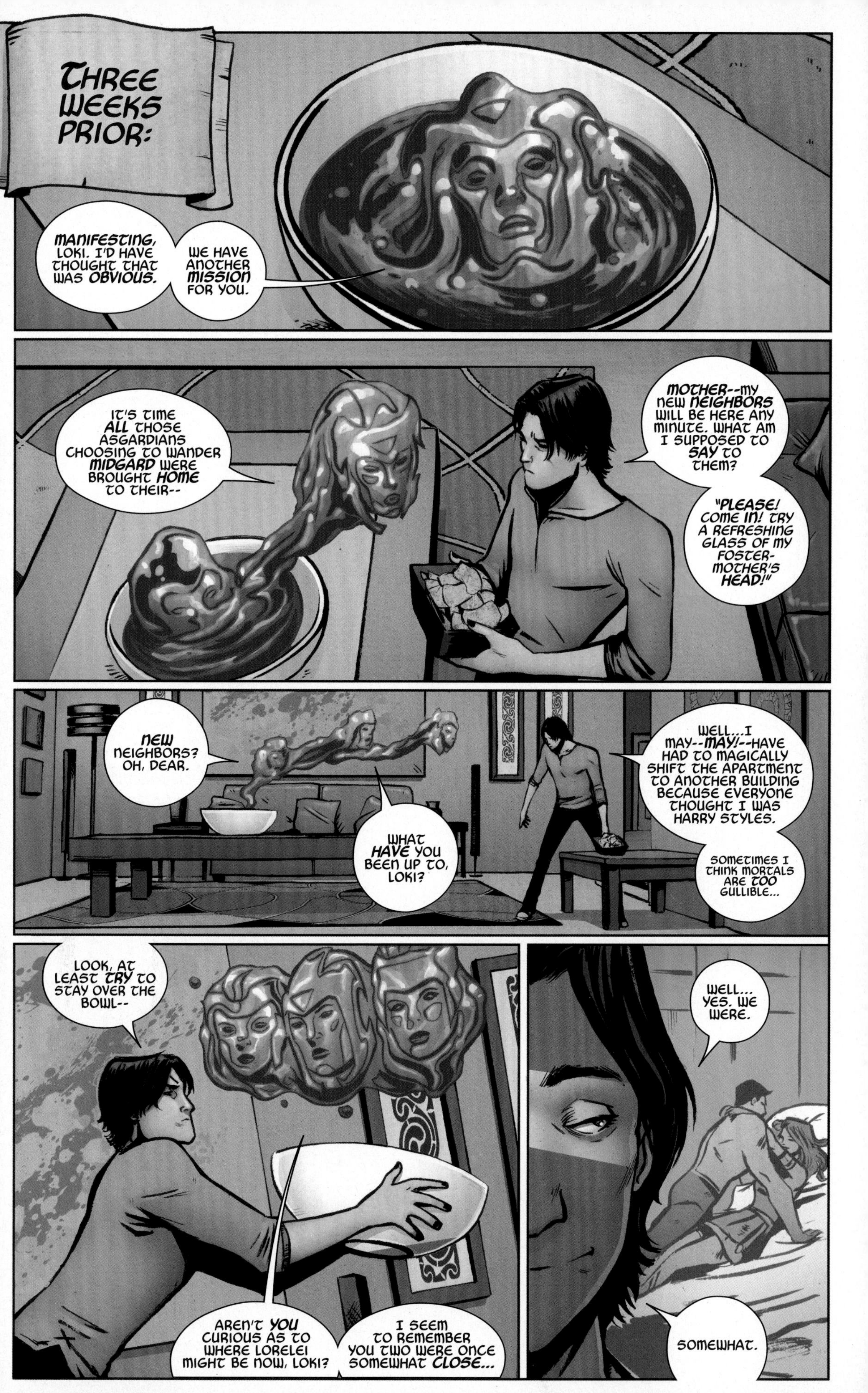
THREE WEEKS PRIOR:
MANIFESTING, LOKI. I'D HAVE THOUGHT THAT WAS OBVIOUS.
WE HAVE ANOTHER MISSION FOR YOU.
IT'S TIME ALL THOSE ASGARDIANS CHOOSING TO WANDER MIDGARD WERE BROUGHT HOME TO THEIR--
MOTHER--my new NEIGHBORS will be here any minute. What am I supposed to SAY to them?
"PLEASE! COME IN! TRY A REFRESHING GLASS OF MY FOSTER-MOTHER'S HEAD!"
NEW NEIGHBORS? OH, DEAR.
WHAT HAVE YOU BEEN UP TO, LOKI?
WELL...I MAY--MAY!--HAVE HAD TO MAGICALLY SHIFT THE APARTMENT TO ANOTHER BUILDING BECAUSE EVERYONE THOUGHT I WAS HARRY STYLES.
SOMETIMES I THINK MORTALS ARE TOO GULLIBLE...
LOOK, AT LEAST TRY TO STAY OVER THE BOWL--
AREN'T YOU CURIOUS AS TO WHERE LORELEI MIGHT BE NOW, LOKI?
I SEEM TO REMEMBER YOU TWO WERE ONCE SOMEWHAT CLOSE...
WELL... YES. WE WERE.
SOMEWHAT.

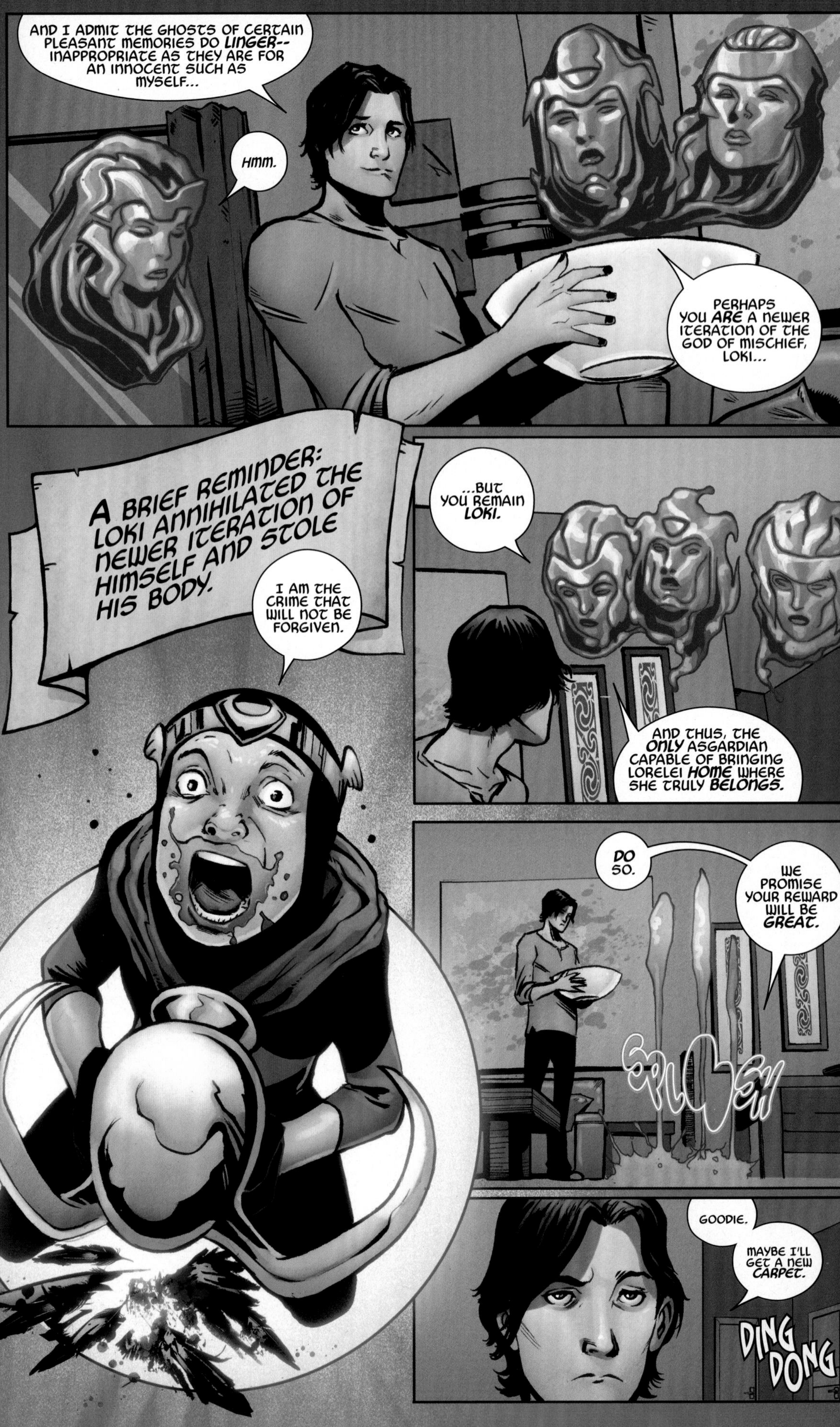
AND I ADMIT THE GHOSTS OF CERTAIN PLEASANT MEMORIES DO LINGER-- INAPPROPRIATE AS THEY ARE FOR AN INNOCENT SUCH AS MYSELF...
HMM.
PERHAPS YOU ARE A NEWER ITERATION OF THE GOD OF MISCHIEF, LOKI...
A BRIEF REMINDER: LOKI ANNIHILATED THE NEWER ITERATION OF HIMSELF AND STOLE HIS BODY.
I AM THE CRIME THAT WILL NOT BE FORGIVEN.
...BUT YOU REMAIN LOKI.
AND THUS, THE ONLY ASGARDIAN CAPABLE OF BRINGING LORELEI HOME WHERE SHE TRULY BELONGS.
DO SO.
WE PROMISE YOUR REWARD WILL BE GREAT.
SPLOOSH
GOODIE.
MAYBE I'LL GET A NEW CARPET.
DING DONG

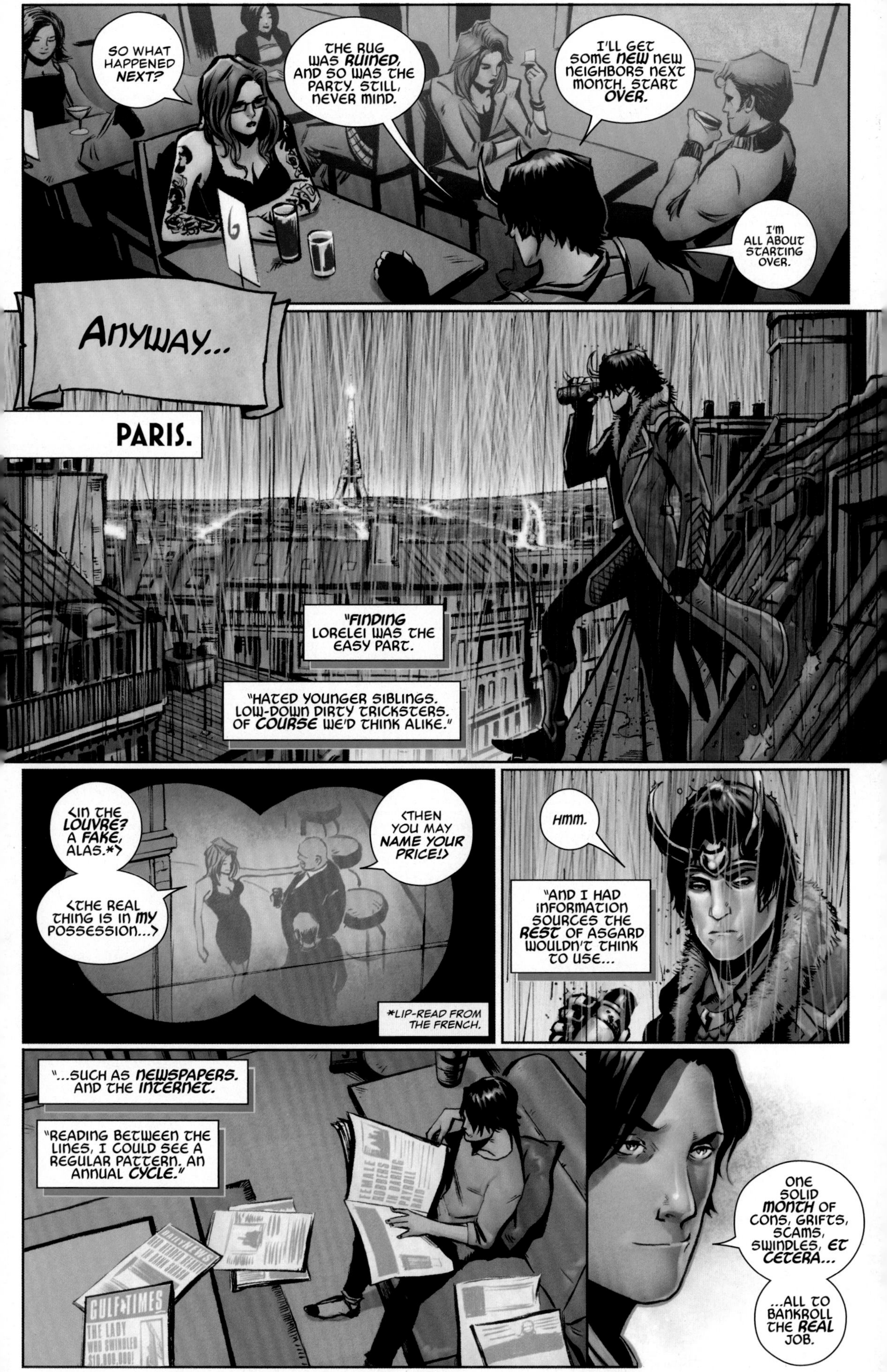
SO WHAT HAPPENED NEXT?
THE RUG WAS RUINED, AND SO WAS THE PARTY. STILL, NEVER MIND.
I'LL GET SOME NEW NEW NEIGHBORS NEXT MONTH. START OVER.
I'M ALL ABOUT STARTING OVER.
ANYWAY...
PARIS.
"FINDING LORELEI WAS THE EASY PART.
"HATED YOUNGER SIBLINGS. LOW-DOWN DIRTY TRICKSTERS. OF COURSE WE'D THINK ALIKE."
<IN THE LOUVRE? A FAKE, ALAS.*>
<THE REAL THING IS IN MY POSSESSION...>
<THEN YOU MAY NAME YOUR PRICE!>
*LIP-READ FROM THE FRENCH.
HMM.
"AND I HAD INFORMATION SOURCES THE REST OF ASGARD WOULDN'T THINK TO USE...
"...SUCH AS NEWSPAPERS. AND THE INTERNET.
"READING BETWEEN THE LINES, I COULD SEE A REGULAR PATTERN. AN ANNUAL CYCLE."
GULF TIMES
THE LADY WHO SWINDLED $10,000,000!
ONE SOLID MONTH OF CONS, GRIFTS, SCAMS, SWINDLES, ET CETERA...
...ALL TO BANKROLL THE REAL JOB.

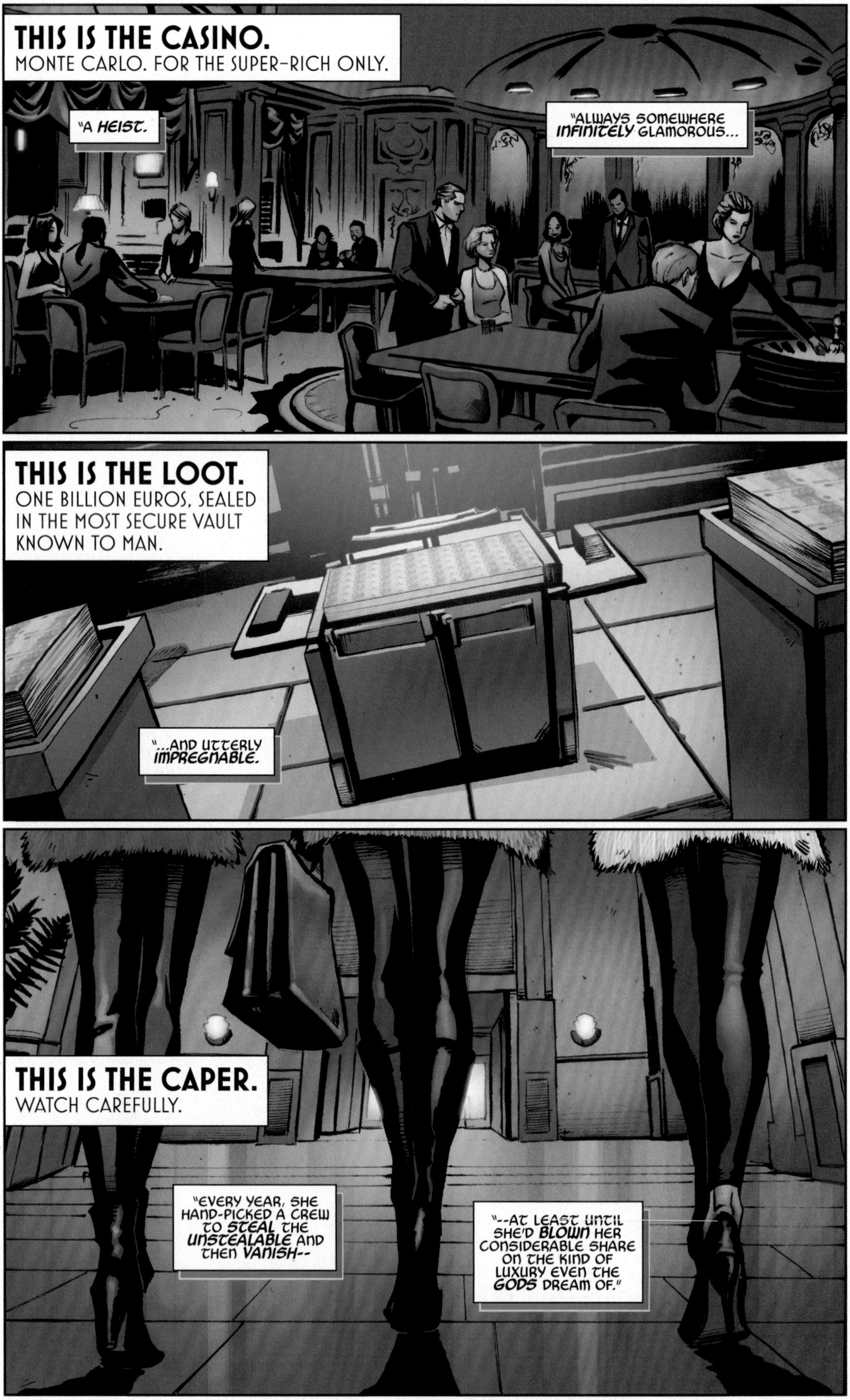
THIS IS THE CASINO.
MONTE CARLO. FOR THE SUPER-RICH ONLY.
"A HEIST.
"ALWAYS SOMEWHERE INFINITELY GLAMOROUS...
THIS IS THE LOOT.
ONE BILLION EUROS, SEALED IN THE MOST SECURE VAULT KNOWN TO MAN.
"...AND UTTERLY IMPREGNABLE.
THIS IS THE CAPER.
WATCH CAREFULLY.
"EVERY YEAR, SHE HAND-PICKED A CREW TO STEAL THE UNSTEALABLE AND THEN VANISH--
"--AT LEAST UNTIL SHE'D BLOWN HER CONSIDERABLE SHARE ON THE KIND OF LUXURY EVEN THE GODS DREAM OF."

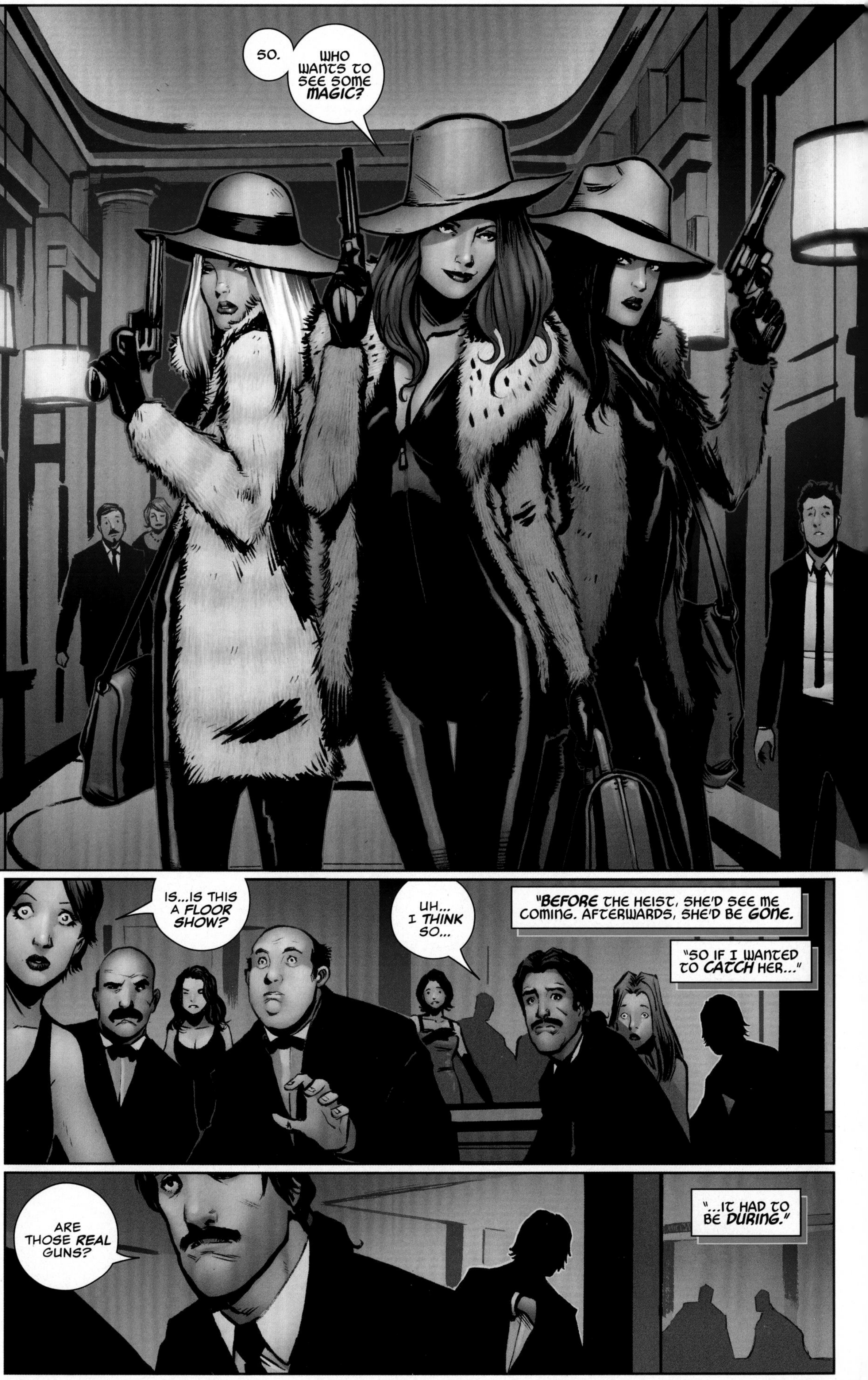

SO.
WHO WANTS TO SEE SOME MAGIC?
IS...IS THIS A FLOOR SHOW?
UH... I THINK SO...
"BEFORE THE HEIST, SHE'D SEE ME COMING. AFTERWARDS, SHE'D BE GONE.
"SO IF I WANTED TO CATCH HER..."
ARE THOSE REAL GUNS?
"...IT HAD TO BE DURING."

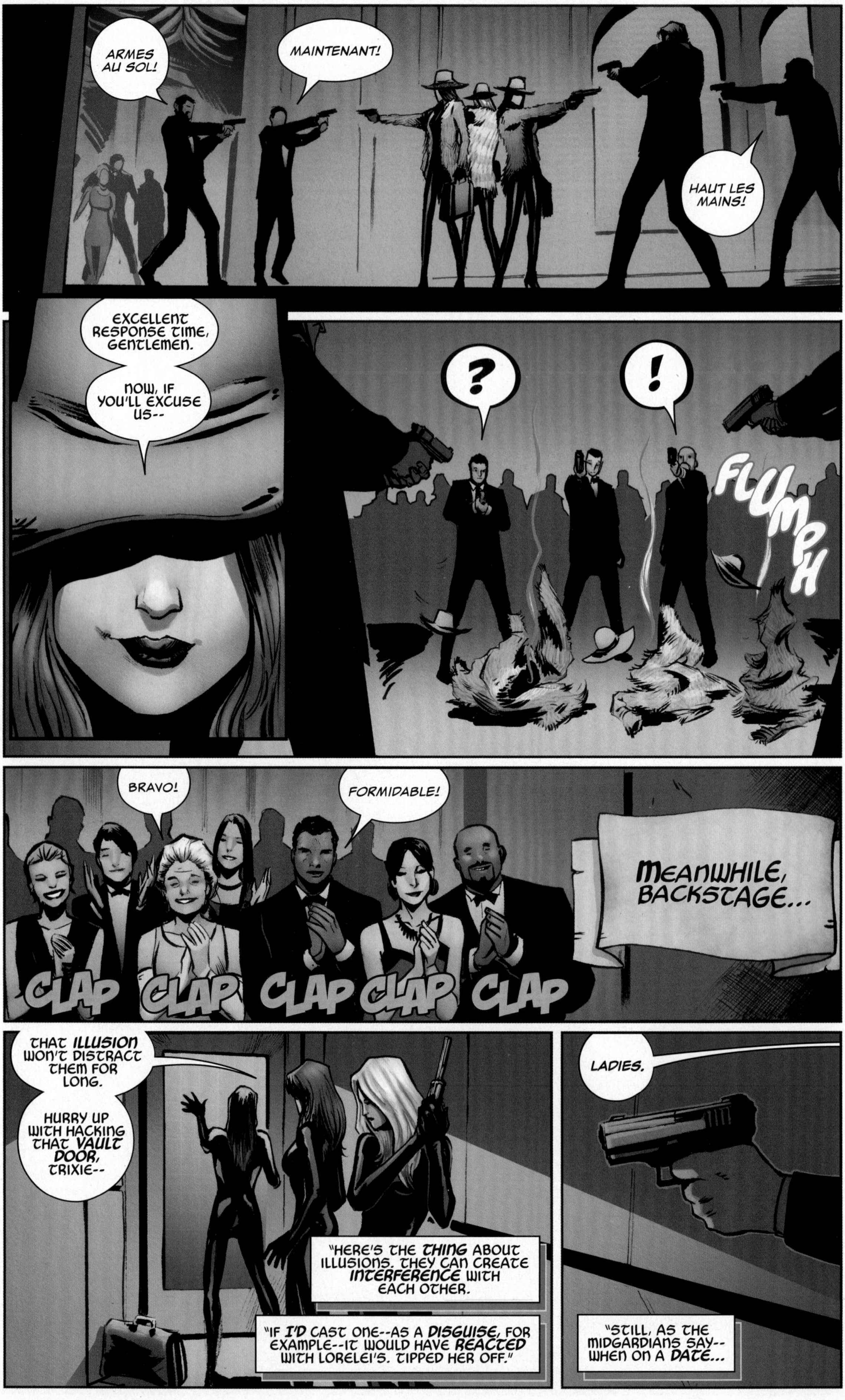
ARMES AU SOL!
MAINTENANT!
HAUT LES MAINS!
EXCELLENT RESPONSE TIME, GENTLEMEN.
NOW, IF YOU'LL EXCUSE US--
?
!
FLUMPH
BRAVO!
FORMIDABLE!
CLAP CLAP CLAP CLAP CLAP
MEANWHILE, BACKSTAGE...
THAT ILLUSION WON'T DISTRACT THEM FOR LONG.
HURRY UP WITH HACKING THAT VAULT DOOR, TRIXIE--
"HERE'S THE THING ABOUT ILLUSIONS. THEY CAN CREATE INTERFERENCE WITH EACH OTHER.
"IF I'D CAST ONE--AS A DISGUISE, FOR EXAMPLE--IT WOULD HAVE REACTED WITH LORELEI'S. TIPPED HER OFF."
LADIES.
"STILL, AS THE MIDGARDIANS SAY-- WHEN ON A DATE...

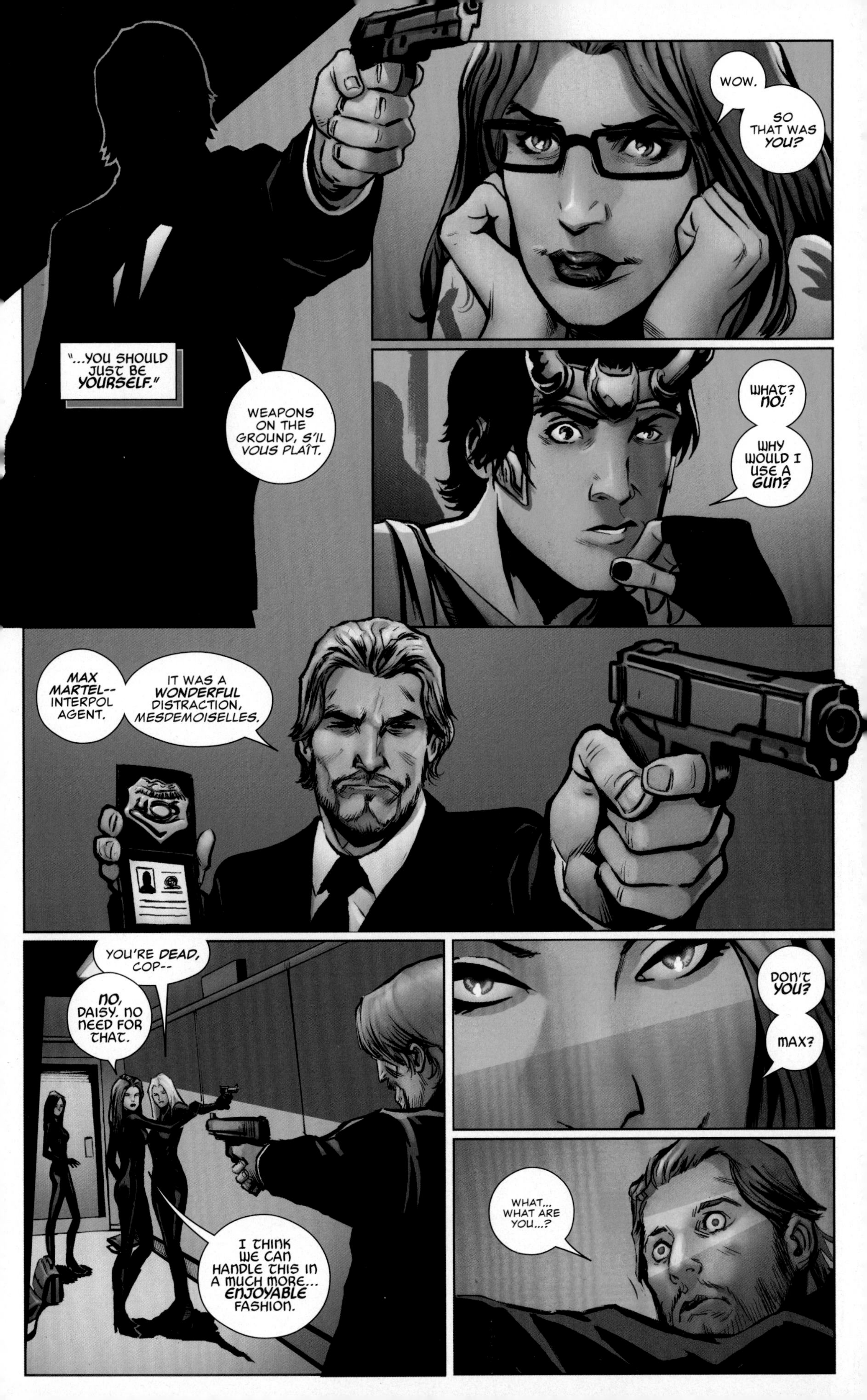
WOW.
SO THAT WAS YOU?
"...YOU SHOULD JUST BE YOURSELF."
WEAPONS ON THE GROUND, S'IL VOUS PLAÎT.
WHAT? NO!
WHY WOULD I USE A GUN?
MAX MARTEL-- INTERPOL AGENT.
IT WAS A WONDERFUL DISTRACTION, MESDEMOISELLES.
YOU'RE DEAD, COP--
NO, DAISY. NO NEED FOR THAT.
I THINK WE CAN HANDLE THIS IN A MUCH MORE... ENJOYABLE FASHION.
DON'T YOU?
MAX?
WHAT... WHAT ARE YOU...?

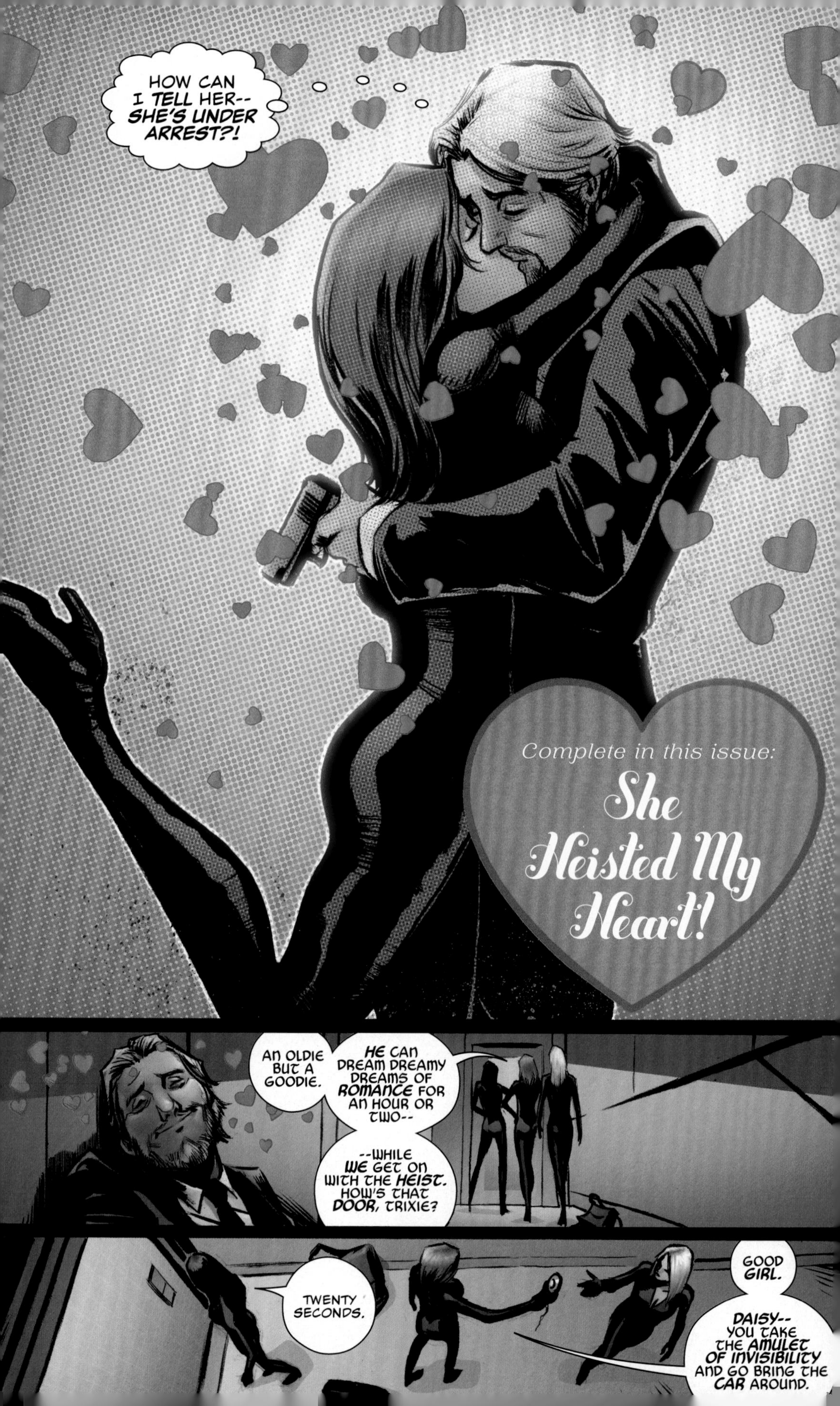
HOW CAN I TELL HER-- SHE'S UNDER ARREST?!
Complete in this issue:
She Heisted My Heart!
AN OLDIE BUT A GOODIE.
HE CAN DREAM DREAMY DREAMS OF ROMANCE FOR AN HOUR OR TWO--
--WHILE WE GET ON WITH THE HEIST. HOW'S THAT DOOR, TRIXIE?
TWENTY SECONDS.
GOOD GIRL.
DAISY-- YOU TAKE THE AMULET OF INVISIBILITY AND GO BRING THE CAR AROUND.

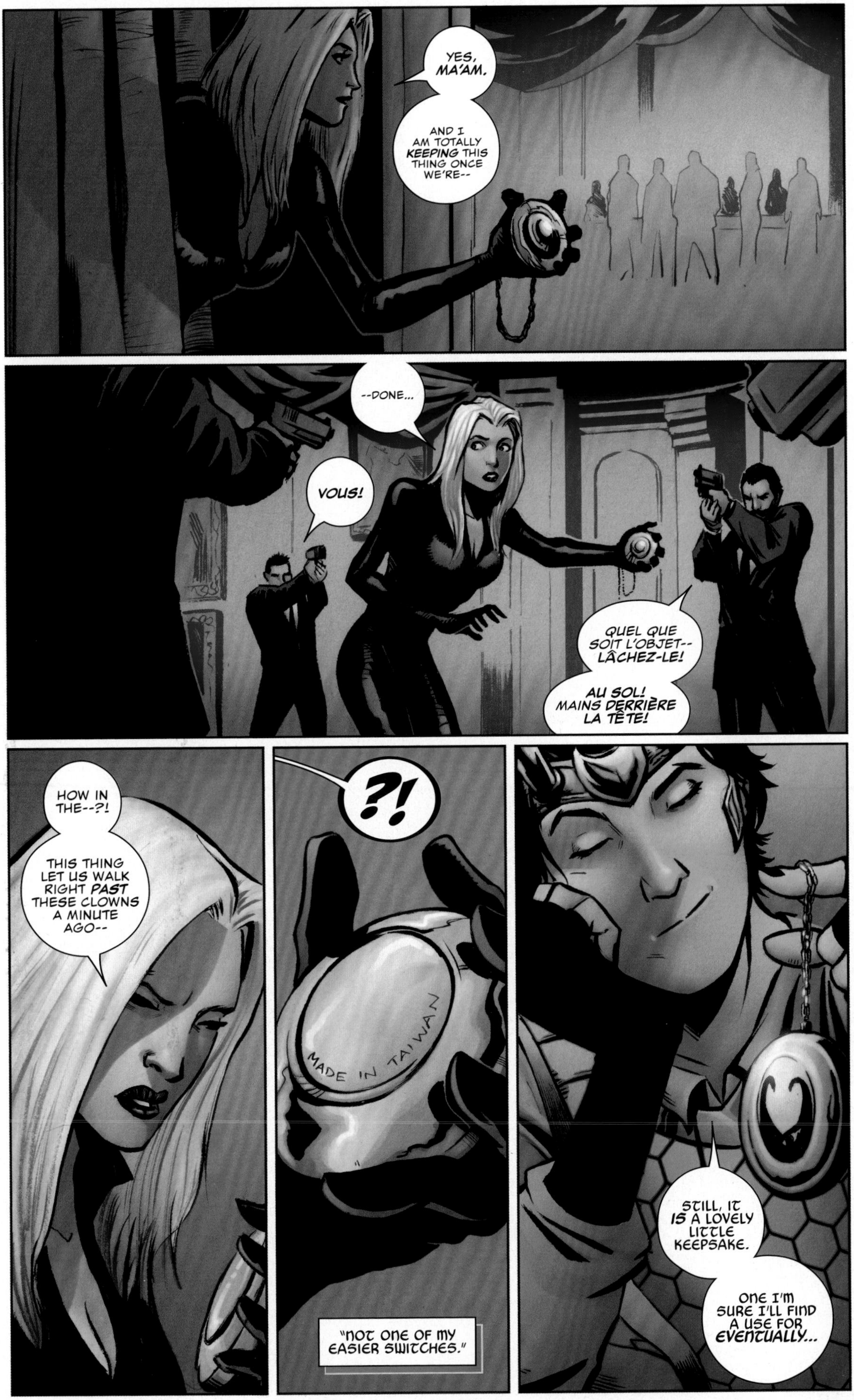
YES, MA'AM.
AND I AM TOTALLY KEEPING THIS THING ONCE WE'RE--
--DONE...
VOUS!
QUEL QUE SOIT L'OBJET-- LÂCHEZ-LE!
AU SOL! MAINS DERRIÈRE LA TÊTE!
HOW IN THE--?!
THIS THING LET US WALK RIGHT PAST THESE CLOWNS A MINUTE AGO--
?!
MADE IN TAIWAN
"NOT ONE OF MY EASIER SWITCHES."
STILL, IT IS A LOVELY LITTLE KEEPSAKE.
ONE I'M SURE I'LL FIND A USE FOR EVENTUALLY...

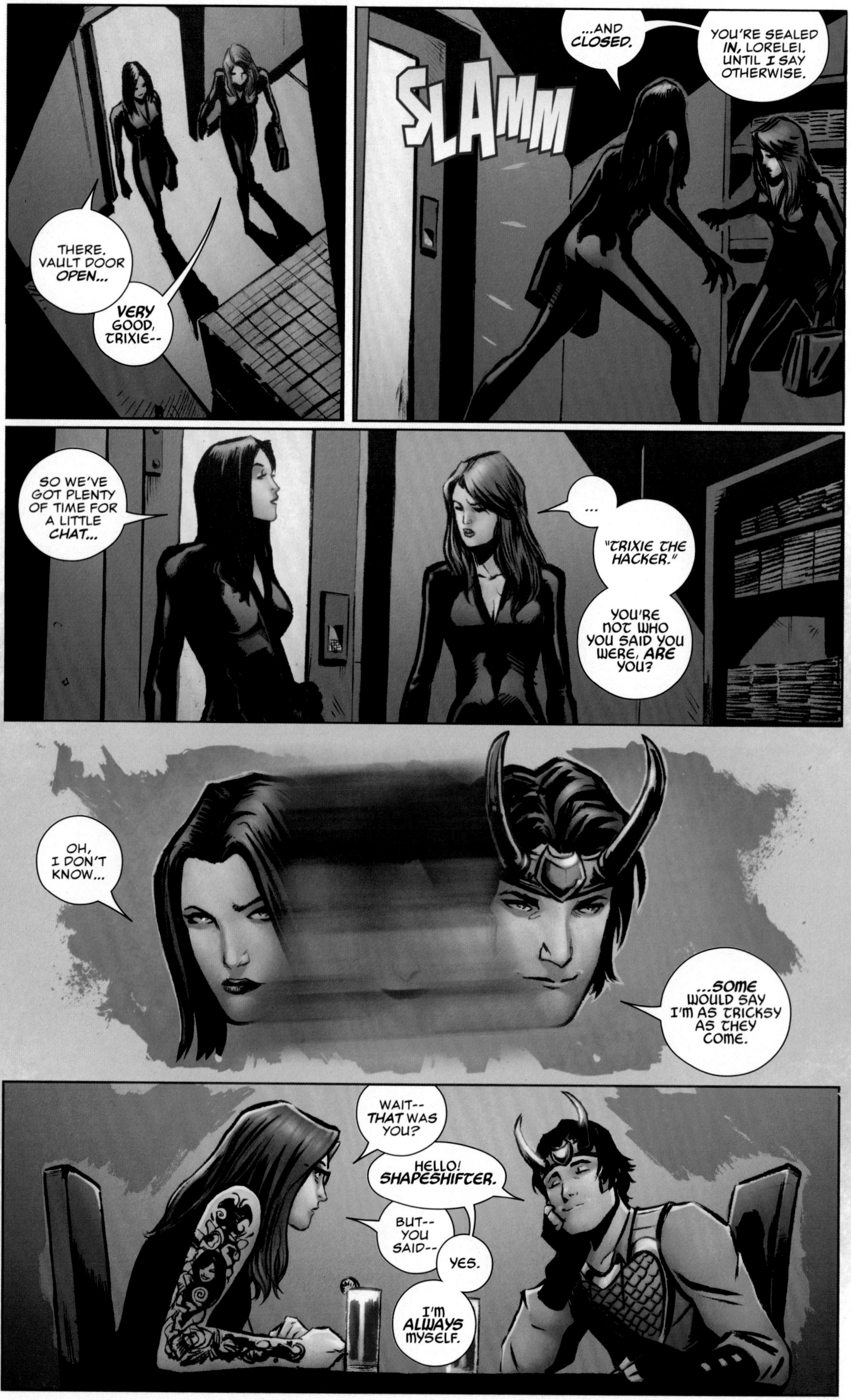

THERE. VAULT DOOR OPEN...
VERY GOOD, TRIXIE--
SLAMM
...AND CLOSED.
YOU'RE SEALED IN, LORELEI. UNTIL I SAY OTHERWISE.
SO WE'VE GOT PLENTY OF TIME FOR A LITTLE CHAT...
...
"TRIXIE THE HACKER."
YOU'RE NOT WHO YOU SAID YOU WERE, ARE YOU?
OH, I DON'T KNOW...
...SOME WOULD SAY I'M AS TRICKSY AS THEY COME.
WAIT-- THAT WAS YOU?
HELLO! SHAPESHIFTER.
BUT-- YOU SAID--
YES.
I'M ALWAYS MYSELF.

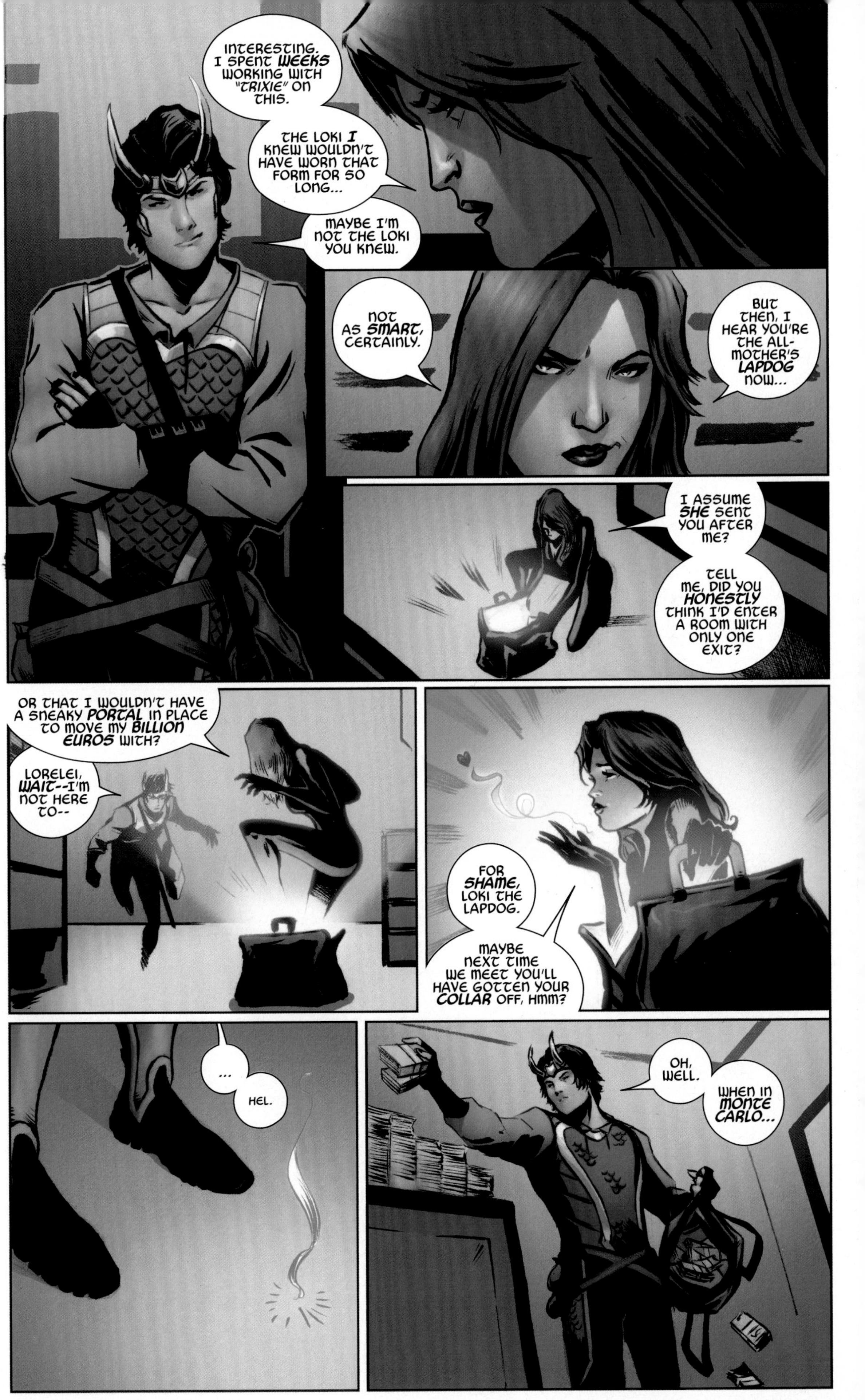

INTERESTING. I SPENT WEEKS WORKING WITH "TRIXIE" ON THIS.
THE LOKI I KNEW WOULDN'T HAVE WORN THAT FORM FOR SO LONG...
MAYBE I'M NOT THE LOKI YOU KNEW.
NOT AS SMART, CERTAINLY.
BUT THEN, I HEAR YOU'RE THE ALL-MOTHER'S LAPDOG NOW...
I ASSUME SHE SENT YOU AFTER ME?
TELL ME, DID YOU HONESTLY THINK I'D ENTER A ROOM WITH ONLY ONE EXIT?
OR THAT I WOULDN'T HAVE A SNEAKY PORTAL IN PLACE TO MOVE MY BILLION EUROS WITH?
LORELEI, WAIT--I'M NOT HERE TO--
FOR SHAME, LOKI THE LAPDOG.
MAYBE NEXT TIME WE MEET YOU'LL HAVE GOTTEN YOUR COLLAR OFF, HMM?
...
HEL.
OH, WELL.
WHEN IN MONTE CARLO...

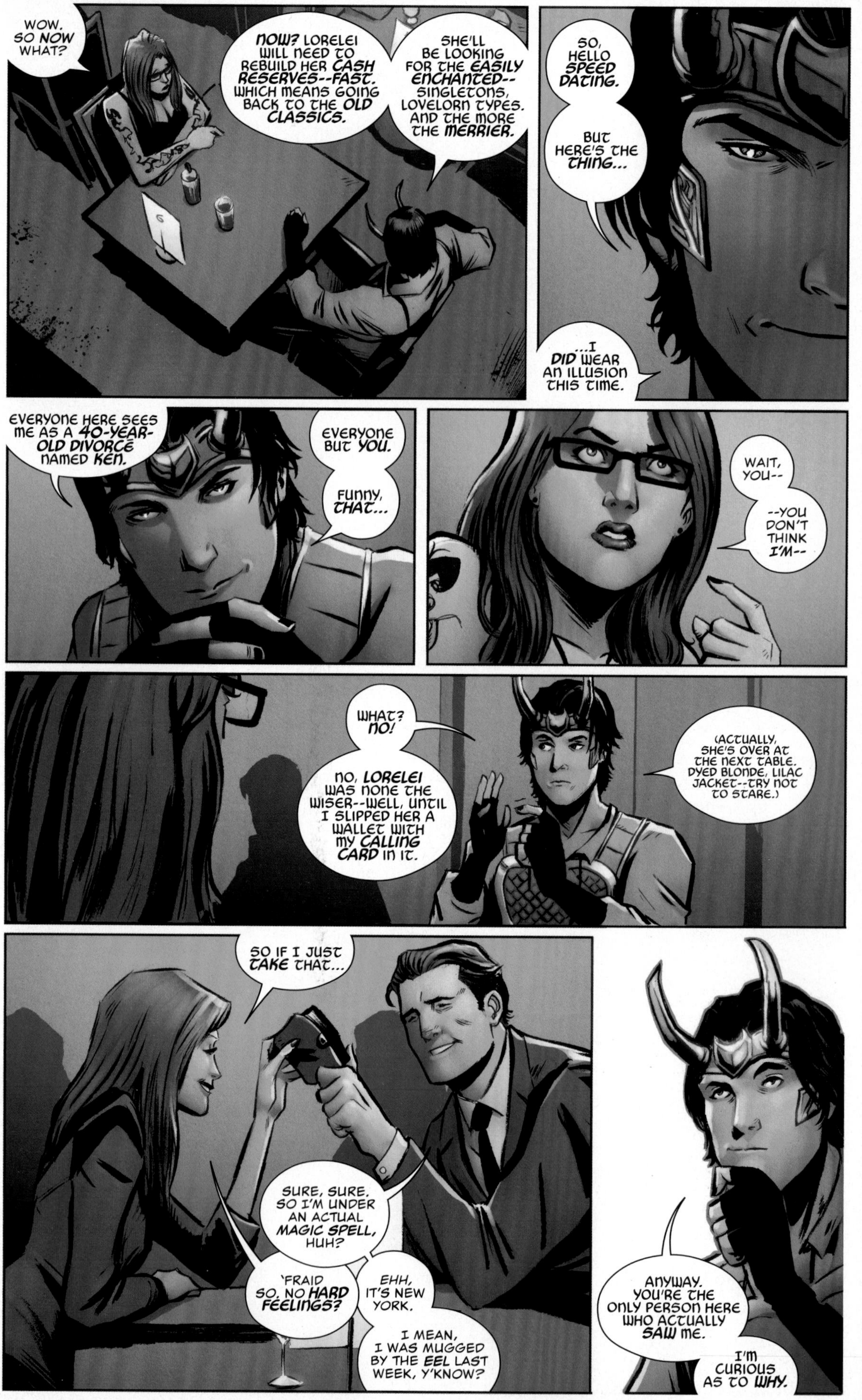
WOW. SO NOW WHAT?
NOW? LORELEI WILL NEED TO REBUILD HER CASH RESERVES--FAST. WHICH MEANS GOING BACK TO THE OLD CLASSICS.
SHE'LL BE LOOKING FOR THE EASILY ENCHANTED--SINGLETONS, LOVELORN TYPES. AND THE MORE THE MERRIER.
SO, HELLO SPEED DATING.
BUT HERE'S THE THING...
...I DID WEAR AN ILLUSION THIS TIME.
EVERYONE HERE SEES ME AS A 40-YEAR-OLD DIVORCÉ NAMED KEN.
EVERYONE BUT YOU.
FUNNY, THAT...
WAIT, YOU--
--YOU DON'T THINK I'M--
WHAT? NO!
NO, LORELEI WAS NONE THE WISER--WELL, UNTIL I SLIPPED HER A WALLET WITH MY CALLING CARD IN IT.
(ACTUALLY, SHE'S OVER AT THE NEXT TABLE. DYED BLONDE, LILAC JACKET--TRY NOT TO STARE.)
SO IF I JUST TAKE THAT...
SURE, SURE. SO I'M UNDER AN ACTUAL MAGIC SPELL, HUH?
'FRAID SO. NO HARD FEELINGS?
EHH, IT'S NEW YORK.
I MEAN, I WAS MUGGED BY THE EEL LAST WEEK, Y'KNOW?
ANYWAY. YOU'RE THE ONLY PERSON HERE WHO ACTUALLY SAW ME.
I'M CURIOUS AS TO WHY.

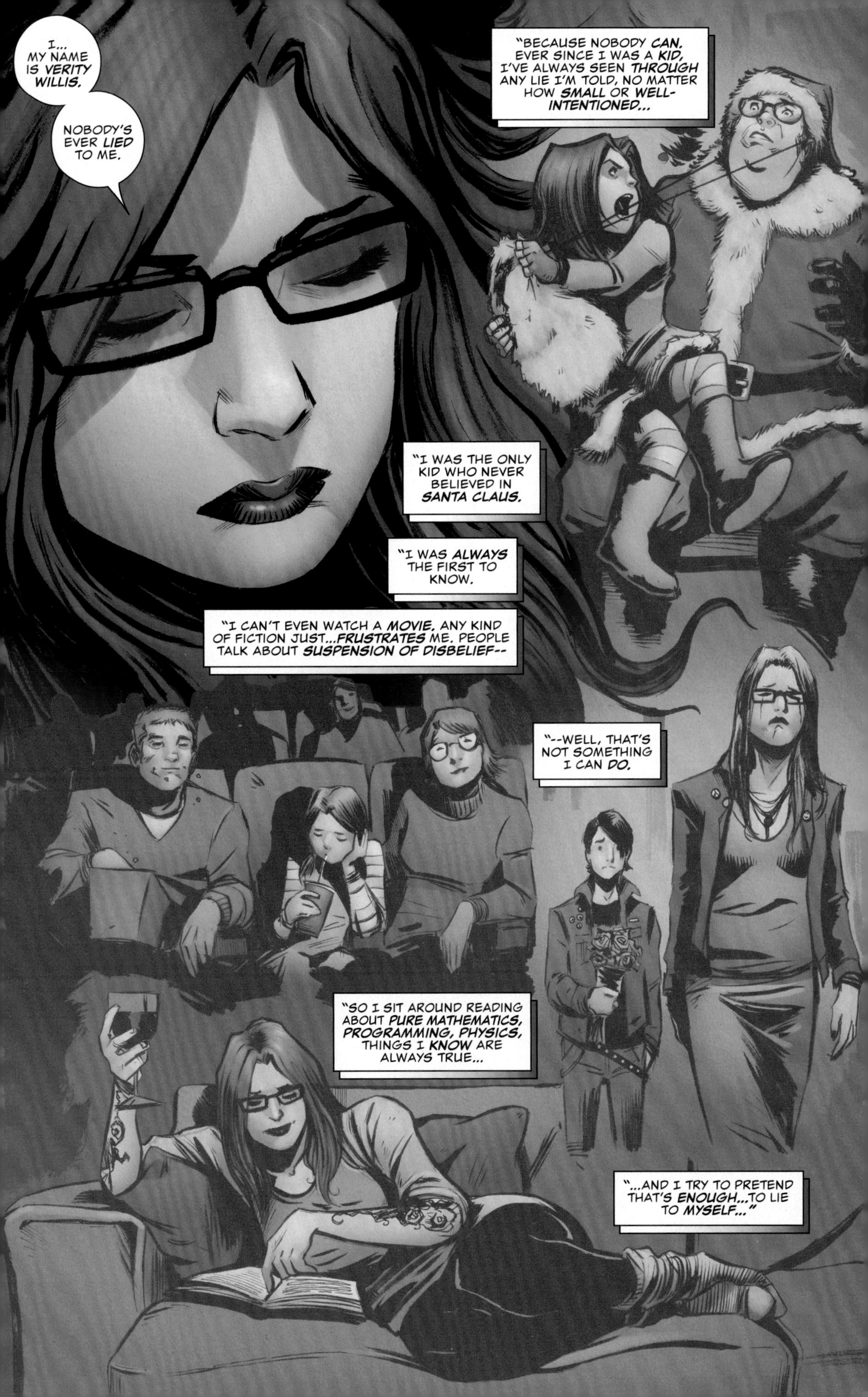
I... MY NAME IS VERITY WILLIS.
NOBODY'S EVER LIED TO ME.
"BECAUSE NOBODY CAN. EVER SINCE I WAS A KID, I'VE ALWAYS SEEN THROUGH ANY LIE I'M TOLD, NO MATTER HOW SMALL OR WELL-INTENTIONED...
"I WAS THE ONLY KID WHO NEVER BELIEVED IN SANTA CLAUS.
"I WAS ALWAYS THE FIRST TO KNOW.
"I CAN'T EVEN WATCH A MOVIE. ANY KIND OF FICTION JUST...FRUSTRATES ME. PEOPLE TALK ABOUT SUSPENSION OF DISBELIEF--
"--WELL, THAT'S NOT SOMETHING I CAN DO.
"SO I SIT AROUND READING ABOUT PURE MATHEMATICS, PROGRAMMING, PHYSICS, THINGS I KNOW ARE ALWAYS TRUE...
"...AND I TRY TO PRETEND THAT'S ENOUGH...TO LIE TO MYSELF..."

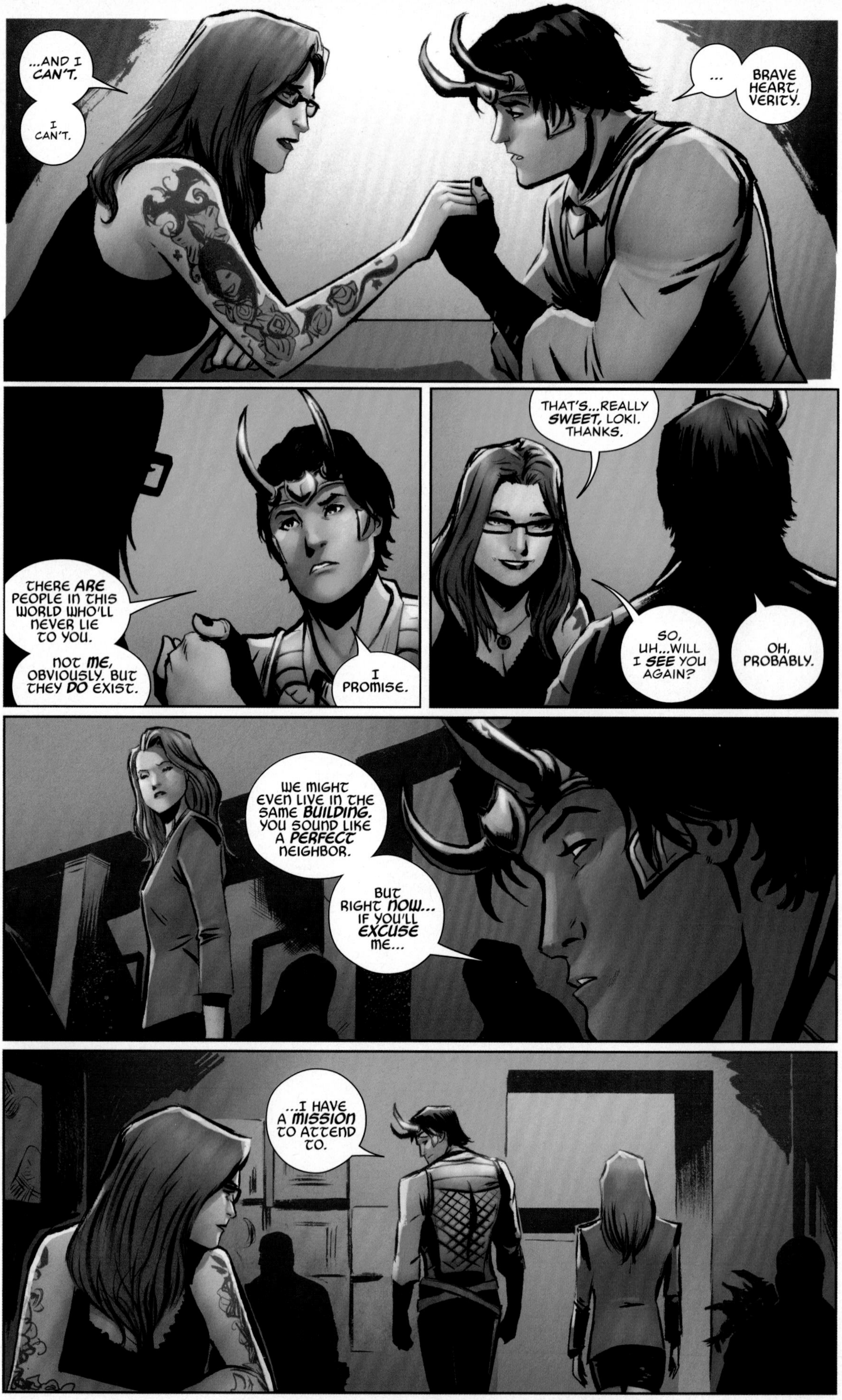
...AND I CAN'T.
I CAN'T.
... BRAVE HEART, VERITY.
THERE ARE PEOPLE IN THIS WORLD WHO'LL NEVER LIE TO YOU.
NOT ME, OBVIOUSLY. BUT THEY DO EXIST.
I PROMISE.
THAT'S...REALLY SWEET, LOKI. THANKS.
SO, UH...WILL I SEE YOU AGAIN?
OH, PROBABLY.
WE MIGHT EVEN LIVE IN THE SAME BUILDING. YOU SOUND LIKE A PERFECT NEIGHBOR.
BUT RIGHT NOW... IF YOU'LL EXCUSE ME...
...I HAVE A MISSION TO ATTEND TO.

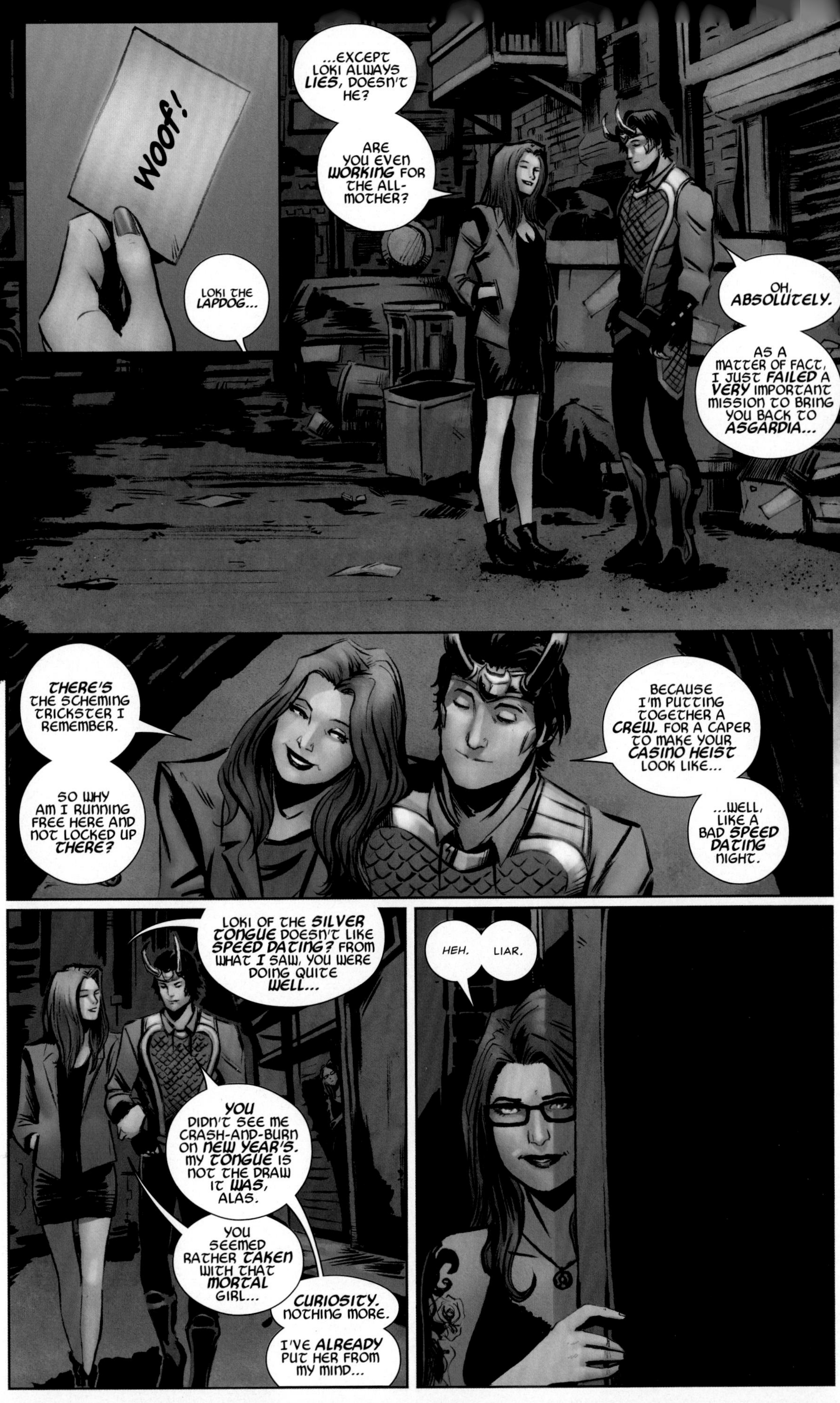

WOOF!
LOKI THE LAPDOG...
...EXCEPT LOKI ALWAYS LIES, DOESN'T HE?
ARE YOU EVEN WORKING FOR THE ALL-MOTHER?
OH, ABSOLUTELY.
AS A MATTER OF FACT, I JUST FAILED A VERY IMPORTANT MISSION TO BRING YOU BACK TO ASGARDIA...
THERE'S THE SCHEMING TRICKSTER I REMEMBER.
SO WHY AM I RUNNING FREE HERE AND NOT LOCKED UP THERE?
BECAUSE I'M PUTTING TOGETHER A CREW. FOR A CAPER TO MAKE YOUR CASINO HEIST LOOK LIKE...
...WELL, LIKE A BAD SPEED DATING NIGHT.
LOKI OF THE SILVER TONGUE DOESN'T LIKE SPEED DATING? FROM WHAT I SAW, YOU WERE DOING QUITE WELL...
YOU DIDN'T SEE ME CRASH-AND-BURN ON NEW YEAR'S. MY TONGUE IS NOT THE DRAW IT WAS, ALAS.
YOU SEEMED RATHER TAKEN WITH THAT MORTAL GIRL...
CURIOSITY. NOTHING MORE.
I'VE ALREADY PUT HER FROM MY MIND...
HEH.
LIAR.

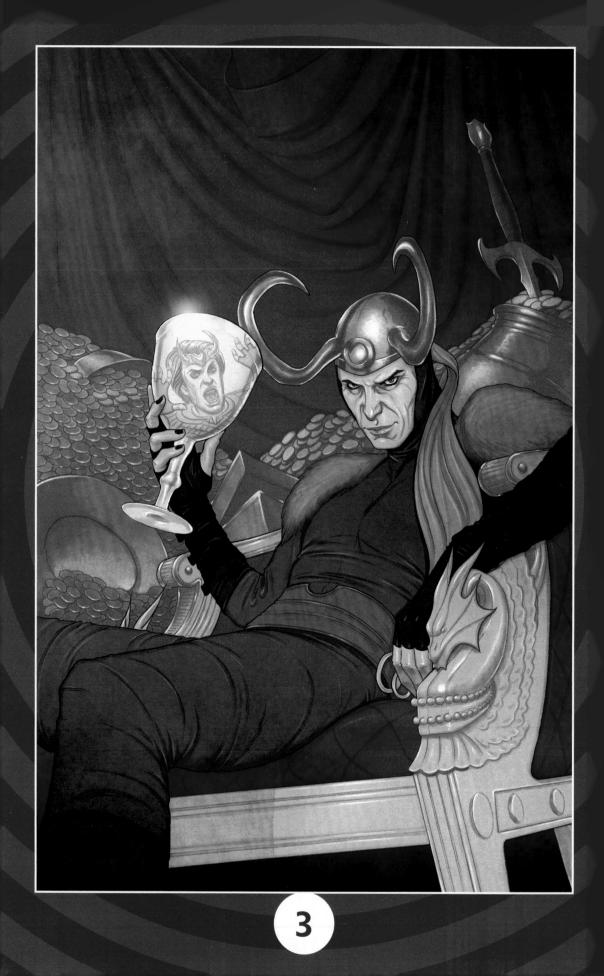

3

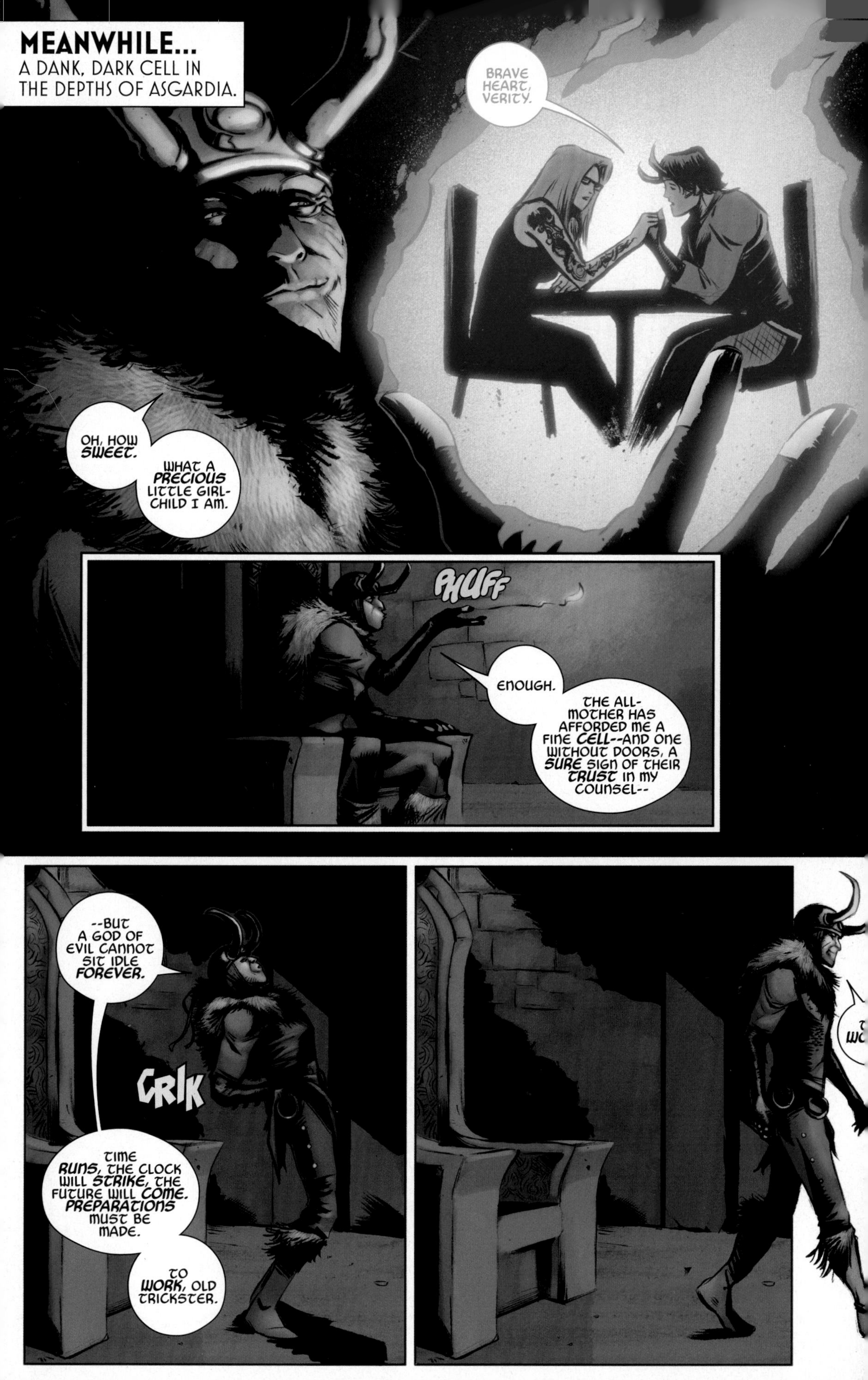
MEANWHILE... A DANK, DARK CELL IN THE DEPTHS OF ASGARDIA.
BRAVE HEART, VERITY.
OH, HOW SWEET.
WHAT A PRECIOUS LITTLE GIRL-CHILD I AM.
PHUFF
ENOUGH.
THE ALL-MOTHER HAS AFFORDED ME A FINE CELL--AND ONE WITHOUT DOORS, A SURE SIGN OF THEIR TRUST IN MY COUNSEL--
--BUT A GOD OF EVIL CANNOT SIT IDLE FOREVER.
CRIK
TIME RUNS, THE CLOCK WILL STRIKE, THE FUTURE WILL COME. PREPARATIONS MUST BE MADE.
TO WORK, OLD TRICKSTER.

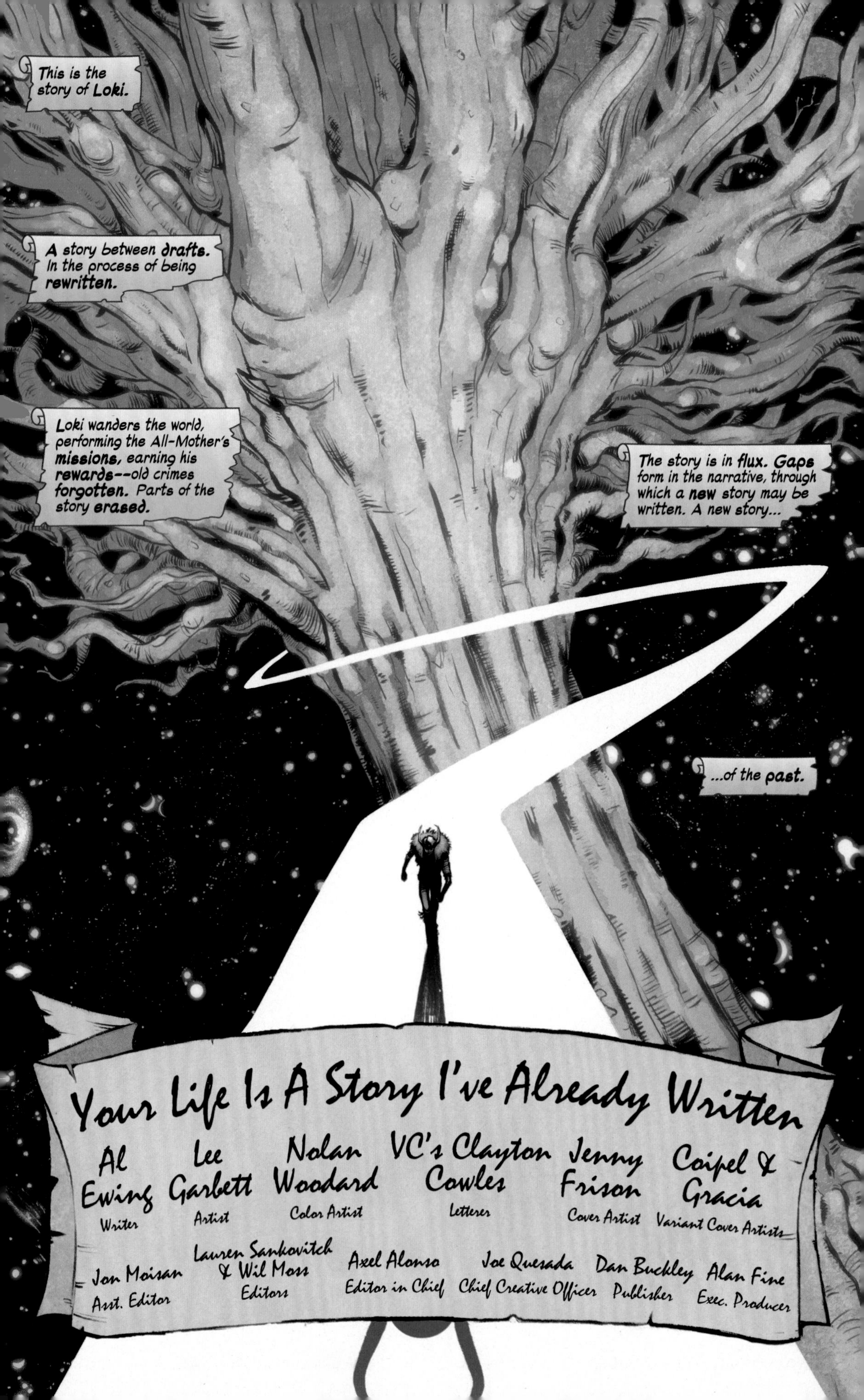
This is the story of Loki.
A story between drafts. In the process of being rewritten.
Loki wanders the world, performing the All-Mother's missions, earning his rewards--old crimes forgotten. Parts of the story erased.
The story is in flux. Gaps form in the narrative, through which a new story may be written. A new story...
...of the past.
Your Life Is A Story I've Already Written
Al Ewing Writer
Lee Garbett Artist
Nolan Woodard Color Artist
VC's Clayton Cowles Letterer
Jenny Frison Cover Artist
Coipel & Gracia Variant Cover Artists
Jon Moisan Asst. Editor
Lauren Sankovitch & Wil Moss Editors
Axel Alonso Editor in Chief
Joe Quesada Chief Creative Officer
Dan Buckley Publisher
Alan Fine Exec. Producer

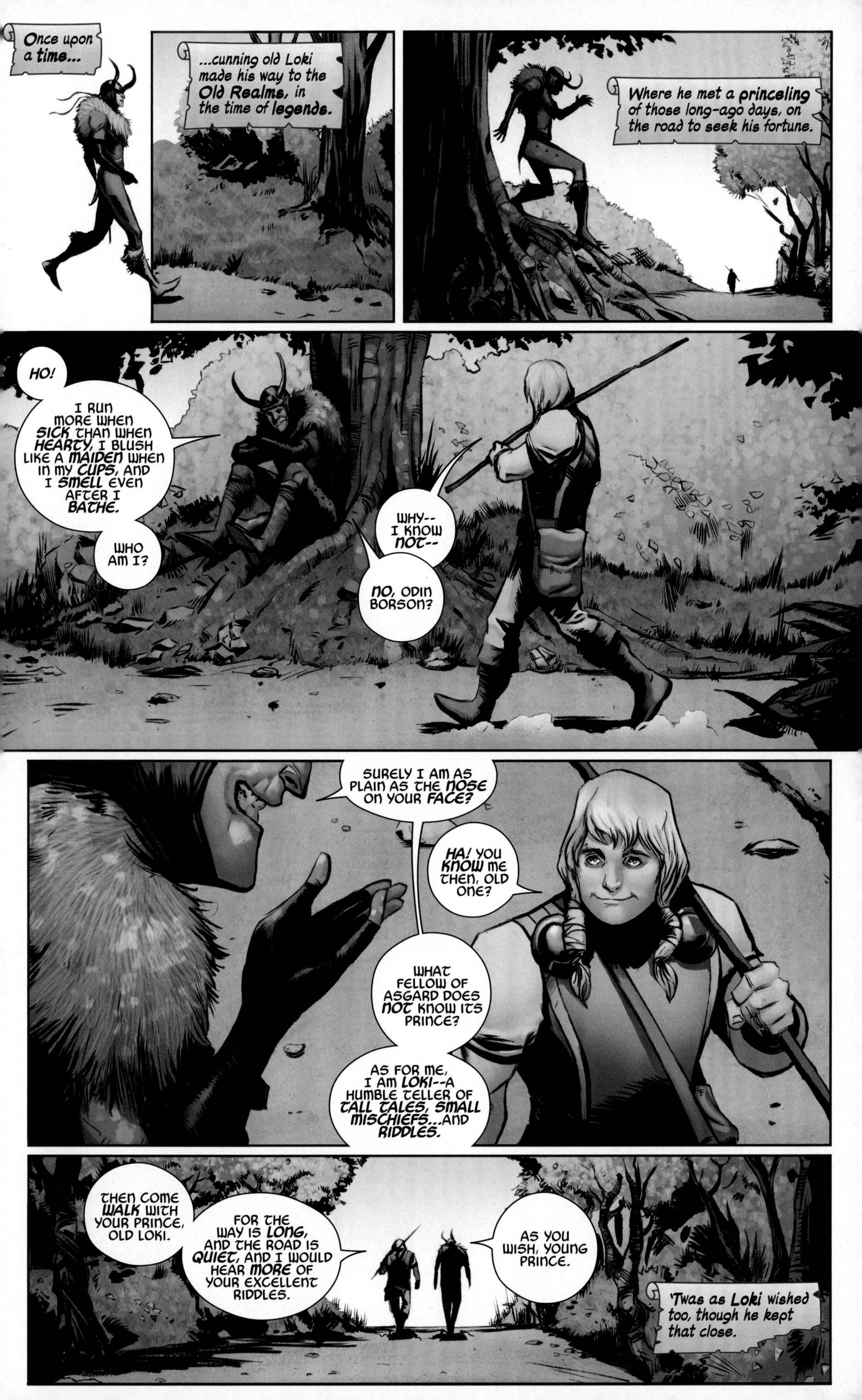

Once upon a time...
...cunning old Loki made his way to the Old Realms, in the time of legends.
Where he met a princeling of those long-ago days, on the road to seek his fortune.
HO!
I RUN MORE WHEN SICK THAN WHEN HEARTY, I BLUSH LIKE A MAIDEN WHEN IN MY CUPS, AND I SMELL EVEN AFTER I BATHE.
WHO AM I?
WHY-- I KNOW NOT--
NO, ODIN BORSON?
SURELY I AM AS PLAIN AS THE NOSE ON YOUR FACE?
HA! YOU KNOW ME THEN, OLD ONE?
WHAT FELLOW OF ASGARD DOES NOT KNOW ITS PRINCE?
AS FOR ME, I AM LOKI--A HUMBLE TELLER OF TALL TALES, SMALL MISCHIEFS...AND RIDDLES.
THEN COME WALK WITH YOUR PRINCE, OLD LOKI.
FOR THE WAY IS LONG, AND THE ROAD IS QUIET, AND I WOULD HEAR MORE OF YOUR EXCELLENT RIDDLES.
AS YOU WISH, YOUNG PRINCE.
'Twas as Loki wished too, though he kept that close.

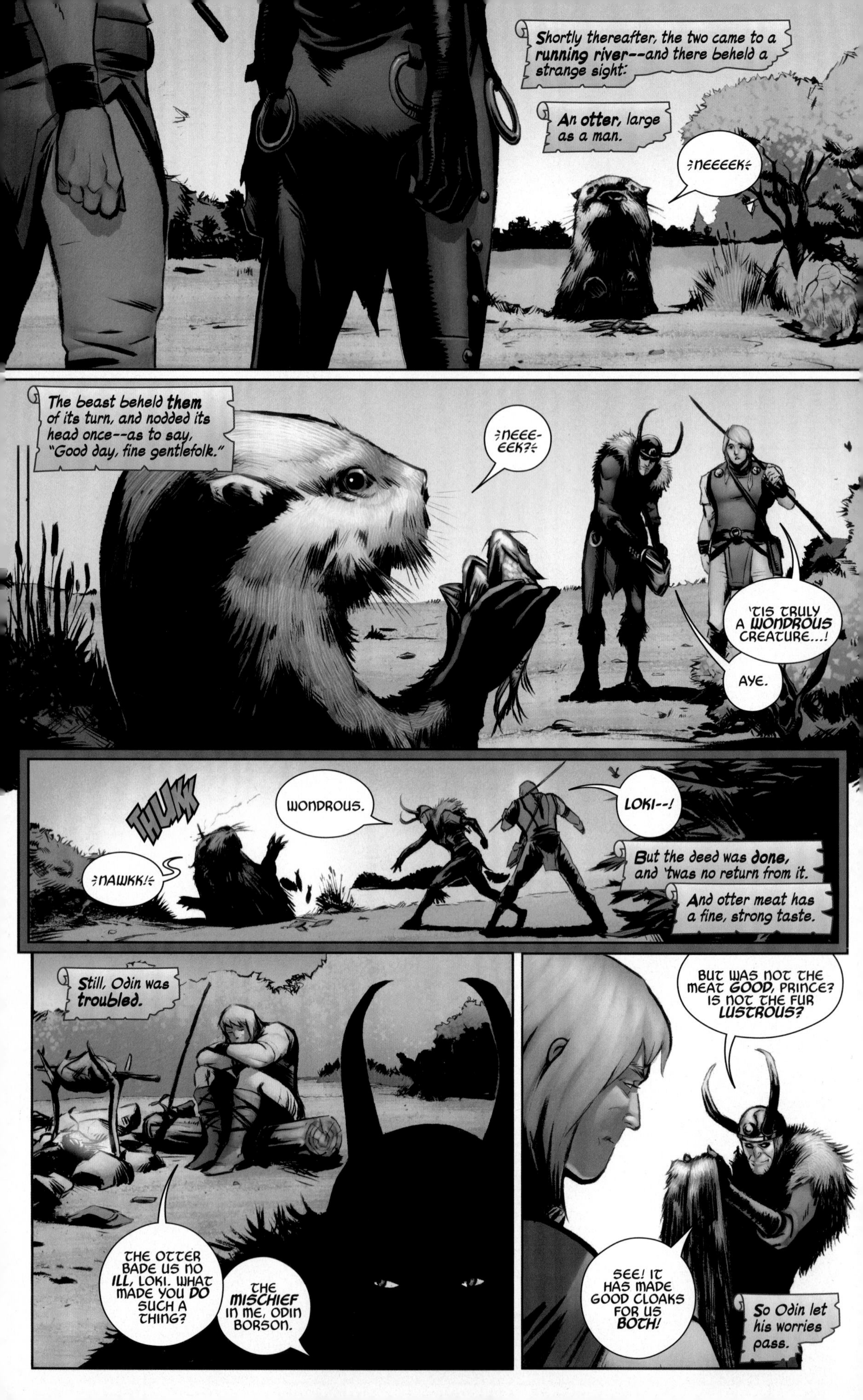
Shortly thereafter, the two came to a running river--and there beheld a strange sight:
An otter, large as a man.
NEEEEK
The beast beheld them of its turn, and nodded its head once--as to say, "Good day, fine gentlefolk."
NEEE-EEK?
'TIS TRULY A WONDROUS CREATURE...!
AYE.
THUKK
NAWKK!
WONDROUS.
LOKI--!
But the deed was done, and 'twas no return from it.
And otter meat has a fine, strong taste.
Still, Odin was troubled.
THE OTTER BADE US NO ILL, LOKI. WHAT MADE YOU DO SUCH A THING?
THE MISCHIEF IN ME, ODIN BORSON.
BUT WAS NOT THE MEAT GOOD, PRINCE? IS NOT THE FUR LUSTROUS?
SEE! IT HAS MADE GOOD CLOAKS FOR US BOTH!
So Odin let his worries pass.

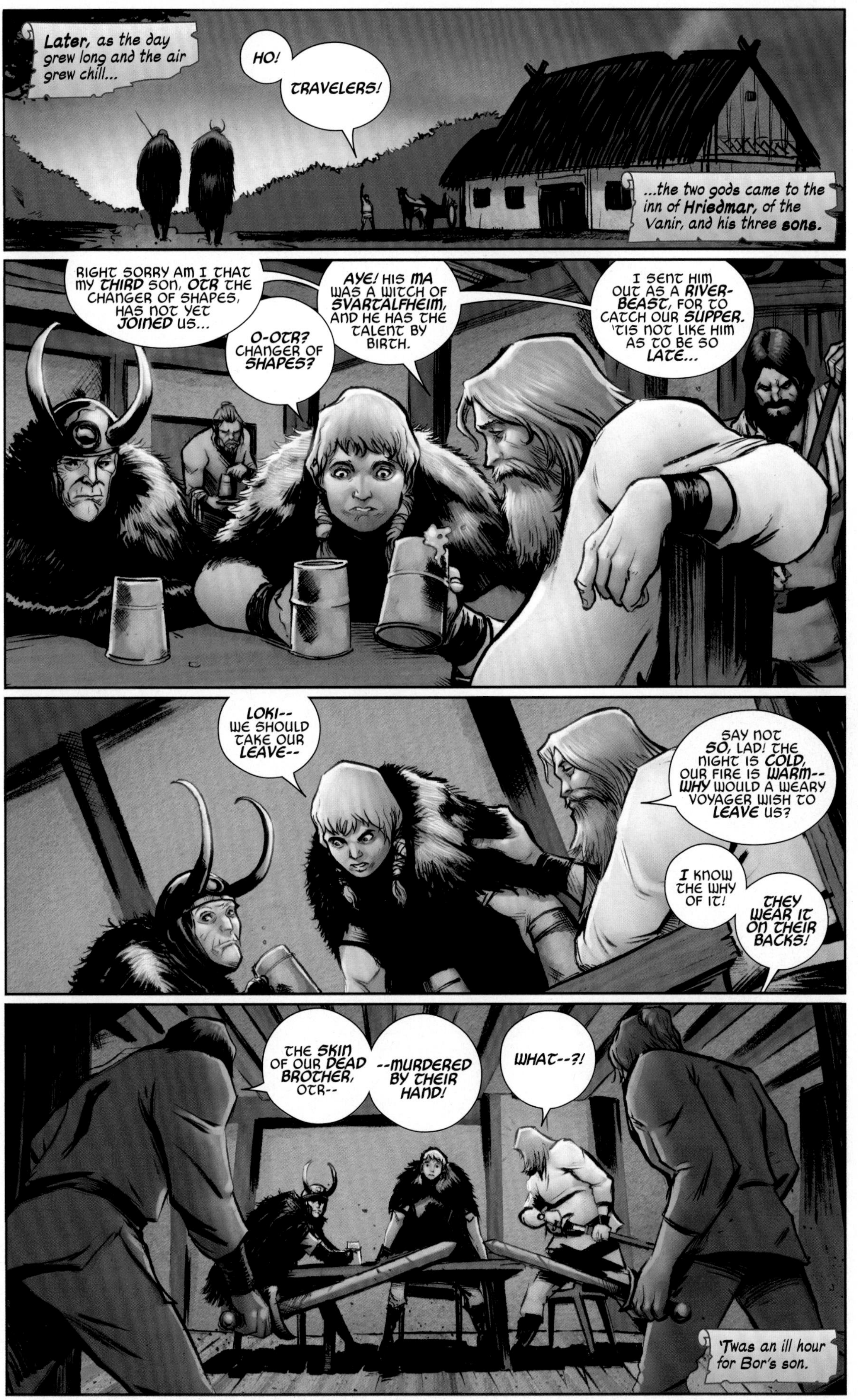
Later, as the day grew long and the air grew chill...
HO!
TRAVELERS!
...the two gods came to the inn of Hriedmar, of the Vanir, and his three sons.
RIGHT SORRY AM I THAT MY THIRD SON, OTR THE CHANGER OF SHAPES, HAS NOT YET JOINED US...
O-OTR? CHANGER OF SHAPES?
AYE! HIS MA WAS A WITCH OF SVARTALFHEIM, AND HE HAS THE TALENT BY BIRTH.
I SENT HIM OUT AS A RIVER-BEAST, FOR TO CATCH OUR SUPPER. 'TIS NOT LIKE HIM AS TO BE SO LATE...
LOKI-- WE SHOULD TAKE OUR LEAVE--
SAY NOT SO, LAD! THE NIGHT IS COLD, OUR FIRE IS WARM-- WHY WOULD A WEARY VOYAGER WISH TO LEAVE US?
I KNOW THE WHY OF IT!
THEY WEAR IT ON THEIR BACKS!
THE SKIN OF OUR DEAD BROTHER, OTR--
--MURDERED BY THEIR HAND!
WHAT--?!
'Twas an ill hour for Bor's son.

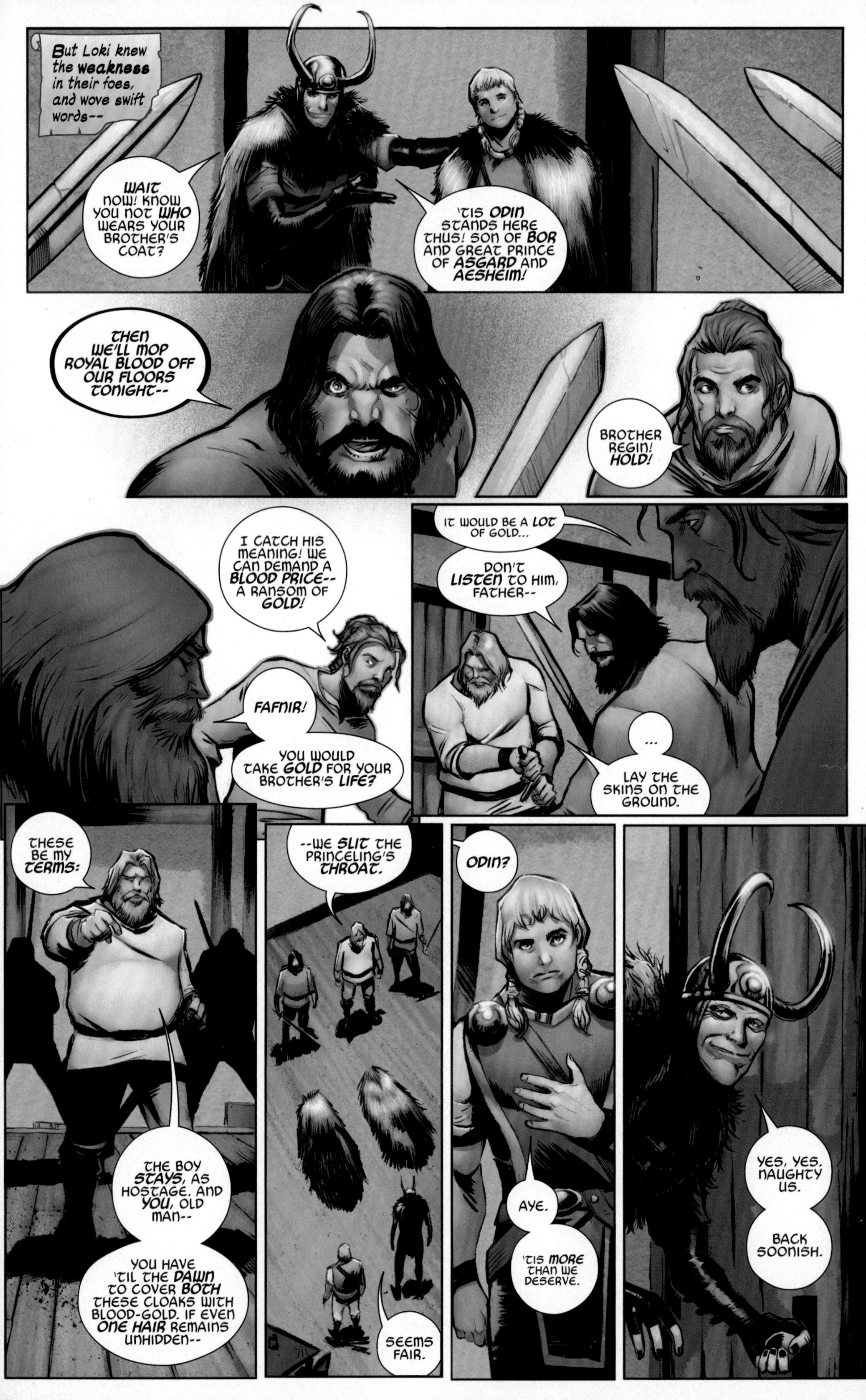
But Loki knew the weakness in their foes, and wove swift words--
WAIT NOW! KNOW YOU NOT WHO WEARS YOUR BROTHER'S COAT?
'TIS ODIN STANDS HERE THUS! SON OF BOR AND GREAT PRINCE OF ASGARD AND AESHEIM!
THEN WE'LL MOP ROYAL BLOOD OFF OUR FLOORS TONIGHT--
BROTHER REGIN! HOLD!
I CATCH HIS MEANING! WE CAN DEMAND A BLOOD PRICE-- A RANSOM OF GOLD!
FAFNIR!
YOU WOULD TAKE GOLD FOR YOUR BROTHER'S LIFE?
IT WOULD BE A LOT OF GOLD...
DON'T LISTEN TO HIM, FATHER--
...
LAY THE SKINS ON THE GROUND.
THESE BE MY TERMS:
THE BOY STAYS, AS HOSTAGE. AND YOU, OLD MAN--
YOU HAVE 'TIL THE DAWN TO COVER BOTH THESE CLOAKS WITH BLOOD-GOLD. IF EVEN ONE HAIR REMAINS UNHIDDEN--
--WE SLIT THE PRINCELING'S THROAT.
SEEMS FAIR.
ODIN?
AYE.
'TIS MORE THAN WE DESERVE.
YES, YES. NAUGHTY US.
BACK SOONISH.

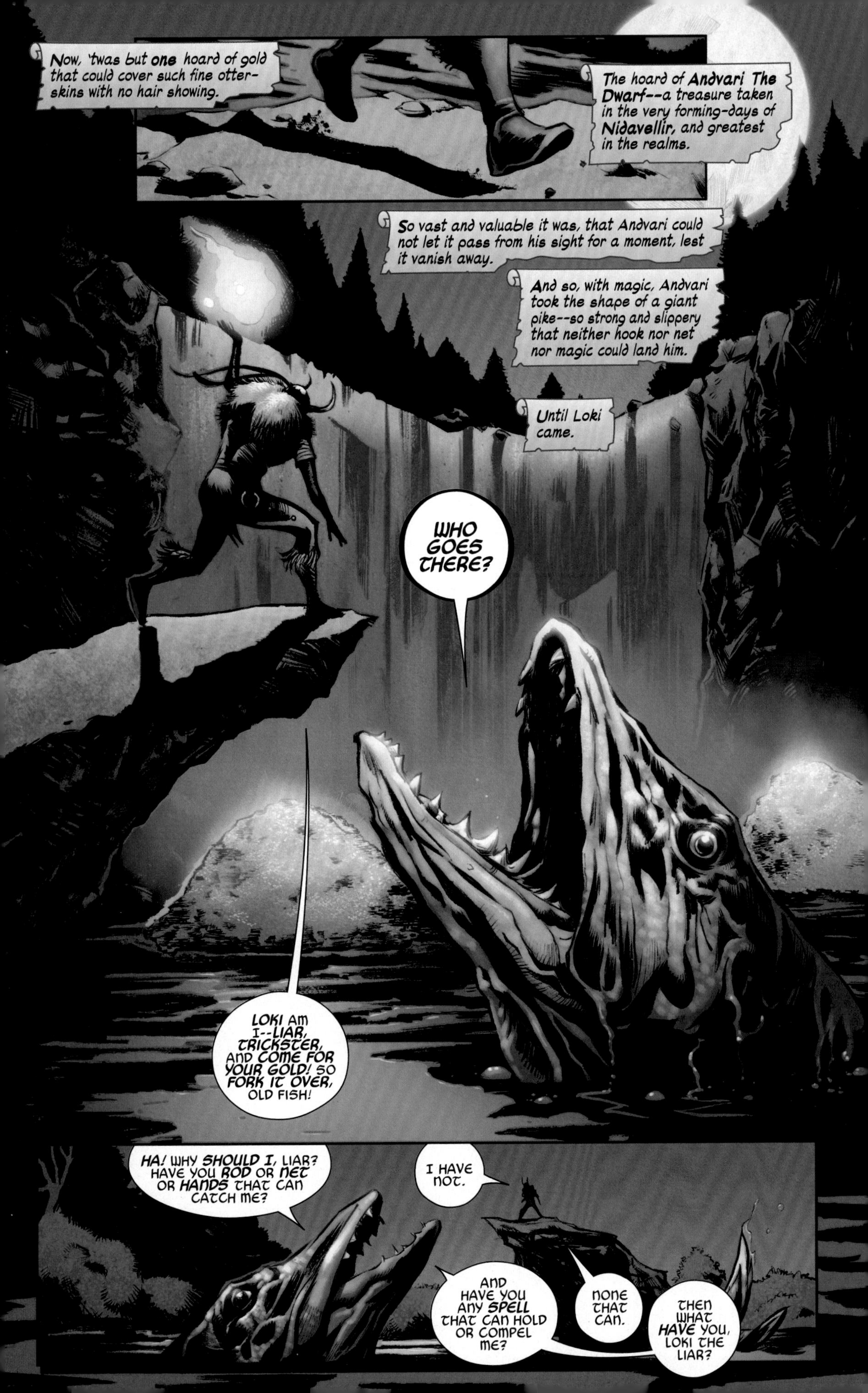
Now, 'twas but one hoard of gold that could cover such fine otter-skins with no hair showing.
The hoard of Andvari The Dwarf--a treasure taken in the very forming-days of Nidavellir, and greatest in the realms.
So vast and valuable it was, that Andvari could not let it pass from his sight for a moment, lest it vanish away.
And so, with magic, Andvari took the shape of a giant pike--so strong and slippery that neither hook nor net nor magic could land him.
Until Loki came.
WHO GOES THERE?
LOKI AM I--LIAR, TRICKSTER, AND COME FOR YOUR GOLD! SO FORK IT OVER, OLD FISH!
HA! WHY SHOULD I, LIAR? HAVE YOU ROD OR NET OR HANDS THAT CAN CATCH ME?
I HAVE NOT.
AND HAVE YOU ANY SPELL THAT CAN HOLD OR COMPEL ME?
NONE THAT CAN.
THEN WHAT HAVE YOU, LOKI THE LIAR?

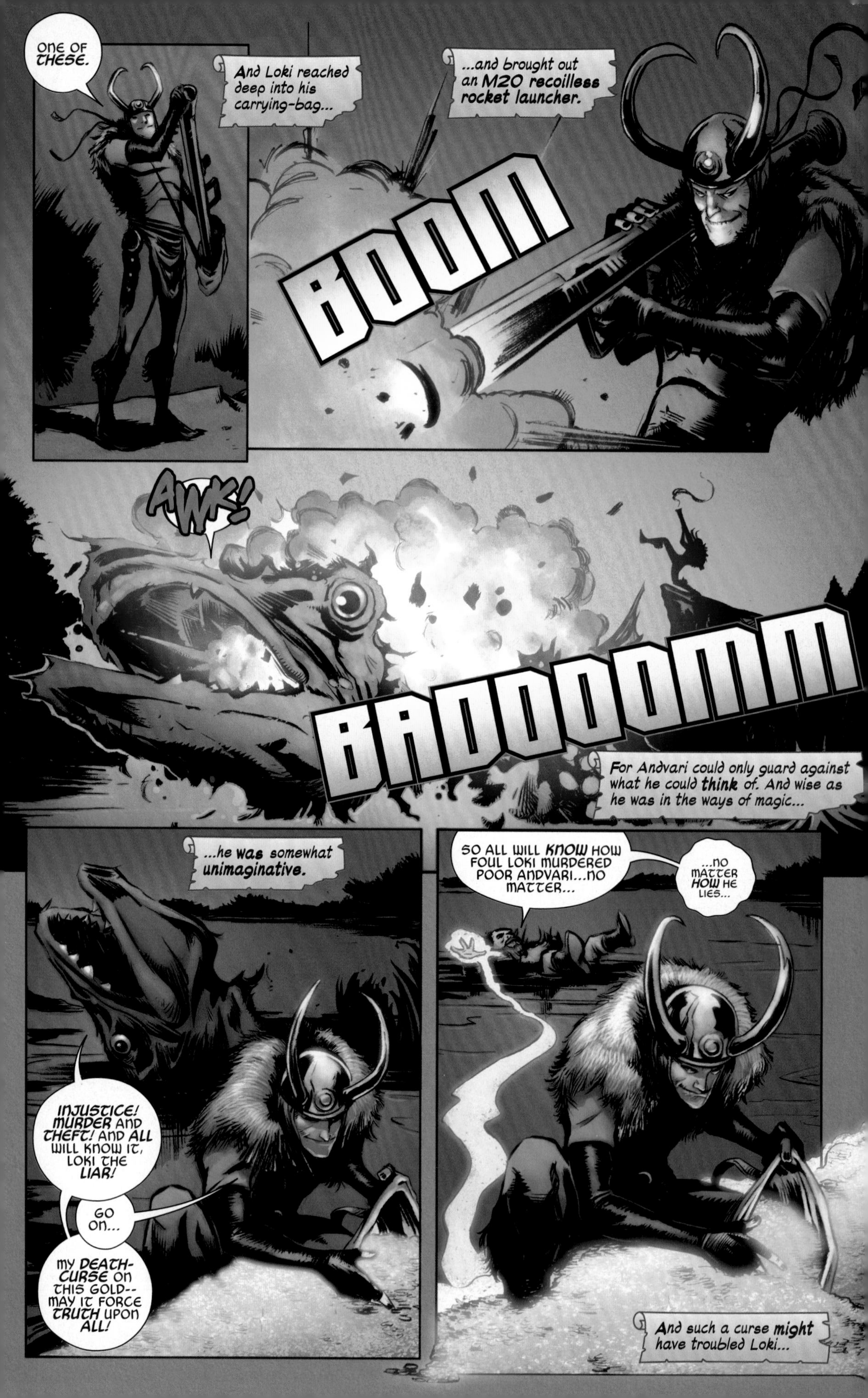

ONE OF THESE.
And Loki reached deep into his carrying-bag...
...and brought out an M20 recoilless rocket launcher.
BOOM
AWK!
BADOOOMM
For Andvari could only guard against what he could think of. And wise as he was in the ways of magic...
...he was somewhat unimaginative.
INJUSTICE! MURDER AND THEFT! AND ALL WILL KNOW IT, LOKI THE LIAR!
GO ON...
MY DEATH-CURSE ON THIS GOLD-- MAY IT FORCE TRUTH UPON ALL!
SO ALL WILL KNOW HOW FOUL LOKI MURDERED POOR ANDVARI...NO MATTER...
...NO MATTER HOW HE LIES...
And such a curse might have troubled Loki...

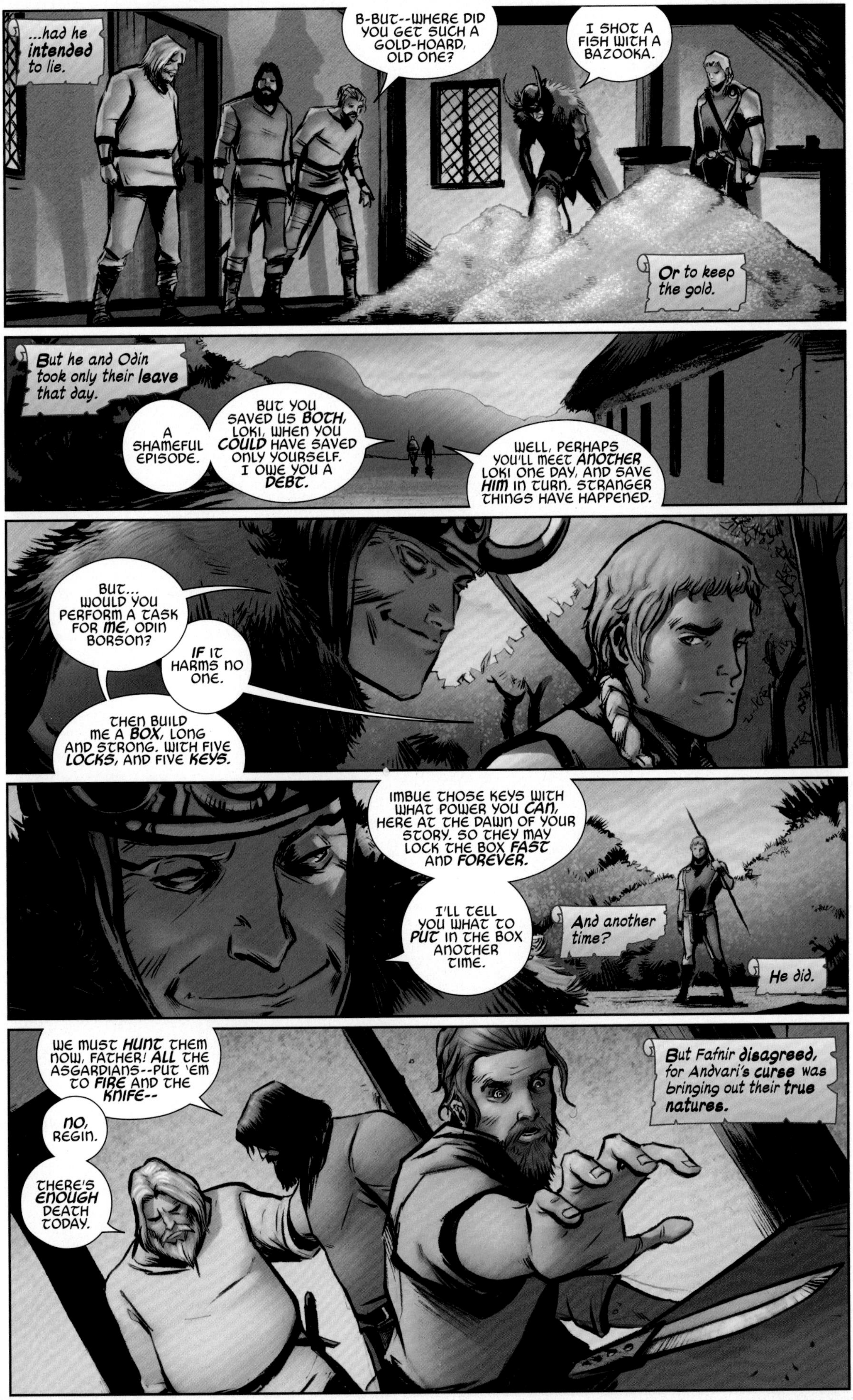

...had he intended to lie.
B-BUT--WHERE DID YOU GET SUCH A GOLD-HOARD, OLD ONE?
I SHOT A FISH WITH A BAZOOKA.
Or to keep the gold.
But he and Odin took only their leave that day.
A SHAMEFUL EPISODE.
BUT YOU SAVED US BOTH, LOKI, WHEN YOU COULD HAVE SAVED ONLY YOURSELF. I OWE YOU A DEBT.
WELL, PERHAPS YOU'LL MEET ANOTHER LOKI ONE DAY, AND SAVE HIM IN TURN. STRANGER THINGS HAVE HAPPENED.
BUT... WOULD YOU PERFORM A TASK FOR ME, ODIN BORSON?
IF IT HARMS NO ONE.
THEN BUILD ME A BOX, LONG AND STRONG. WITH FIVE LOCKS, AND FIVE KEYS.
IMBUE THOSE KEYS WITH WHAT POWER YOU CAN, HERE AT THE DAWN OF YOUR STORY. SO THEY MAY LOCK THE BOX FAST AND FOREVER.
I'LL TELL YOU WHAT TO PUT IN THE BOX ANOTHER TIME.
And another time?
He did.
WE MUST HUNT THEM NOW, FATHER! ALL THE ASGARDIANS--PUT 'EM TO FIRE AND THE KNIFE--
NO, REGIN.
THERE'S ENOUGH DEATH TODAY.
But Fafnir disagreed, for Andvari's curse was bringing out their true natures.

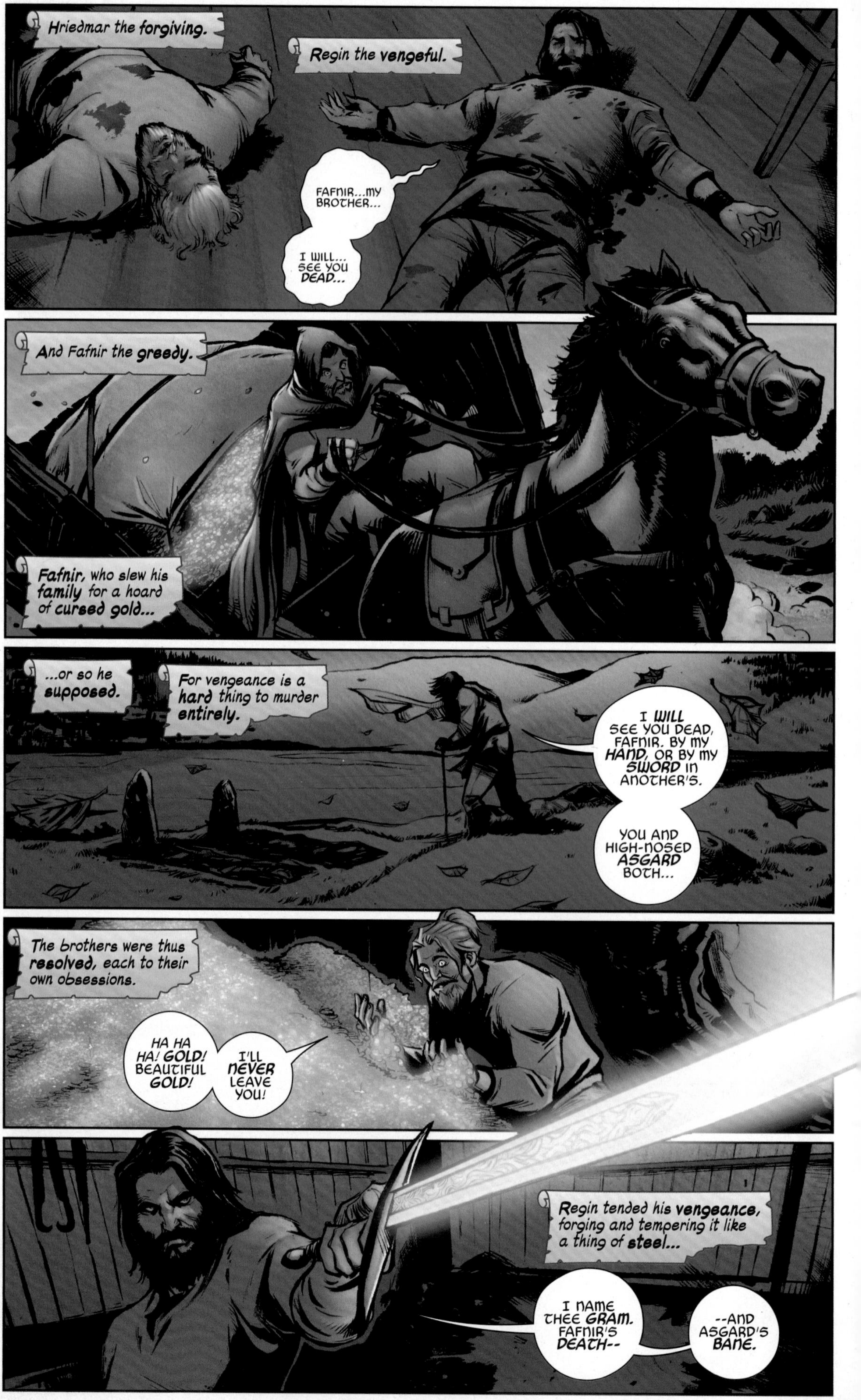
Hriedmar the forgiving.
Regin the vengeful.
FAFNIR...MY BROTHER...
I WILL... SEE YOU DEAD...
And Fafnir the greedy.
Fafnir, who slew his family for a hoard of cursed gold...
...or so he supposed.
For vengeance is a hard thing to murder entirely.
I WILL SEE YOU DEAD, FAFNIR. BY MY HAND, OR BY MY SWORD IN ANOTHER'S.
YOU AND HIGH-NOSED ASGARD BOTH...
The brothers were thus resolved, each to their own obsessions.
HA HA HA! GOLD! BEAUTIFUL GOLD!
I'LL NEVER LEAVE YOU!
Regin tended his vengeance, forging and tempering it like a thing of steel...
I NAME THEE GRAM. FAFNIR'S DEATH--
--AND ASGARD'S BANE.

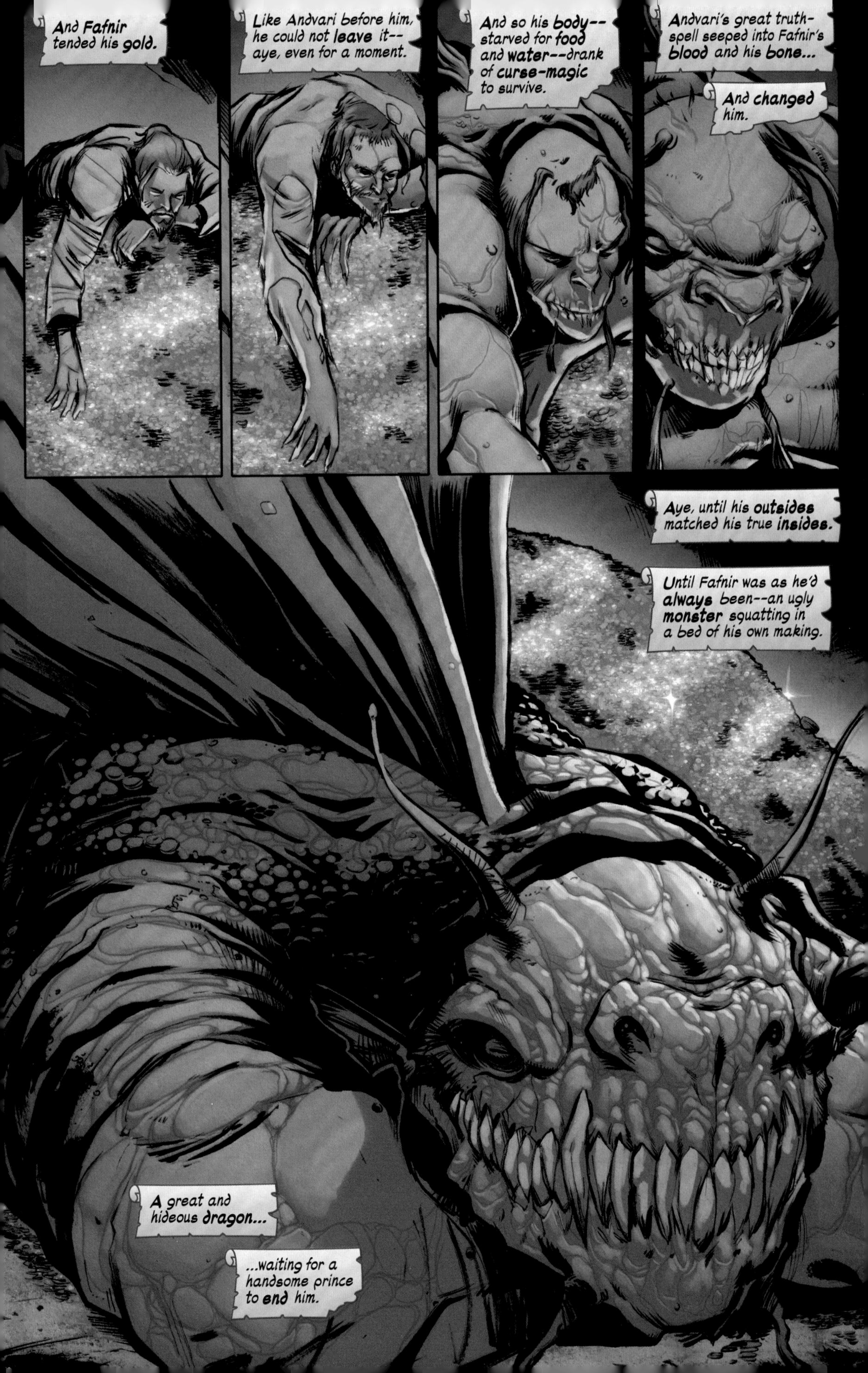
And Fafnir tended his gold.
Like Andvari before him, he could not leave it--aye, even for a moment.
And so his body--starved for food and water--drank of curse-magic to survive.
Andvari's great truth-spell seeped into Fafnir's blood and his bone...
And changed him.
Aye, until his outsides matched his true insides.
Until Fafnir was as he'd always been--an ugly monster squatting in a bed of his own making.
A great and hideous dragon...
...waiting for a handsome prince to end him.

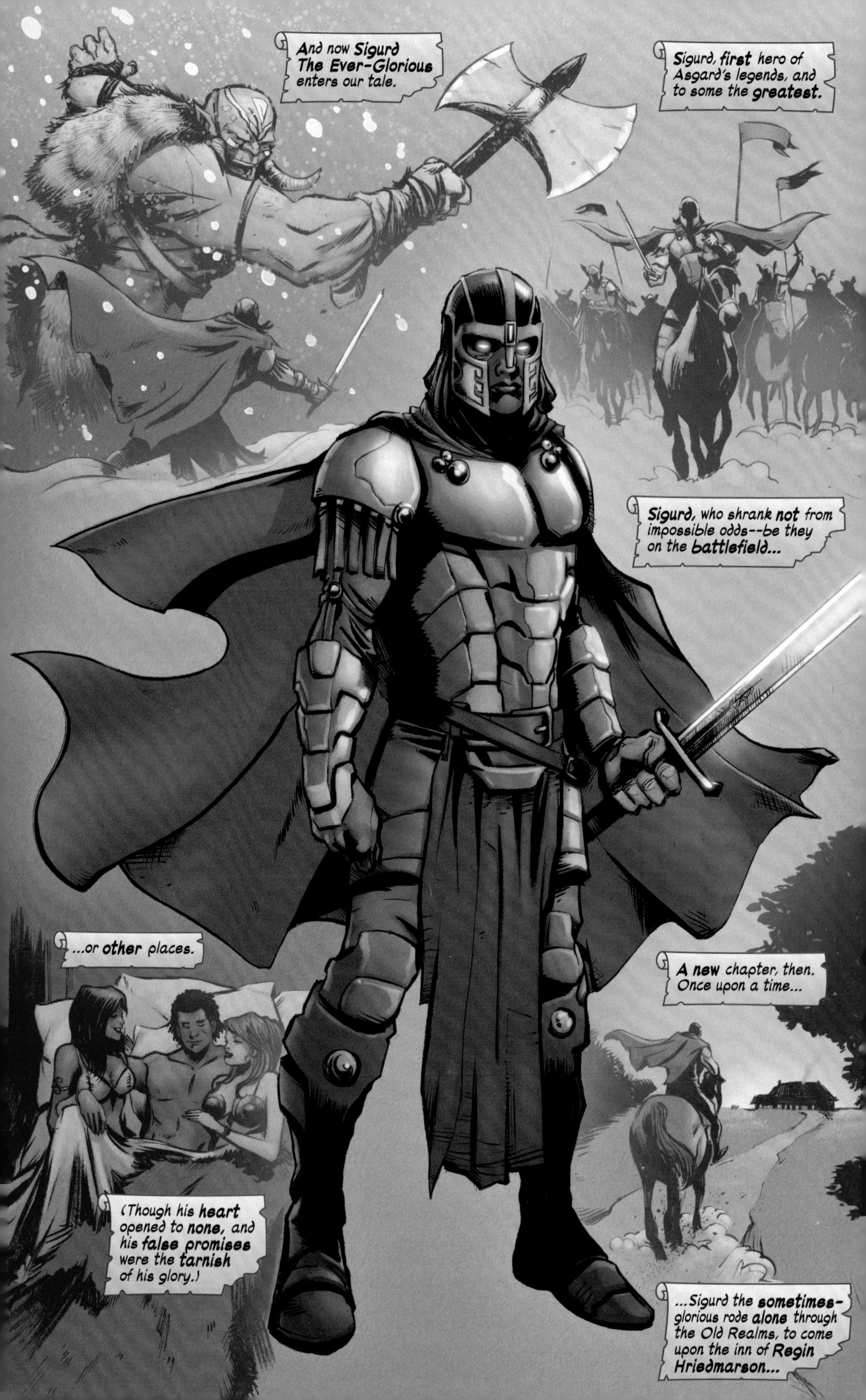
And now Sigurd The Ever-Glorious enters our tale.
Sigurd, first hero of Asgard's legends, and to some the greatest.
Sigurd, who shrank not from impossible odds--be they on the battlefield...
...or other places.
(Though his heart opened to none, and his false promises were the tarnish of his glory.)
A new chapter, then. Once upon a time...
...Sigurd the sometimes-glorious rode alone through the Old Realms, to come upon the inn of Regin Hriedmarson...

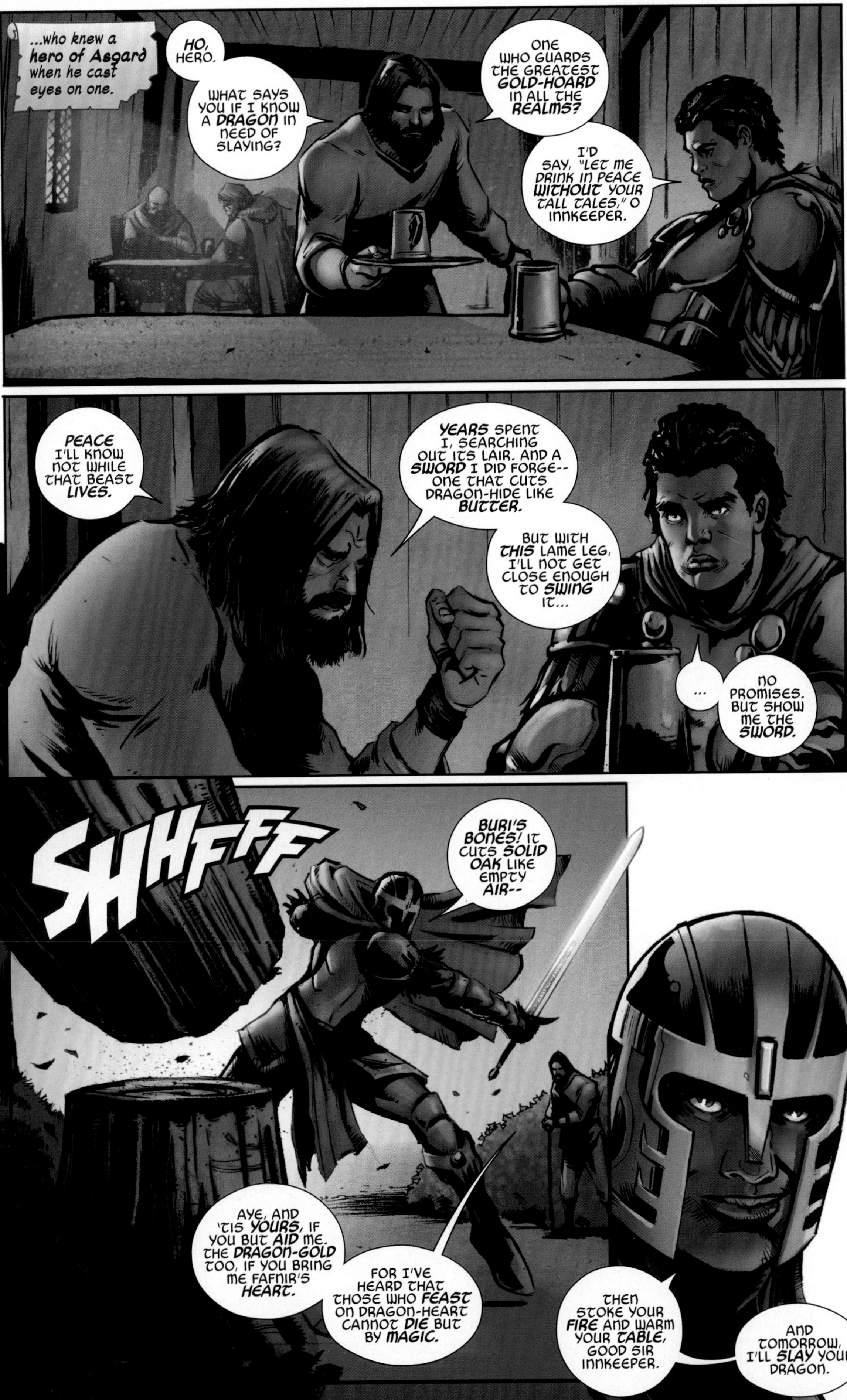
...who knew a hero of Asgard when he cast eyes on one.
HO, HERO.
WHAT SAYS YOU IF I KNOW A DRAGON IN NEED OF SLAYING?
ONE WHO GUARDS THE GREATEST GOLD-HOARD IN ALL THE REALMS?
I'D SAY, "LET ME DRINK IN PEACE WITHOUT YOUR TALL TALES," O INNKEEPER.
PEACE I'LL KNOW NOT WHILE THAT BEAST LIVES.
YEARS SPENT I, SEARCHING OUT ITS LAIR. AND A SWORD I DID FORGE-- ONE THAT CUTS DRAGON-HIDE LIKE BUTTER.
BUT WITH THIS LAME LEG, I'LL NOT GET CLOSE ENOUGH TO SWING IT...
...
NO PROMISES. BUT SHOW ME THE SWORD.
SHHFFF
BURI'S BONES! IT CUTS SOLID OAK LIKE EMPTY AIR--
AYE, AND 'TIS YOURS, IF YOU BUT AID ME. THE DRAGON-GOLD TOO, IF YOU BRING ME FAFNIR'S HEART.
FOR I'VE HEARD THAT THOSE WHO FEAST ON DRAGON-HEART CANNOT DIE BUT BY MAGIC.
THEN STOKE YOUR FIRE AND WARM YOUR TABLE, GOOD SIR INNKEEPER.
AND TOMORROW, I'LL SLAY YOUR DRAGON.

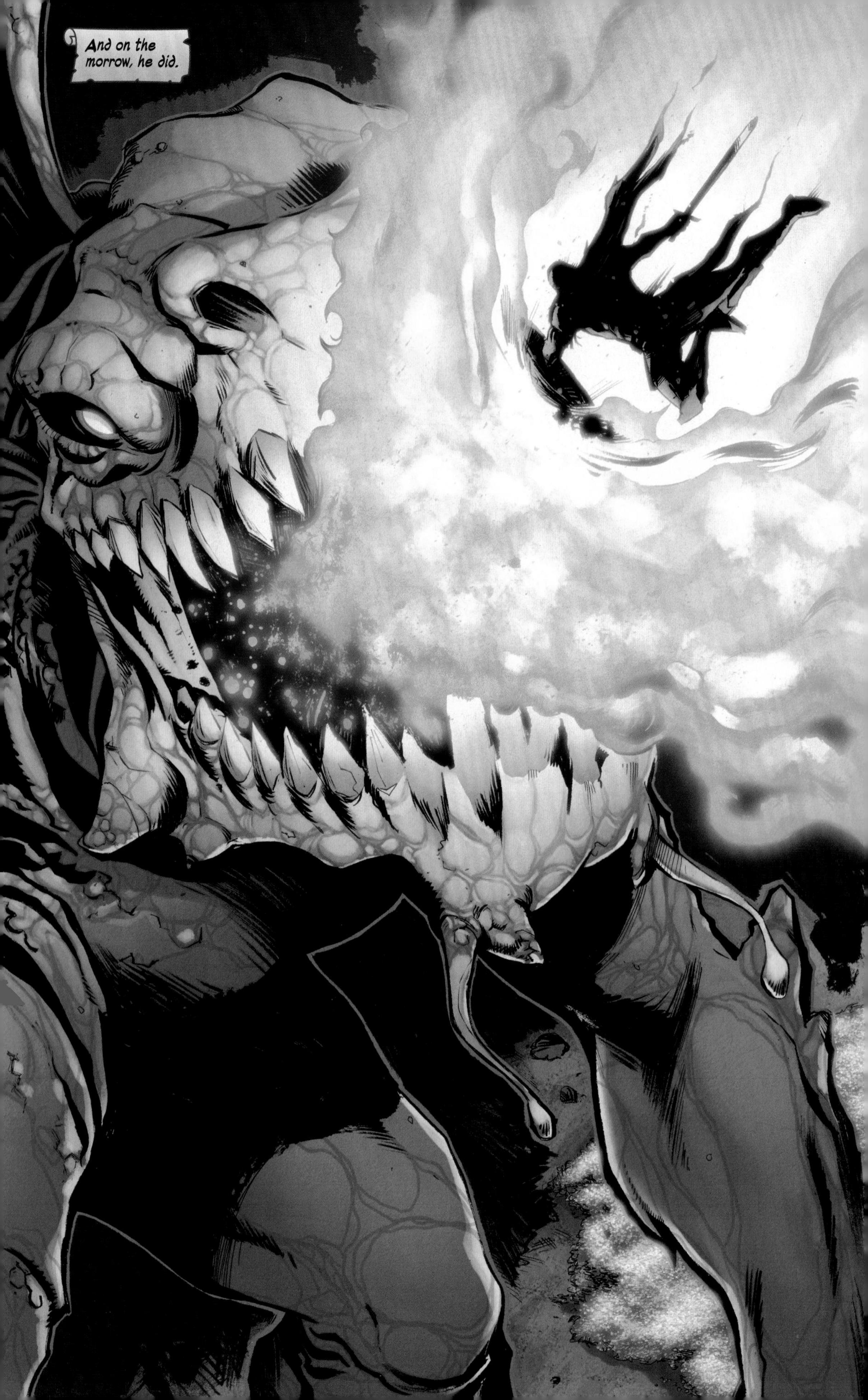
And on the morrow, he did.

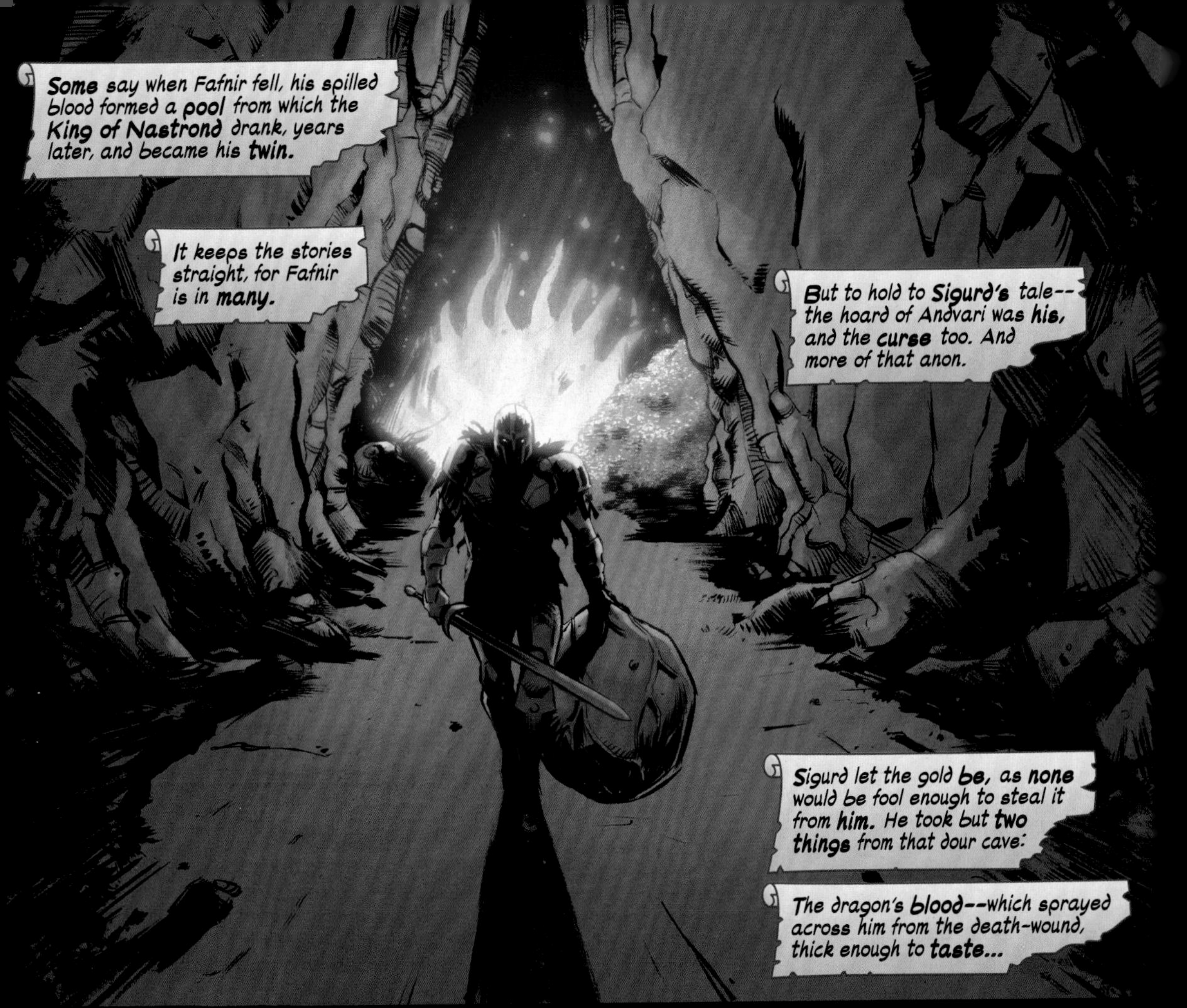
Some say when Fafnir fell, his spilled blood formed a pool from which the King of Nastrond drank, years later, and became his twin.
It keeps the stories straight, for Fafnir is in many.
But to hold to Sigurd's tale--the hoard of Andvari was his, and the curse too. And more of that anon.
Sigurd let the gold be, as none would be fool enough to steal it from him. He took but two things from that dour cave:
The dragon's blood--which sprayed across him from the death-wound, thick enough to taste...

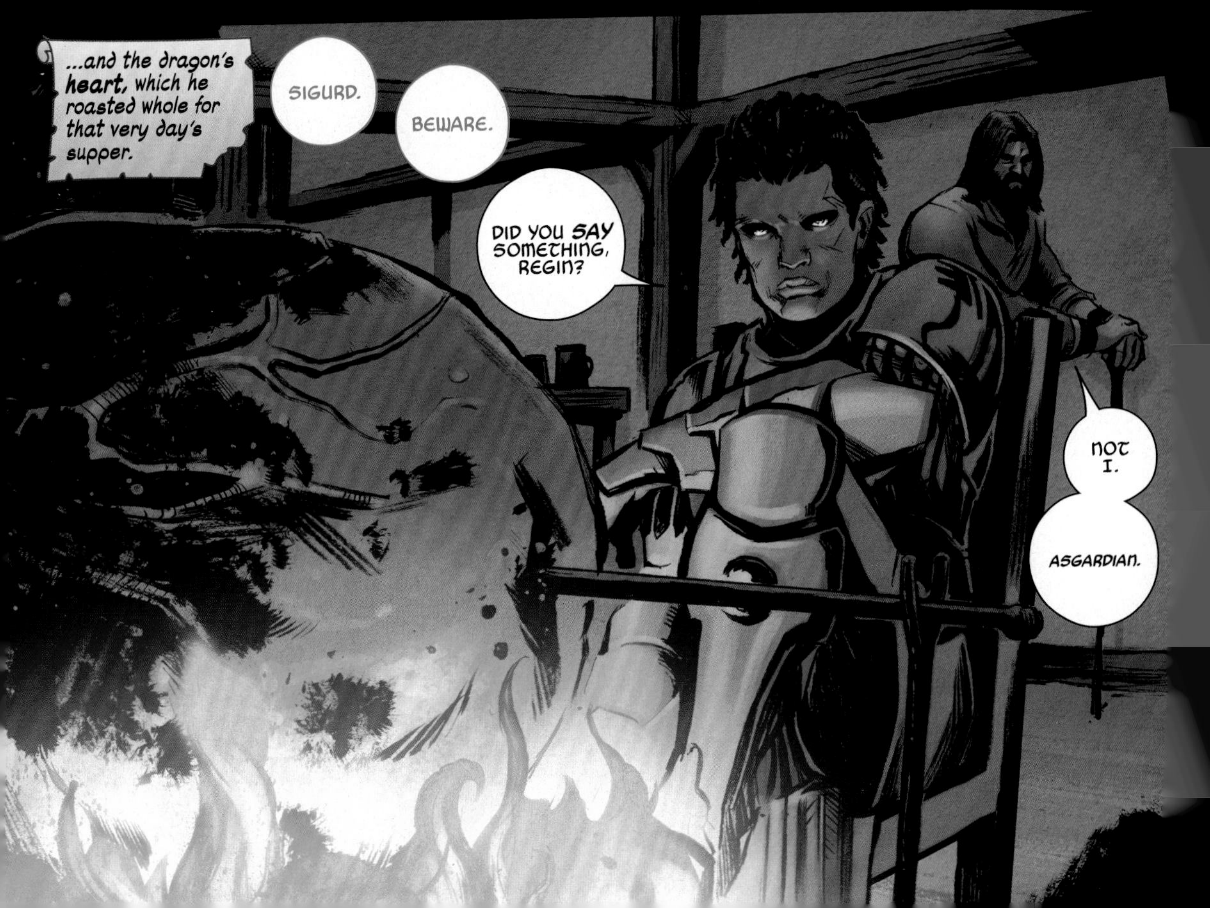
...and the dragon's heart, which he roasted whole for that very day's supper.
SIGURD.
BEWARE.
DID YOU SAY SOMETHING, REGIN?
NOT I.
ASGARDIAN.

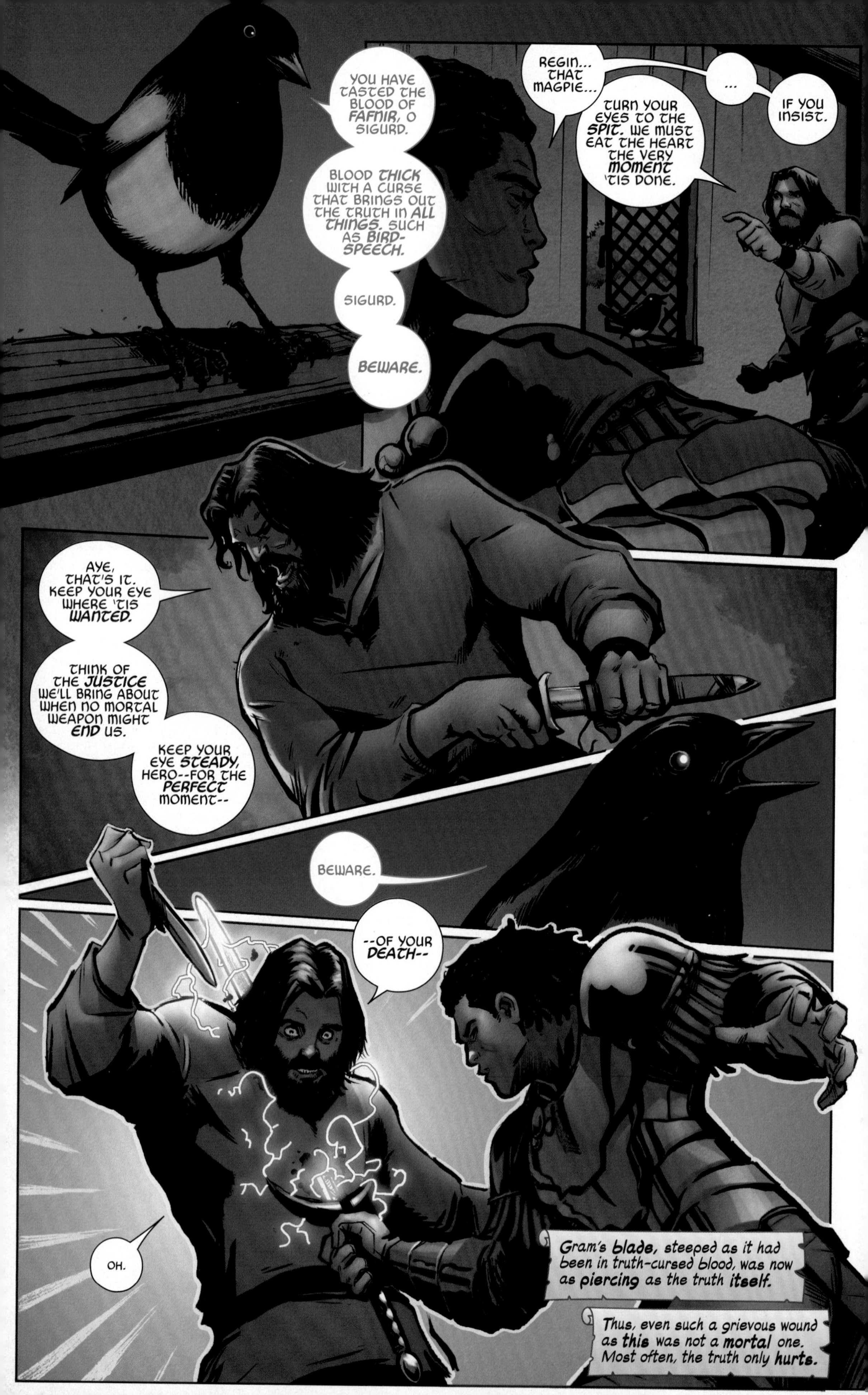
YOU HAVE TASTED THE BLOOD OF FAFNIR, O SIGURD.
BLOOD THICK WITH A CURSE THAT BRINGS OUT THE TRUTH IN ALL THINGS. SUCH AS BIRD-SPEECH.
SIGURD.
BEWARE.
REGIN... THAT MAGPIE...
TURN YOUR EYES TO THE SPIT. WE MUST EAT THE HEART THE VERY MOMENT 'TIS DONE.
...
IF YOU INSIST.
AYE, THAT'S IT. KEEP YOUR EYE WHERE 'TIS WANTED.
THINK OF THE JUSTICE WE'LL BRING ABOUT WHEN NO MORTAL WEAPON MIGHT END US.
KEEP YOUR EYE STEADY, HERO--FOR THE PERFECT MOMENT--
BEWARE.
--OF YOUR DEATH--
OH.
Gram's blade, steeped as it had been in truth-cursed blood, was now as piercing as the truth itself.
Thus, even such a grievous wound as this was not a mortal one. Most often, the truth only hurts.

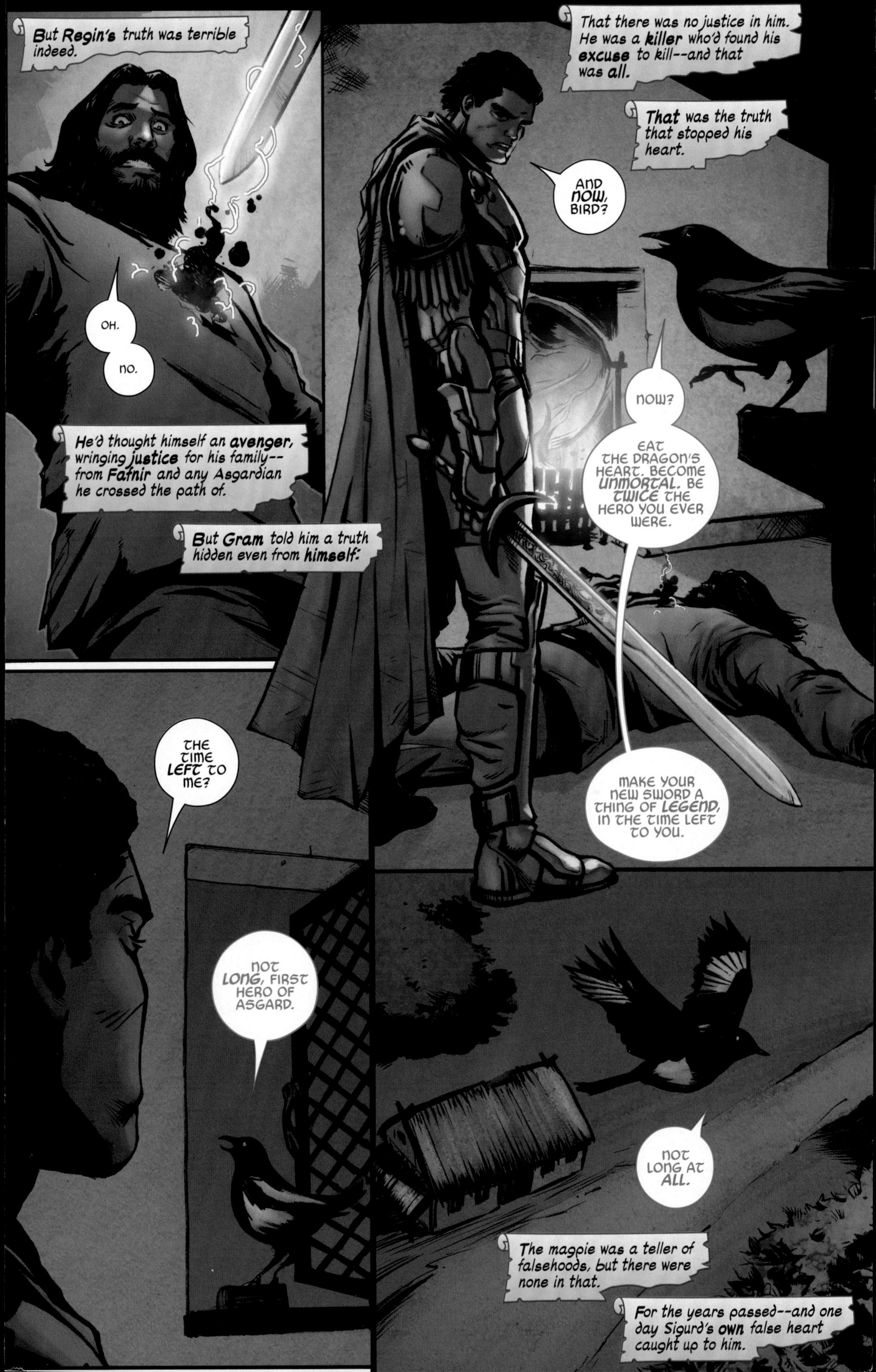
But Regin's truth was terrible indeed.
OH.
NO.
He'd thought himself an avenger, wringing justice for his family--from Fafnir and any Asgardian he crossed the path of.
But Gram told him a truth hidden even from himself:
That there was no justice in him. He was a killer who'd found his excuse to kill--and that was all.
That was the truth that stopped his heart.
AND NOW, BIRD?
NOW?
EAT THE DRAGON'S HEART. BECOME UNMORTAL. BE TWICE THE HERO YOU EVER WERE.
MAKE YOUR NEW SWORD A THING OF LEGEND, IN THE TIME LEFT TO YOU.
THE TIME LEFT TO ME?
NOT LONG, FIRST HERO OF ASGARD.
NOT LONG AT ALL.
The magpie was a teller of falsehoods, but there were none in that.
For the years passed--and one day Sigurd's own false heart caught up to him.

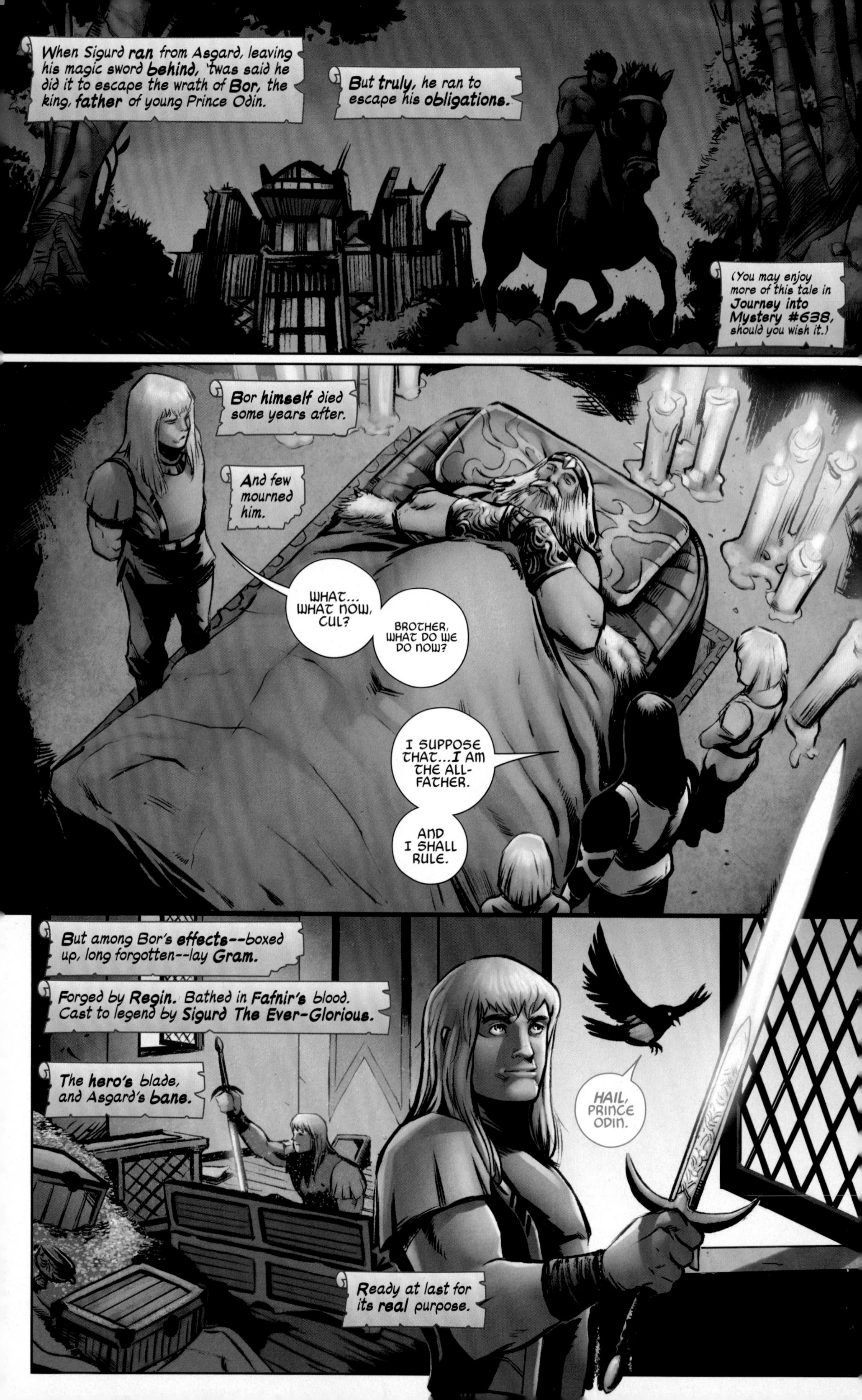

When Sigurd ran from Asgard, leaving his magic sword behind, 'twas said he did it to escape the wrath of Bor, the king, father of young Prince Odin.
But truly, he ran to escape his obligations.
(You may enjoy more of this tale in Journey into Mystery #638, should you wish it.)
Bor himself died some years after.
And few mourned him.
WHAT... WHAT NOW, CUL?
BROTHER, WHAT DO WE DO NOW?
I SUPPOSE THAT...I AM THE ALL-FATHER.
AND I SHALL RULE.
But among Bor's effects--boxed up, long forgotten--lay Gram.
Forged by Regin. Bathed in Fafnir's blood. Cast to legend by Sigurd The Ever-Glorious.
The hero's blade, and Asgard's bane.
HAIL, PRINCE ODIN.
Ready at last for its real purpose.

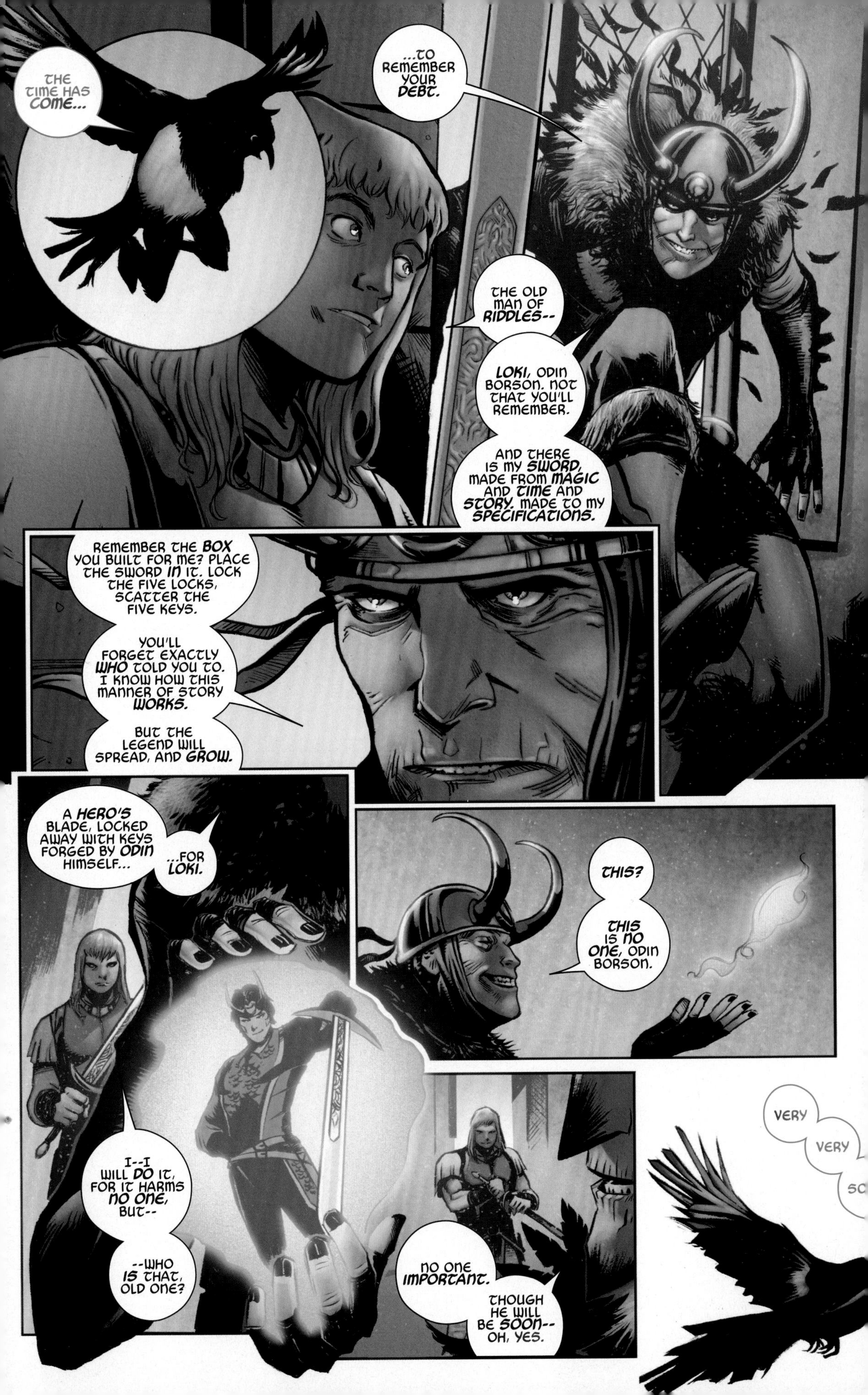

THE TIME HAS COME...
...TO REMEMBER YOUR DEBT.
THE OLD MAN OF RIDDLES--
LOKI, ODIN BORSON. NOT THAT YOU'LL REMEMBER.
AND THERE IS MY SWORD, MADE FROM MAGIC AND TIME AND STORY. MADE TO MY SPECIFICATIONS.
REMEMBER THE BOX YOU BUILT FOR ME? PLACE THE SWORD IN IT. LOCK THE FIVE LOCKS, SCATTER THE FIVE KEYS.
YOU'LL FORGET EXACTLY WHO TOLD YOU TO. I KNOW HOW THIS MANNER OF STORY WORKS.
BUT THE LEGEND WILL SPREAD, AND GROW.
A HERO'S BLADE, LOCKED AWAY WITH KEYS FORGED BY ODIN HIMSELF...
...FOR LOKI.
THIS?
THIS IS NO ONE, ODIN BORSON.
I--I WILL DO IT, FOR IT HARMS NO ONE, BUT--
--WHO IS THAT, OLD ONE?
NO ONE IMPORTANT.
THOUGH HE WILL BE SOON--OH, YES.
VERY
VERY

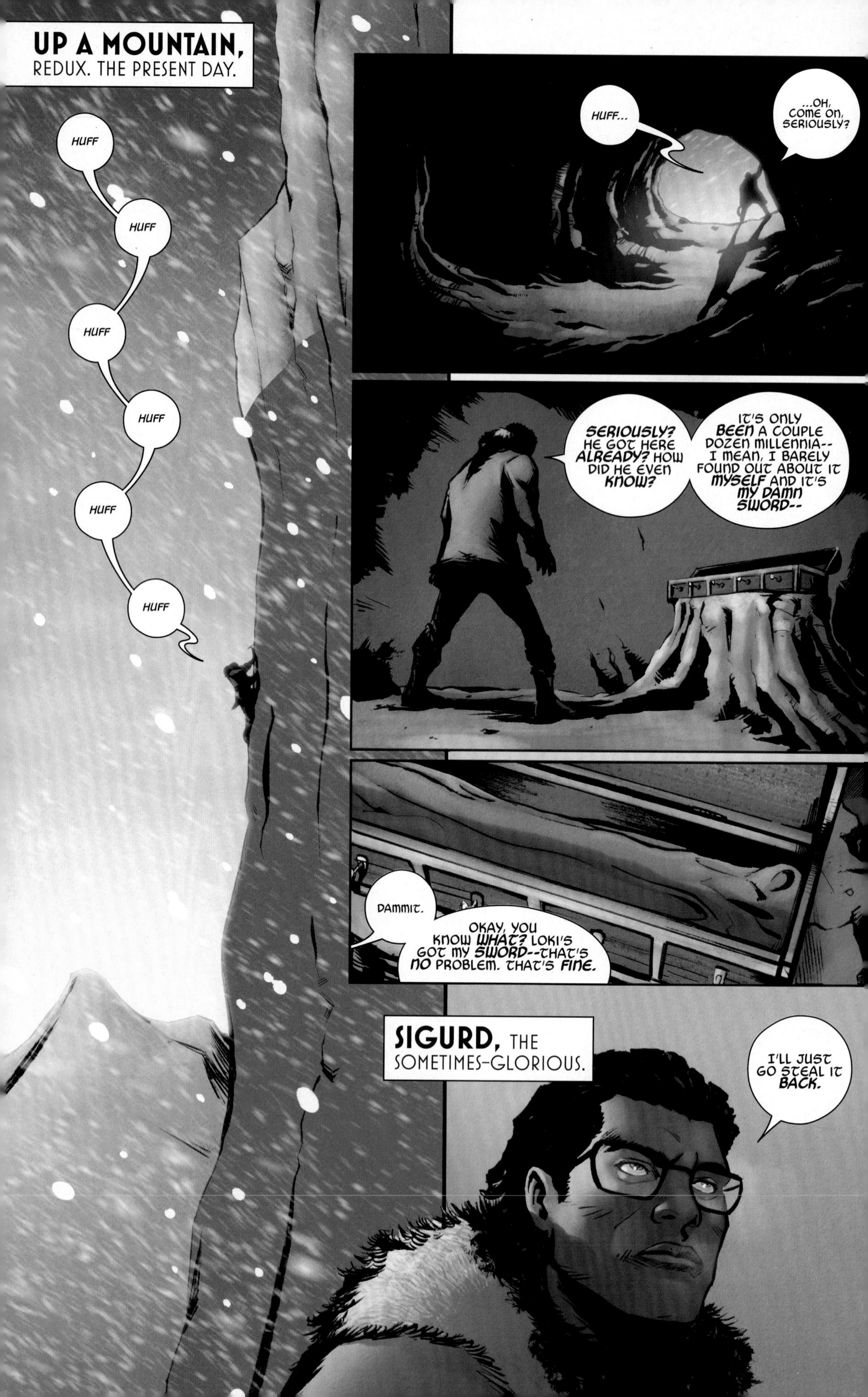
UP A MOUNTAIN, REDUX. THE PRESENT DAY.
HUFF
HUFF
HUFF
HUFF
HUFF
HUFF
HUFF...
...OH, COME ON, SERIOUSLY?
SERIOUSLY? HE GOT HERE ALREADY? HOW DID HE EVEN KNOW?
IT'S ONLY BEEN A COUPLE DOZEN MILLENNIA-- I MEAN, I BARELY FOUND OUT ABOUT IT MYSELF AND IT'S MY DAMN SWORD--
DAMMIT.
OKAY, YOU KNOW WHAT? LOKI'S GOT MY SWORD--THAT'S NO PROBLEM. THAT'S FINE.
SIGURD, THE SOMETIMES-GLORIOUS.
I'LL JUST GO STEAL IT BACK.

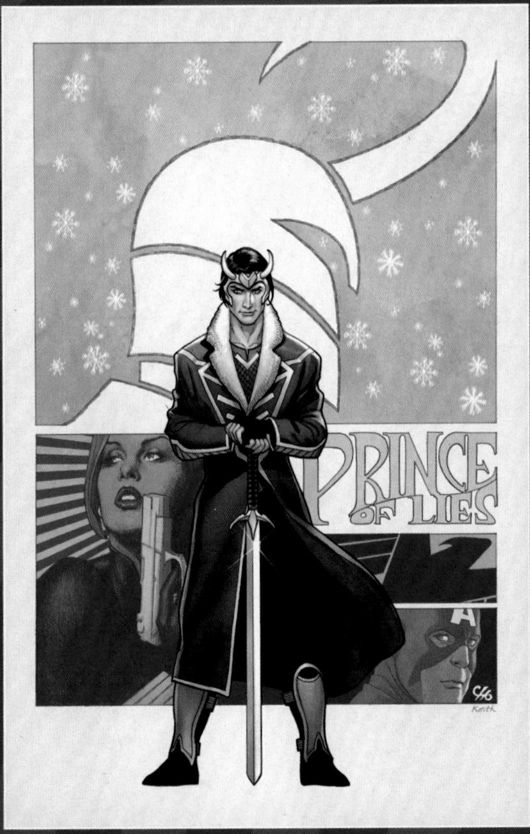
PRINCE
OF LIES

#1 VARIANT
BY FRANK CHO & JASON KEITH

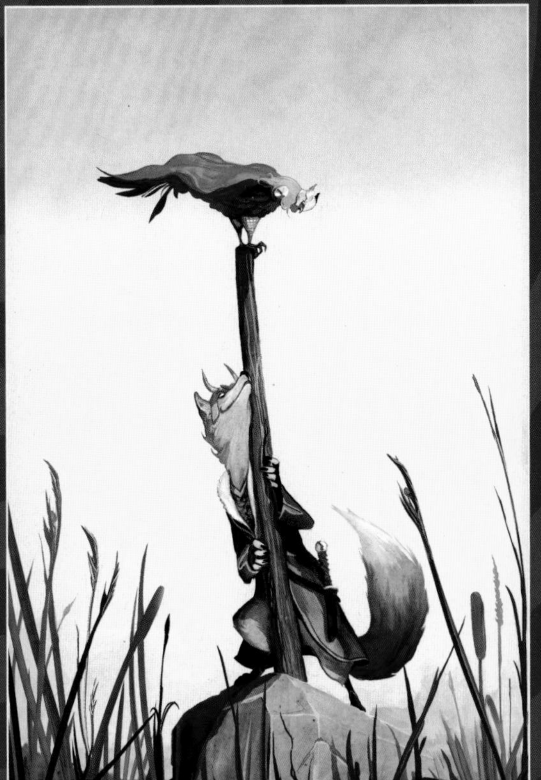

#1 ANIMAL VARIANT
BY MIKE DEL MUNDO

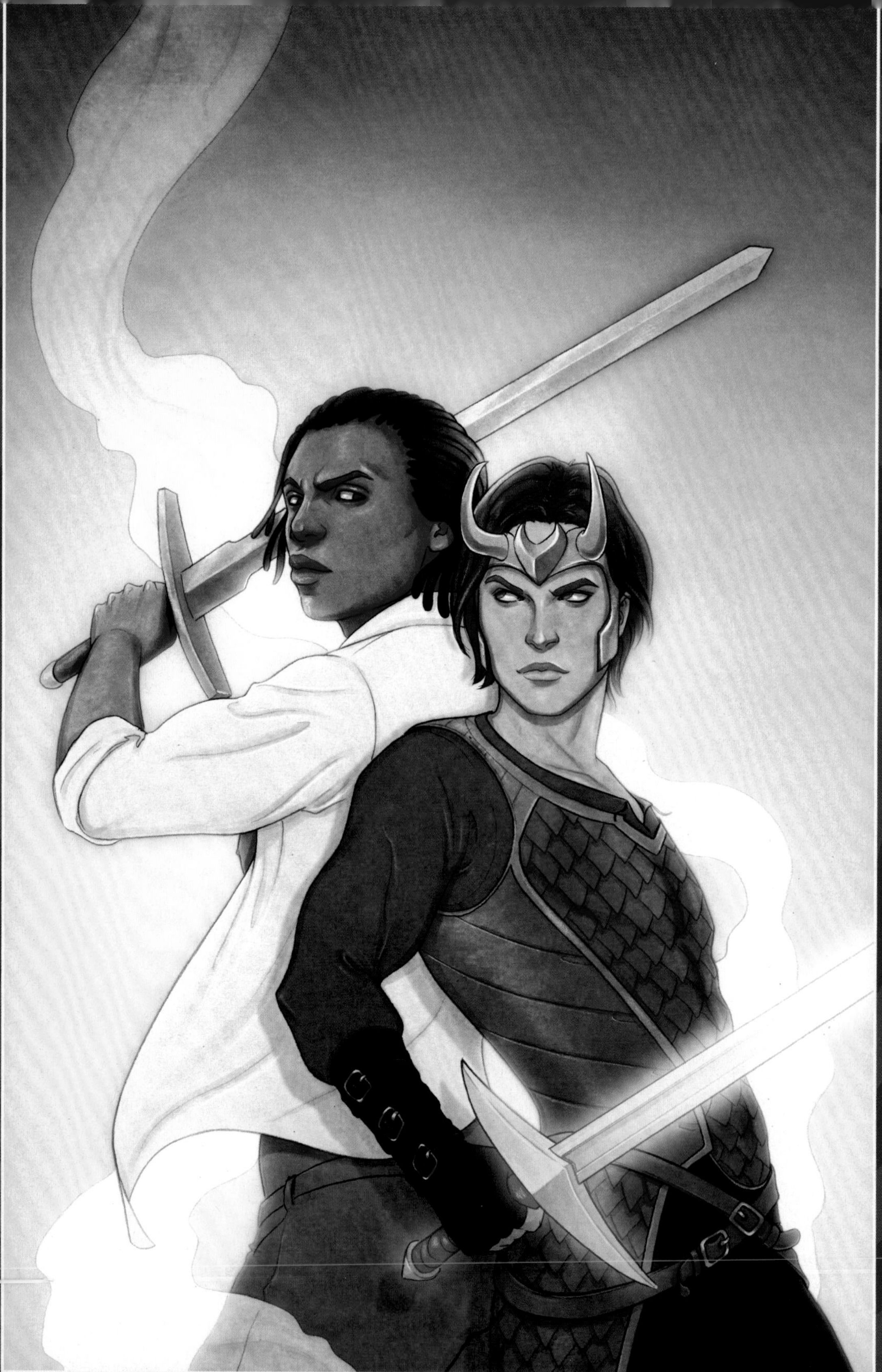

4

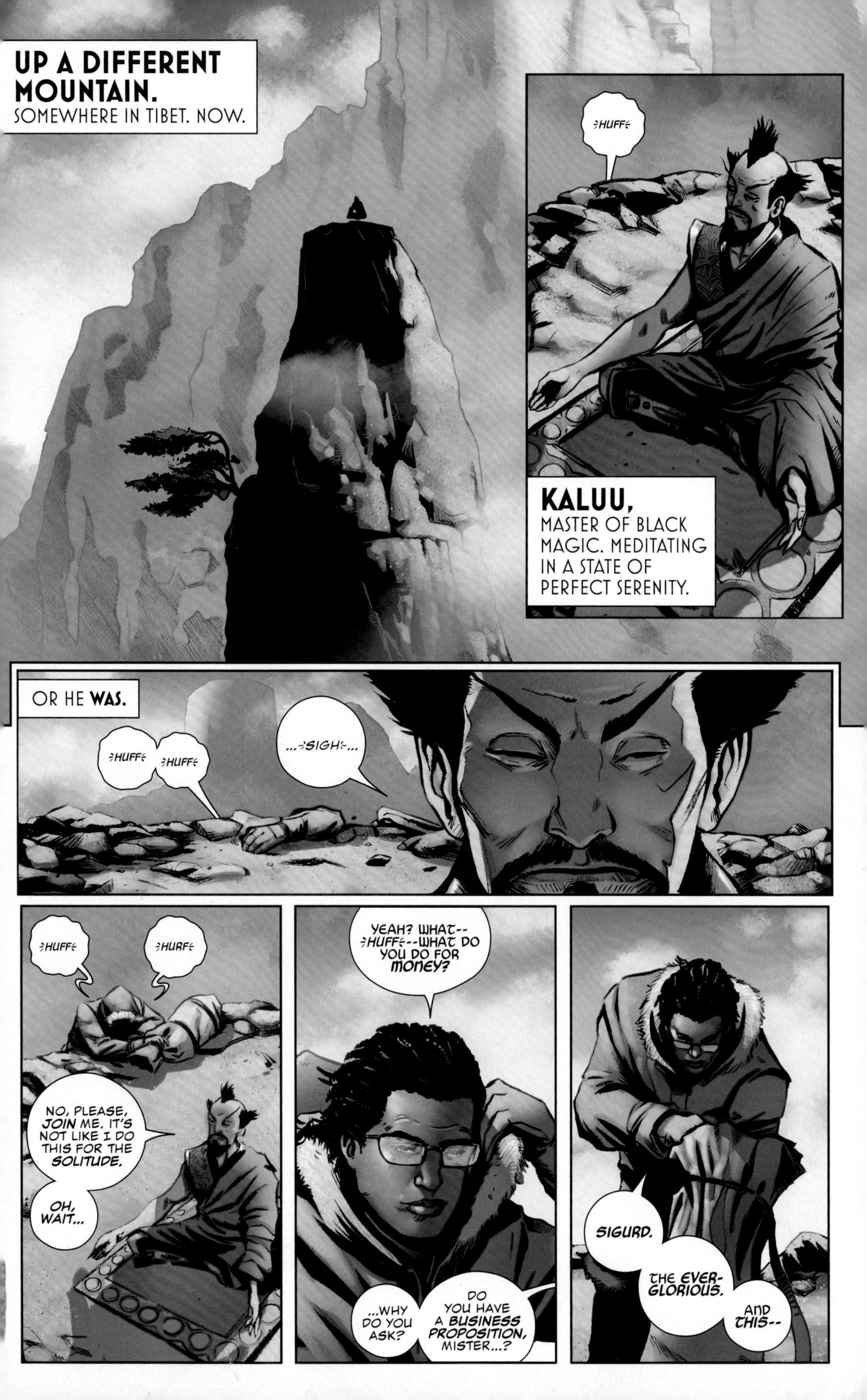
UP A DIFFERENT MOUNTAIN.
SOMEWHERE IN TIBET. NOW.
HUFF
KALUU, MASTER OF BLACK MAGIC. MEDITATING IN A STATE OF PERFECT SERENITY.
OR HE WAS.
HUFF
HUFF
...SIGH...
HUFF
HURF
NO, PLEASE, JOIN ME. IT'S NOT LIKE I DO THIS FOR THE SOLITUDE.
OH, WAIT...
YEAH? WHAT-- HUFF --WHAT DO YOU DO FOR MONEY?
...WHY DO YOU ASK?
DO YOU HAVE A BUSINESS PROPOSITION, MISTER...?
SIGURD.
THE EVER-GLORIOUS.
AND THIS--

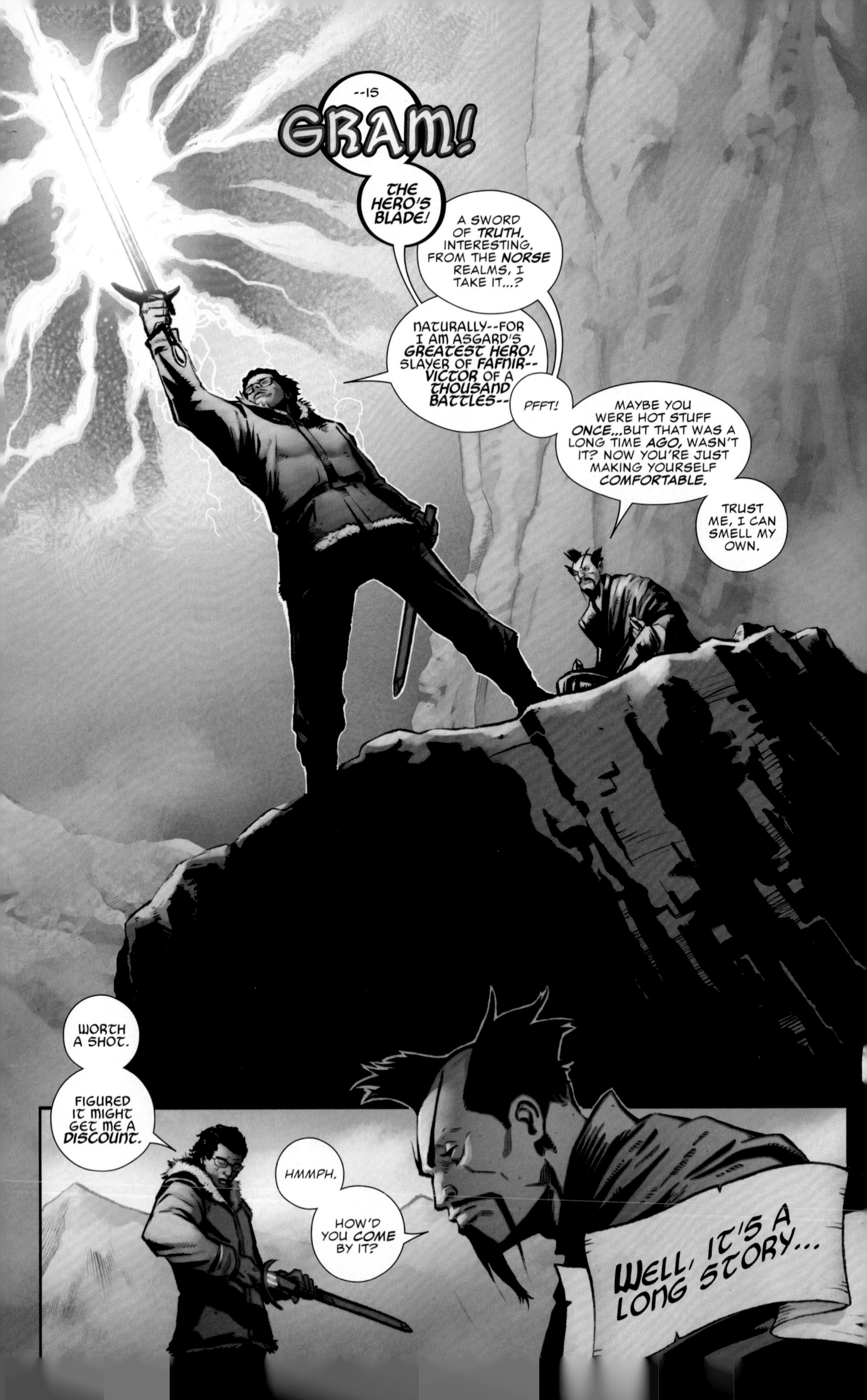
--IS
GRAM!
THE HERO'S BLADE!
A SWORD OF TRUTH. INTERESTING. FROM THE NORSE REALMS, I TAKE IT...?
NATURALLY--FOR I AM ASGARD'S GREATEST HERO! SLAYER OF FAFNIR--VICTOR OF A THOUSAND BATTLES--
PFFT!
MAYBE YOU WERE HOT STUFF ONCE...BUT THAT WAS A LONG TIME AGO, WASN'T IT? NOW YOU'RE JUST MAKING YOURSELF COMFORTABLE.
TRUST ME, I CAN SMELL MY OWN.
WORTH A SHOT.
FIGURED IT MIGHT GET ME A DISCOUNT.
HMMPH.
HOW'D YOU COME BY IT?
WELL, IT'S A LONG STORY...

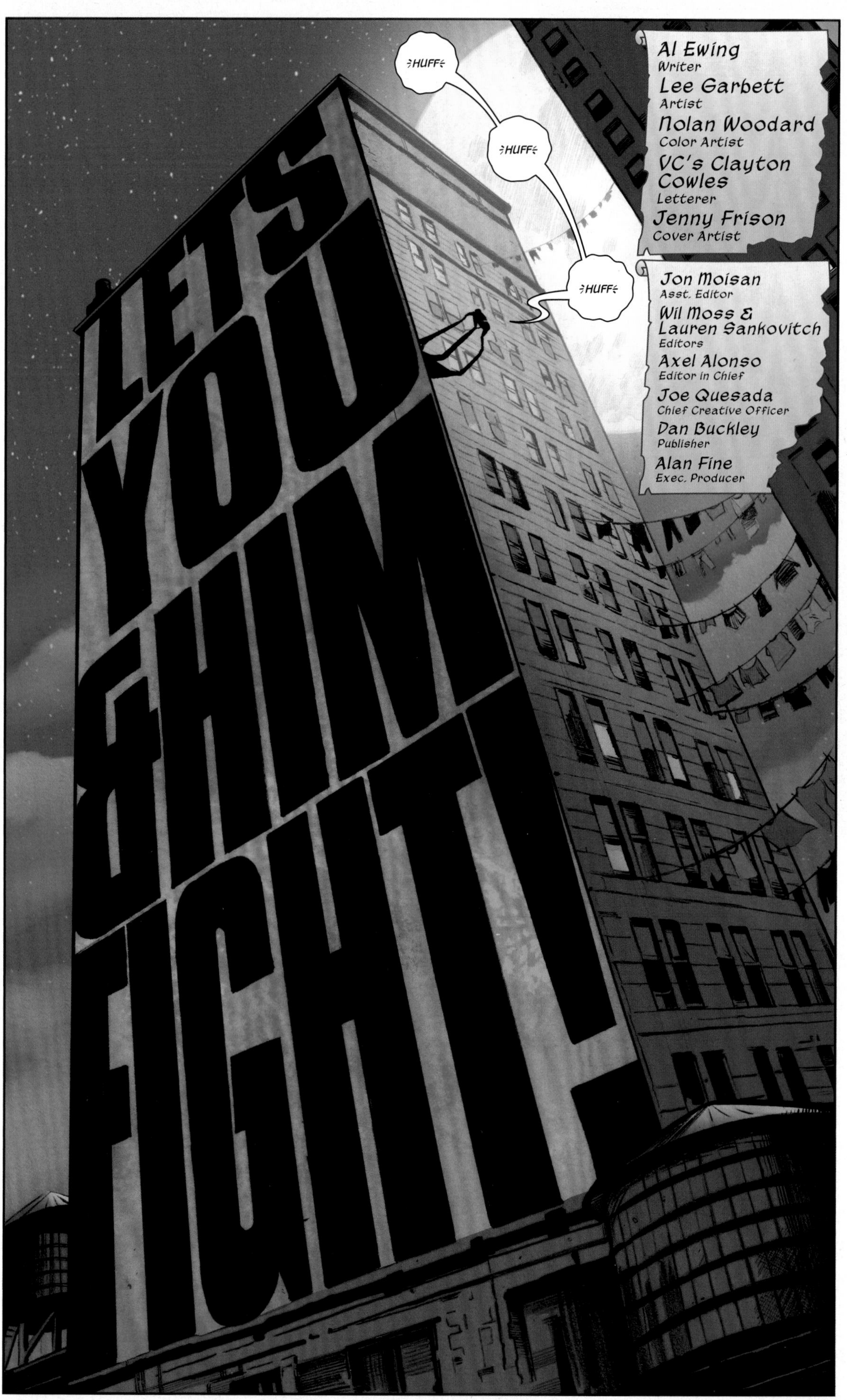

HUFF
HUFF
HUFF
LET'S YOU & HIM FIGHT!
Al Ewing Writer
Lee Garbett Artist
Nolan Woodard Color Artist
VC's Clayton Cowles Letterer
Jenny Frison Cover Artist
Jon Moisan Asst. Editor
Wil Moss & Lauren Sankovitch Editors
Axel Alonso Editor in Chief
Joe Quesada Chief Creative Officer
Dan Buckley Publisher
Alan Fine Exec. Producer

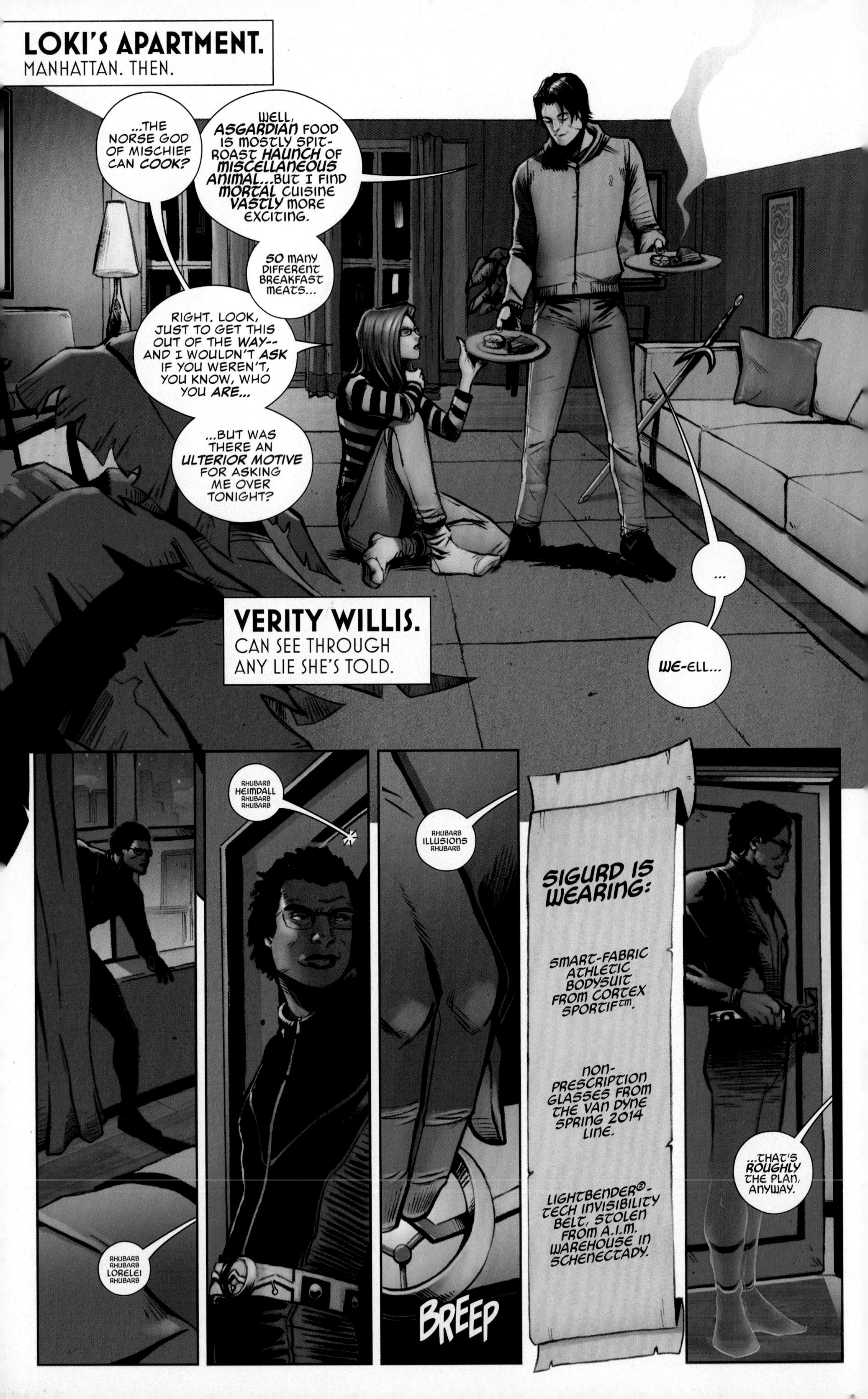
LOKI'S APARTMENT.
MANHATTAN. THEN.
...THE NORSE GOD OF MISCHIEF CAN COOK?
WELL, ASGARDIAN FOOD IS MOSTLY SPIT-ROAST HAUNCH OF MISCELLANEOUS ANIMAL...BUT I FIND MORTAL CUISINE VASTLY MORE EXCITING.
SO MANY DIFFERENT BREAKFAST MEATS...
RIGHT. LOOK, JUST TO GET THIS OUT OF THE WAY-- AND I WOULDN'T ASK IF YOU WEREN'T, YOU KNOW, WHO YOU ARE...
...BUT WAS THERE AN ULTERIOR MOTIVE FOR ASKING ME OVER TONIGHT?
...
WE-ELL...
VERITY WILLIS.
CAN SEE THROUGH ANY LIE SHE'S TOLD.
RHUBARB RHUBARB LORELEI RHUBARB
RHUBARB HEIMDALL RHUBARB RHUBARB
RHUBARB ILLUSIONS RHUBARB
BREEP
SIGURD IS WEARING:
SMART-FABRIC ATHLETIC BODYSUIT FROM CORTEX SPORTIF™.
NON-PRESCRIPTION GLASSES FROM THE VAN DYNE SPRING 2014 LINE.
LIGHTBENDER®-TECH INVISIBILITY BELT, STOLEN FROM A.I.M. WAREHOUSE IN SCHENECTADY.
...THAT'S ROUGHLY THE PLAN, ANYWAY.

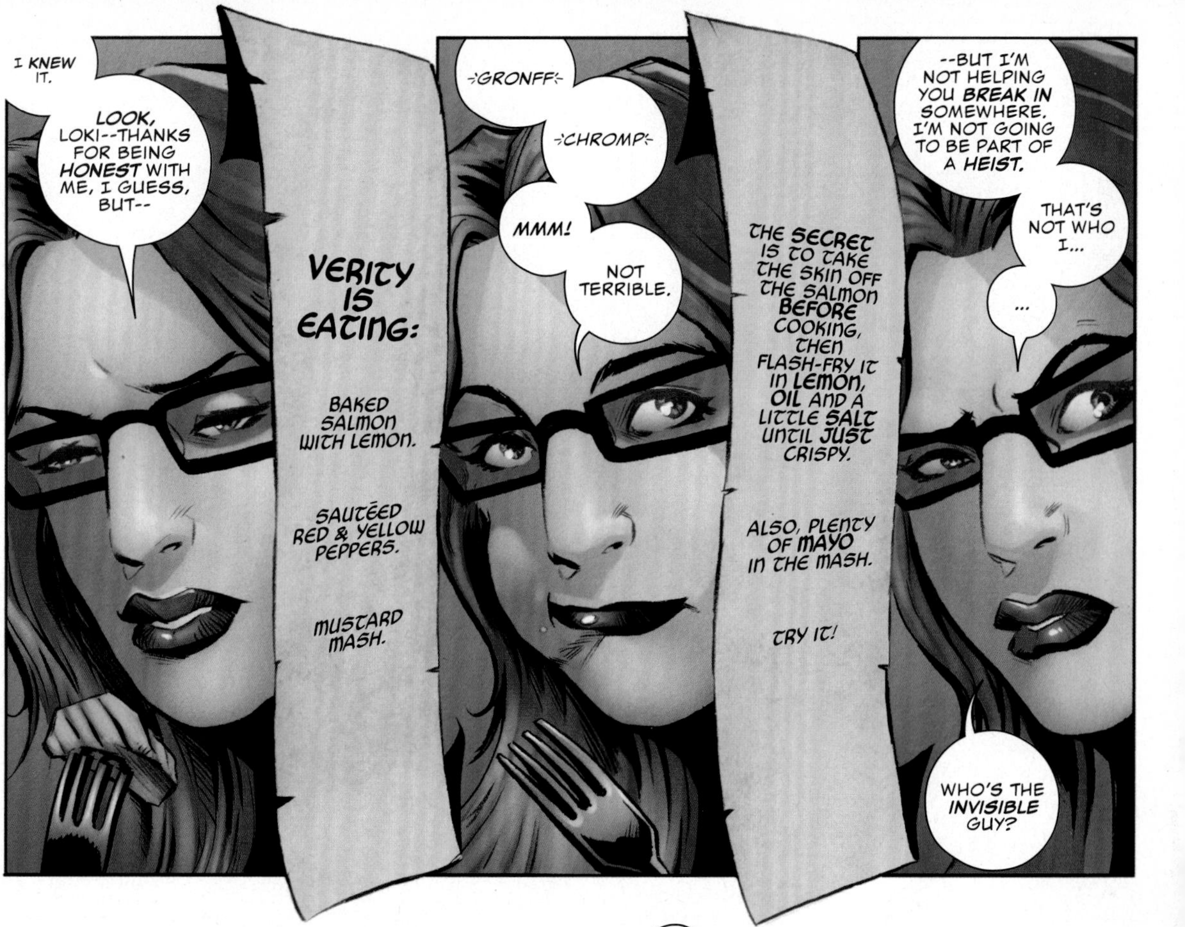
I KNEW IT.
LOOK, LOKI--THANKS FOR BEING HONEST WITH ME, I GUESS, BUT--
VERITY IS EATING:
BAKED SALMON WITH LEMON.
SAUTÉED RED & YELLOW PEPPERS.
MUSTARD MASH.
-GRONFF-
-CHROMP-
MMM!
NOT TERRIBLE.
THE SECRET IS TO TAKE THE SKIN OFF THE SALMON BEFORE COOKING, THEN FLASH-FRY IT IN LEMON, OIL AND A LITTLE SALT UNTIL JUST CRISPY.
ALSO, PLENTY OF MAYO IN THE MASH.
TRY IT!
--BUT I'M NOT HELPING YOU BREAK IN SOMEWHERE. I'M NOT GOING TO BE PART OF A HEIST.
THAT'S NOT WHO I...
...
WHO'S THE INVISIBLE GUY?

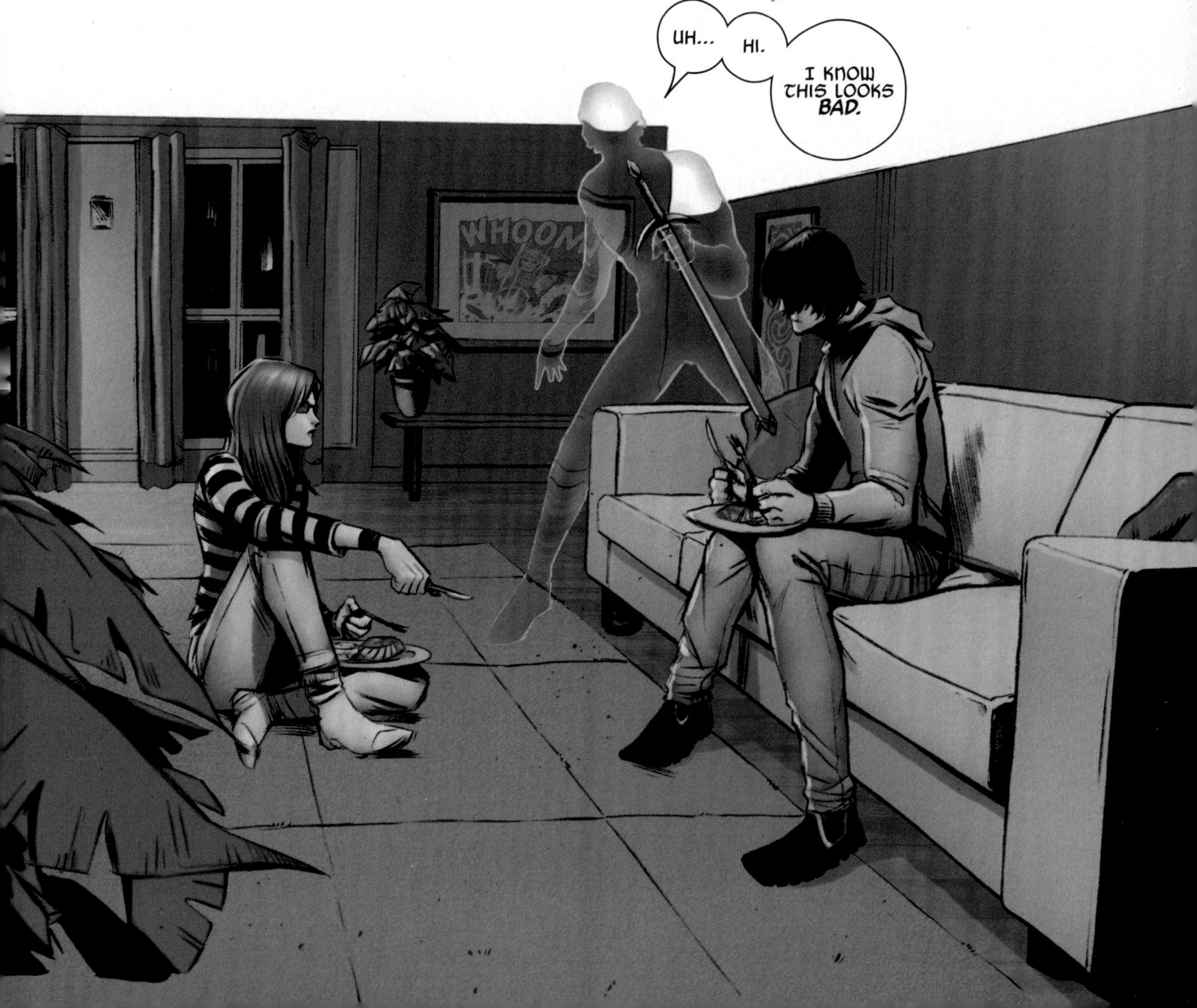
UH...
HI.
I KNOW THIS LOOKS BAD.
WHOOM

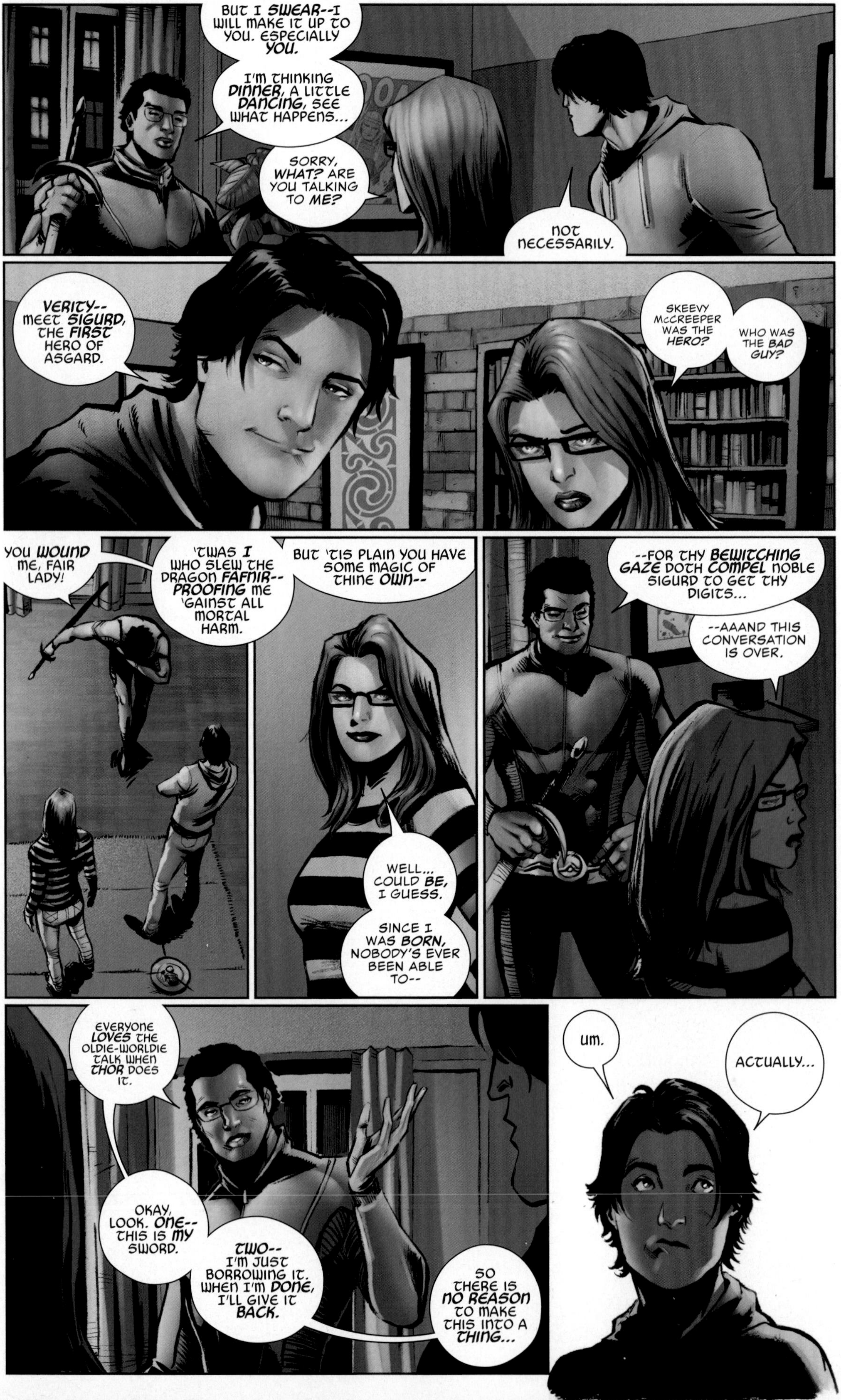
BUT I SWEAR--I WILL MAKE IT UP TO YOU. ESPECIALLY YOU.
I'M THINKING DINNER, A LITTLE DANCING, SEE WHAT HAPPENS...
SORRY, WHAT? ARE YOU TALKING TO ME?
NOT NECESSARILY.
VERITY-- MEET SIGURD, THE FIRST HERO OF ASGARD.
SKEEVY McCREEPER WAS THE HERO?
WHO WAS THE BAD GUY?
YOU WOUND ME, FAIR LADY!
'TWAS I WHO SLEW THE DRAGON FAFNIR-- PROOFING ME 'GAINST ALL MORTAL HARM.
BUT 'TIS PLAIN YOU HAVE SOME MAGIC OF THINE OWN--
WELL... COULD BE, I GUESS.
SINCE I WAS BORN, NOBODY'S EVER BEEN ABLE TO--
--FOR THY BEWITCHING GAZE DOTH COMPEL NOBLE SIGURD TO GET THY DIGITS...
--AAAND THIS CONVERSATION IS OVER.
EVERYONE LOVES THE OLDIE-WORLDIE TALK WHEN THOR DOES IT.
OKAY, LOOK. ONE-- THIS IS MY SWORD.
TWO-- I'M JUST BORROWING IT. WHEN I'M DONE, I'LL GIVE IT BACK.
SO THERE IS NO REASON TO MAKE THIS INTO A THING...
UM.
ACTUALLY...

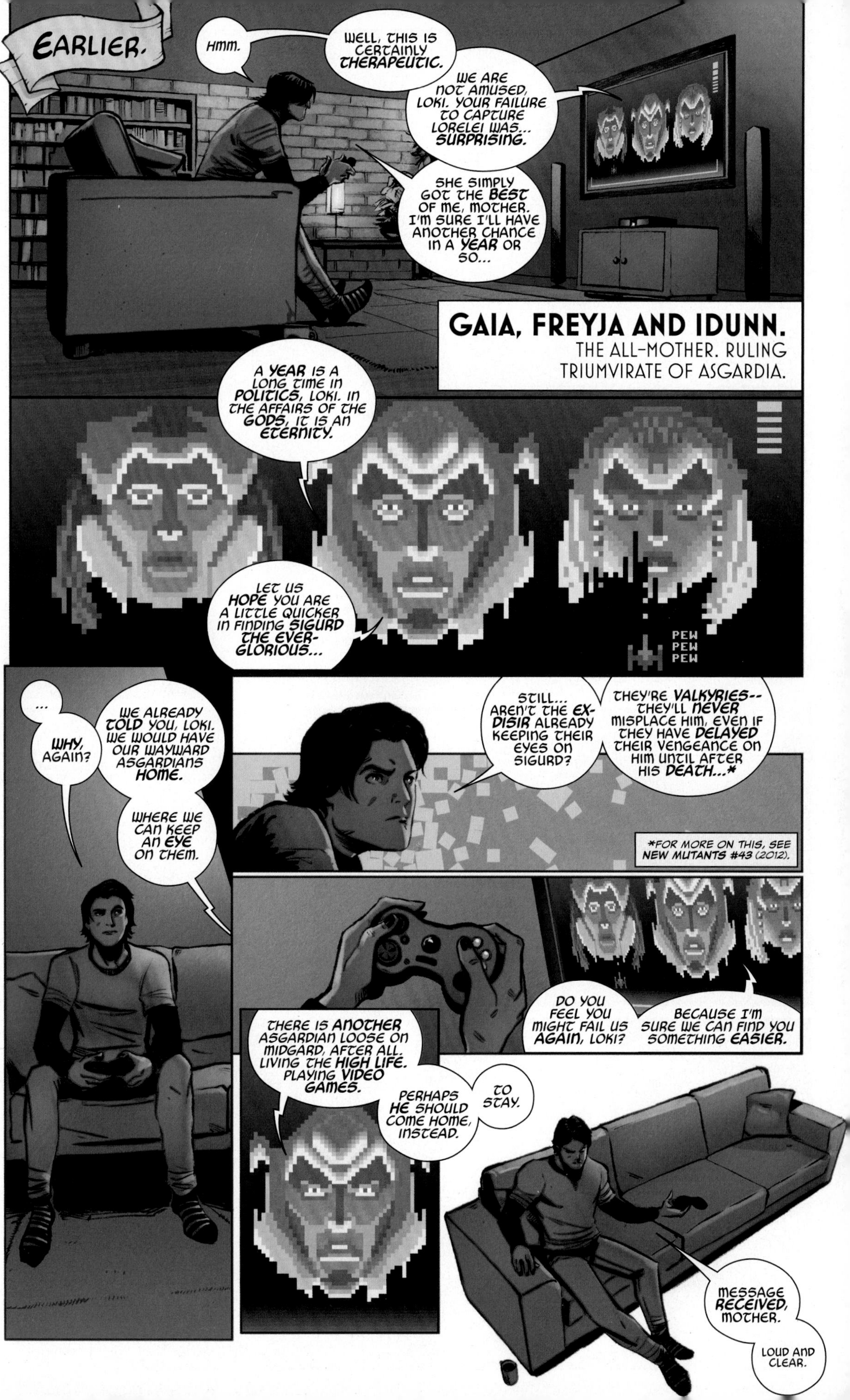
EARLIER.
HMM.
WELL, THIS IS CERTAINLY THERAPEUTIC.
WE ARE NOT AMUSED, LOKI. YOUR FAILURE TO CAPTURE LORELEI WAS... SURPRISING.
SHE SIMPLY GOT THE BEST OF ME, MOTHER. I'M SURE I'LL HAVE ANOTHER CHANCE IN A YEAR OR SO...
GAIA, FREYJA AND IDUNN.
THE ALL-MOTHER. RULING TRIUMVIRATE OF ASGARDIA.
A YEAR IS A LONG TIME IN POLITICS, LOKI. IN THE AFFAIRS OF THE GODS, IT IS AN ETERNITY.
LET US HOPE YOU ARE A LITTLE QUICKER IN FINDING SIGURD THE EVER-GLORIOUS...
PEW PEW PEW
...
WHY, AGAIN?
WE ALREADY TOLD YOU, LOKI. WE WOULD HAVE OUR WAYWARD ASGARDIANS HOME.
WHERE WE CAN KEEP AN EYE ON THEM.
STILL... AREN'T THE EX-DISIR ALREADY KEEPING THEIR EYES ON SIGURD?
THEY'RE VALKYRIES--THEY'LL NEVER MISPLACE HIM, EVEN IF THEY HAVE DELAYED THEIR VENGEANCE ON HIM UNTIL AFTER HIS DEATH...*
*FOR MORE ON THIS, SEE NEW MUTANTS #43 (2012).
DO YOU FEEL YOU MIGHT FAIL US AGAIN, LOKI?
BECAUSE I'M SURE WE CAN FIND YOU SOMETHING EASIER.
THERE IS ANOTHER ASGARDIAN LOOSE ON MIDGARD, AFTER ALL. LIVING THE HIGH LIFE. PLAYING VIDEO GAMES.
PERHAPS HE SHOULD COME HOME, INSTEAD.
TO STAY.
MESSAGE RECEIVED, MOTHER.
LOUD AND CLEAR.

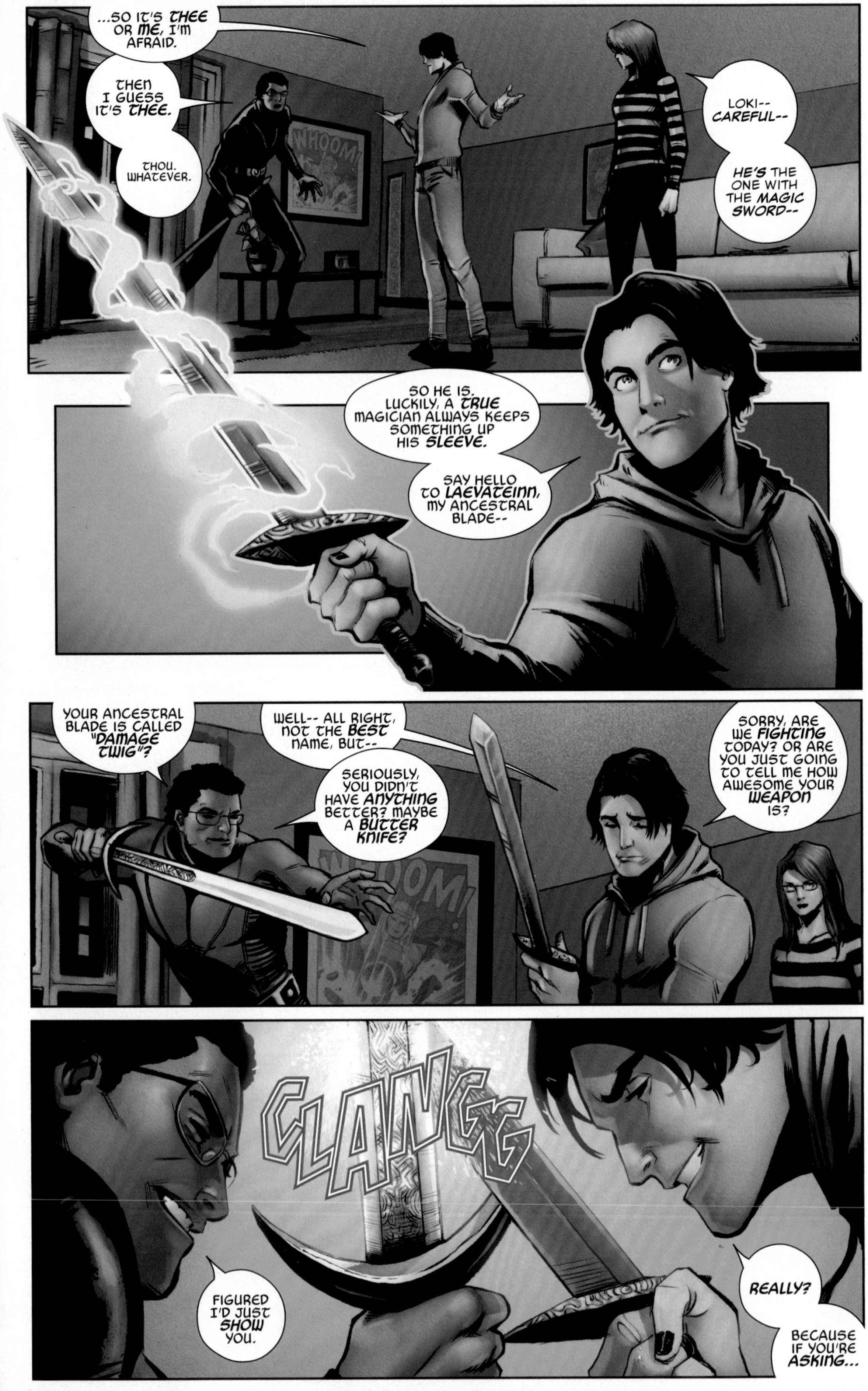
...SO IT'S THEE OR ME, I'M AFRAID.
THEN I GUESS IT'S THEE.
THOU. WHATEVER.
LOKI-- CAREFUL--
HE'S THE ONE WITH THE MAGIC SWORD--
SO HE IS. LUCKILY, A TRUE MAGICIAN ALWAYS KEEPS SOMETHING UP HIS SLEEVE.
SAY HELLO TO LAEVATEINN, MY ANCESTRAL BLADE--
YOUR ANCESTRAL BLADE IS CALLED "DAMAGE TWIG"?
WELL-- ALL RIGHT, NOT THE BEST NAME, BUT--
SERIOUSLY, YOU DIDN'T HAVE ANYTHING BETTER? MAYBE A BUTTER KNIFE?
SORRY, ARE WE FIGHTING TODAY? OR ARE YOU JUST GOING TO TELL ME HOW AWESOME YOUR WEAPON IS?
CLANGG
FIGURED I'D JUST SHOW YOU.
REALLY?
BECAUSE IF YOU'RE ASKING...

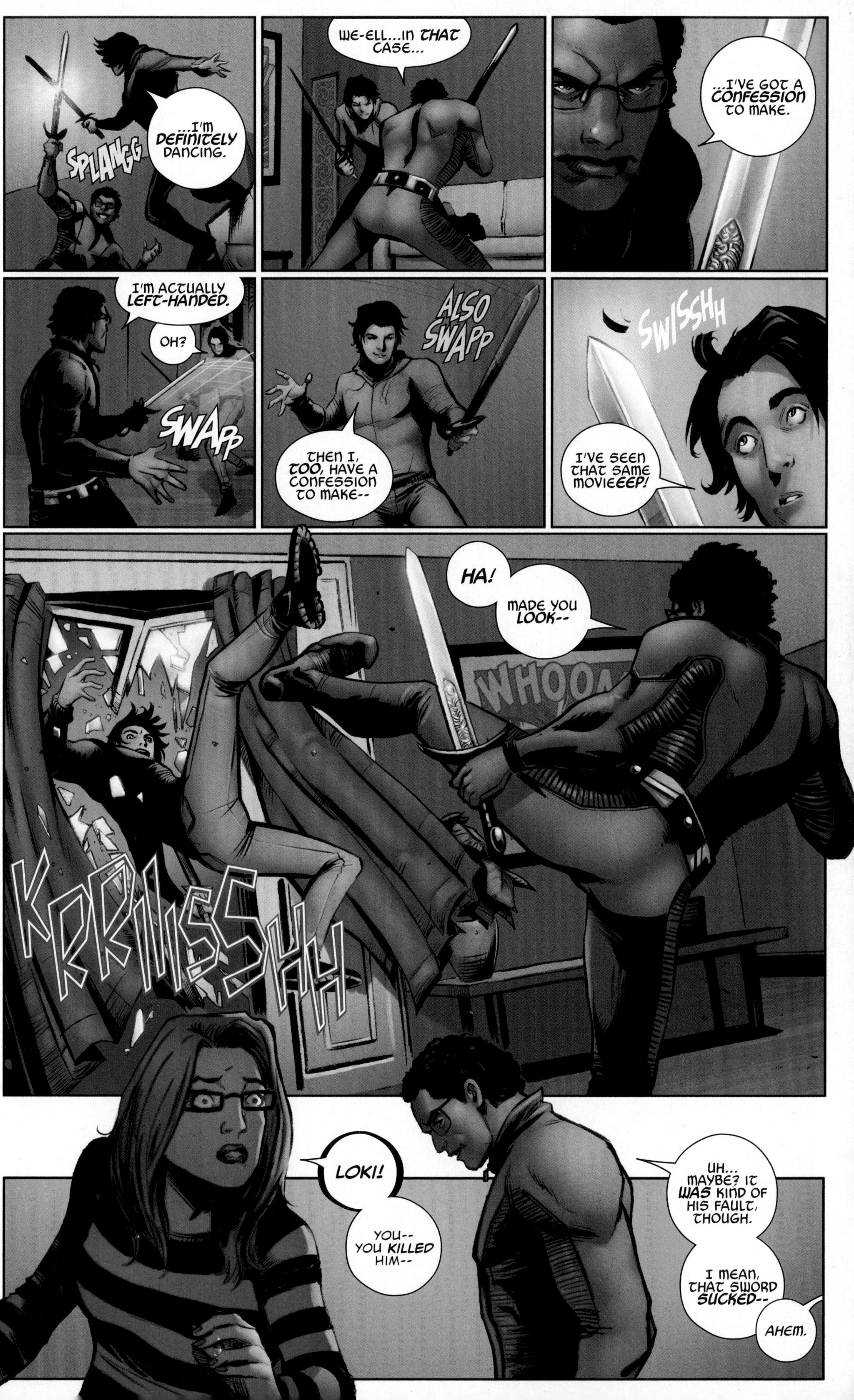
SPLANGG
...I'M DEFINITELY DANCING.
WE-ELL...IN THAT CASE...
...I'VE GOT A CONFESSION TO MAKE.
I'M ACTUALLY LEFT-HANDED.
OH?
SWAPP
ALSO SWAPP
THEN I, TOO, HAVE A CONFESSION TO MAKE--
SWISSHH
I'VE SEEN THAT SAME MOVIEEEP!
HA!
MADE YOU LOOK--
KRRISSHH
LOKI!
YOU-- YOU KILLED HIM--
UH... MAYBE? IT WAS KIND OF HIS FAULT, THOUGH.
I MEAN, THAT SWORD SUCKED--
AHEM.

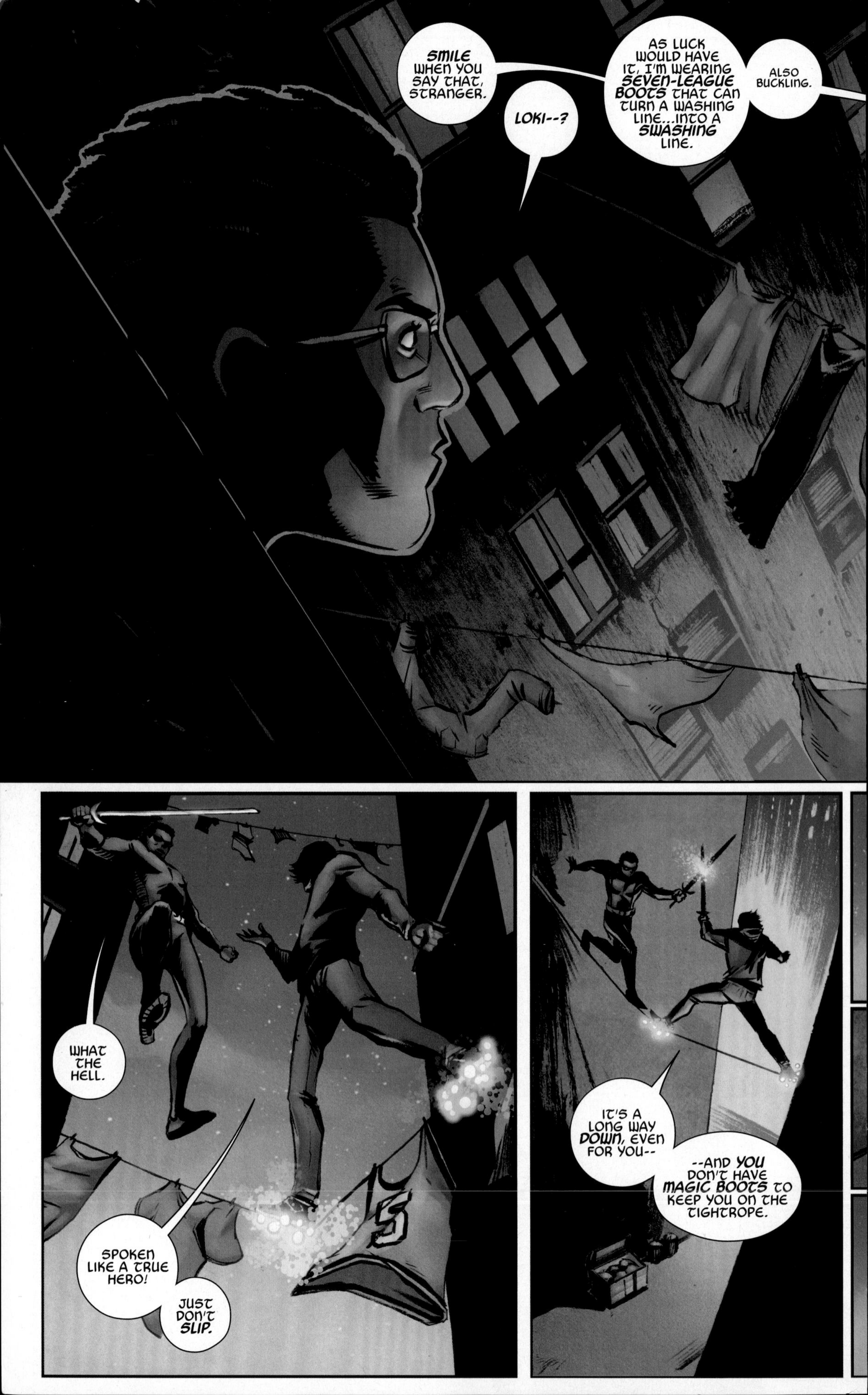
SMILE WHEN YOU SAY THAT, STRANGER.
LOKI--?
AS LUCK WOULD HAVE IT, I'M WEARING SEVEN-LEAGUE BOOTS THAT CAN TURN A WASHING LINE...INTO A SWASHING LINE.
ALSO BUCKLING.
WHAT THE HELL.
SPOKEN LIKE A TRUE HERO!
JUST DON'T SLIP.
IT'S A LONG WAY DOWN, EVEN FOR YOU--
--AND YOU DON'T HAVE MAGIC BOOTS TO KEEP YOU ON THE TIGHTROPE.

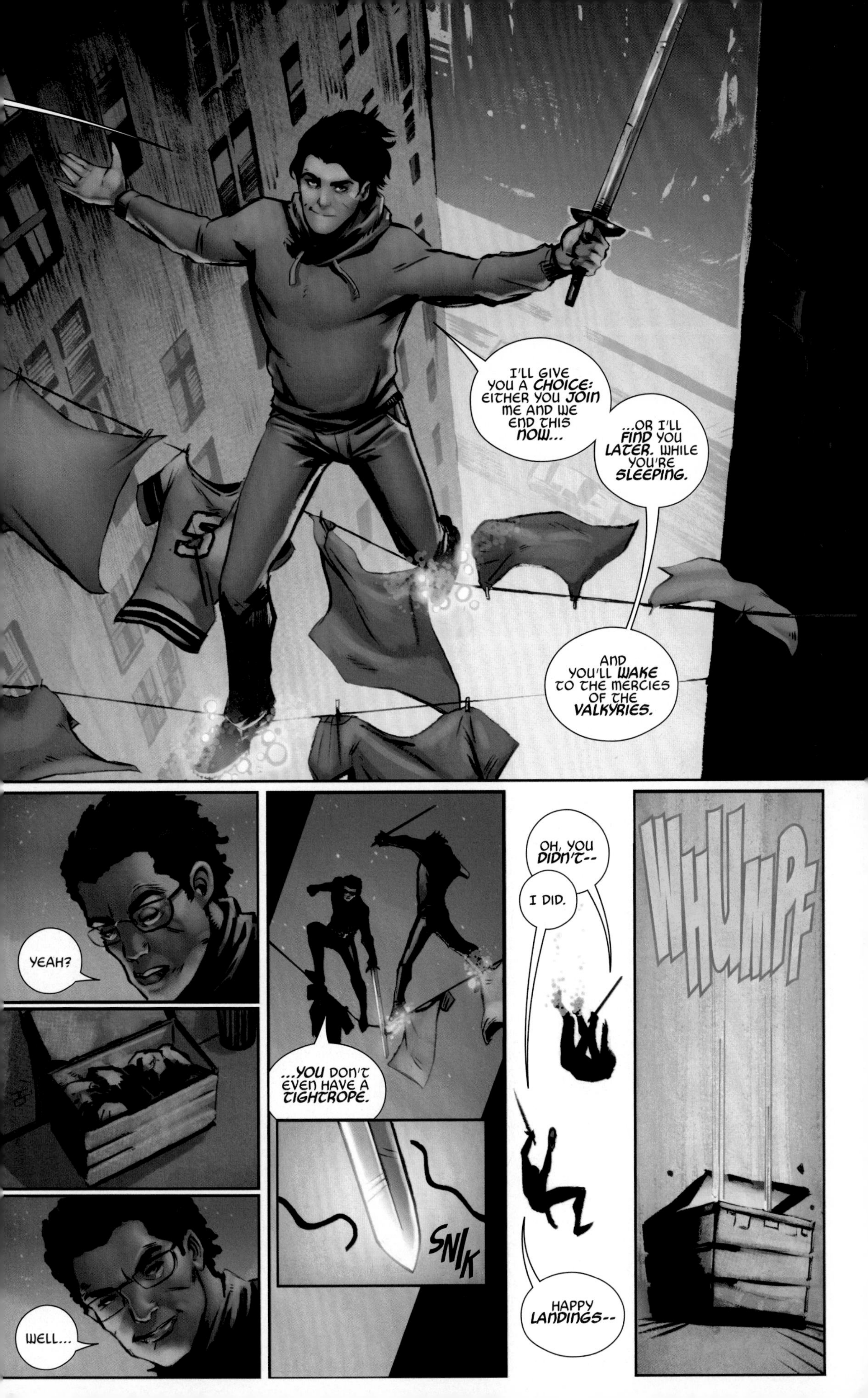
I'LL GIVE YOU A CHOICE: EITHER YOU JOIN ME AND WE END THIS NOW...
...OR I'LL FIND YOU LATER. WHILE YOU'RE SLEEPING.
AND YOU'LL WAKE TO THE MERCIES OF THE VALKYRIES.
YEAH?
WELL...
...YOU DON'T EVEN HAVE A TIGHTROPE.
SNIK
OH, YOU DIDN'T--
I DID.
HAPPY LANDINGS--
WHUMPF

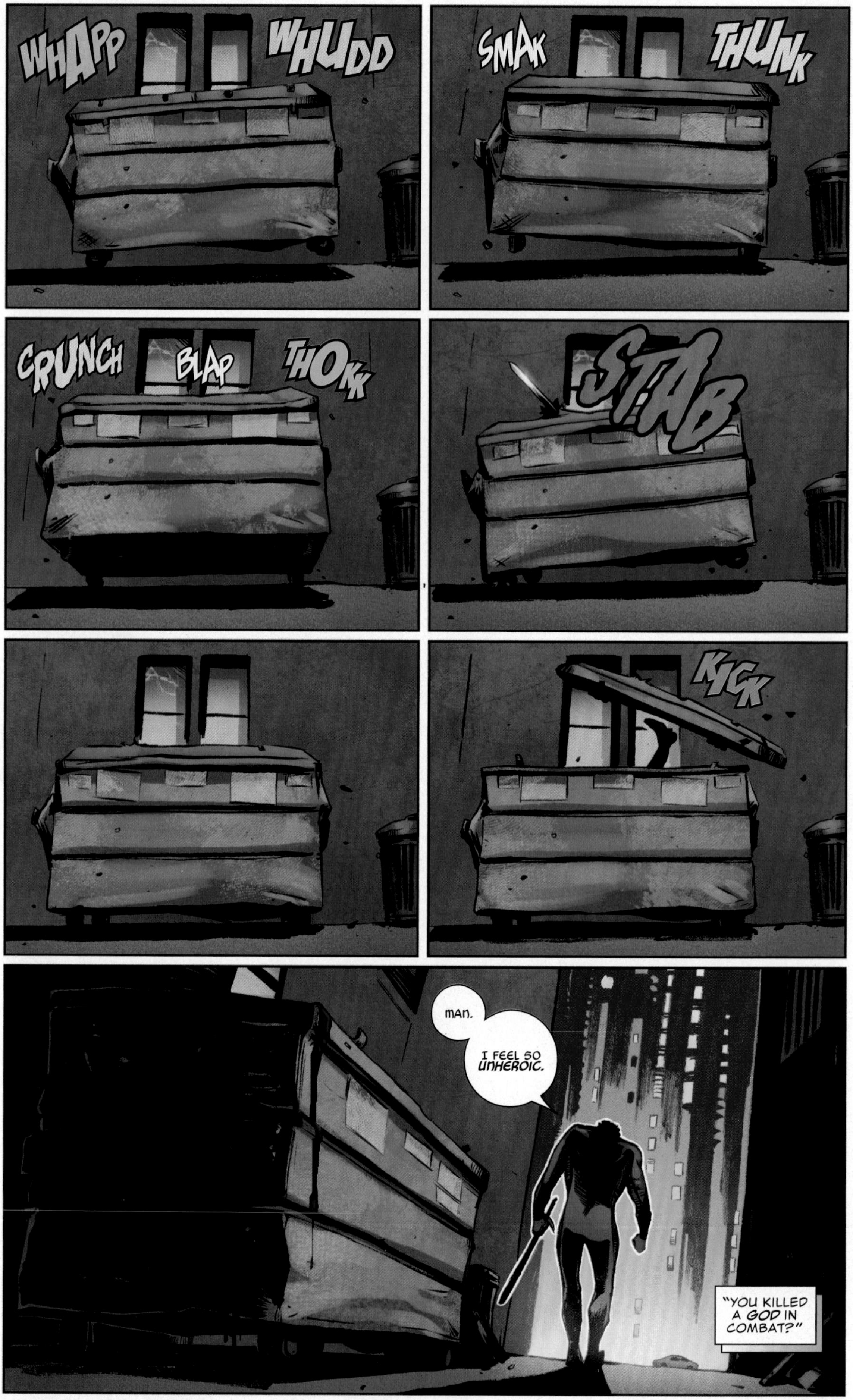
WHAPP
WHUDD
SMAK
THUNK
CRUNCH
BLAP
THOKK
STAB
KICK
MAN.
I FEEL SO UNHEROIC.
"YOU KILLED A GOD IN COMBAT?"

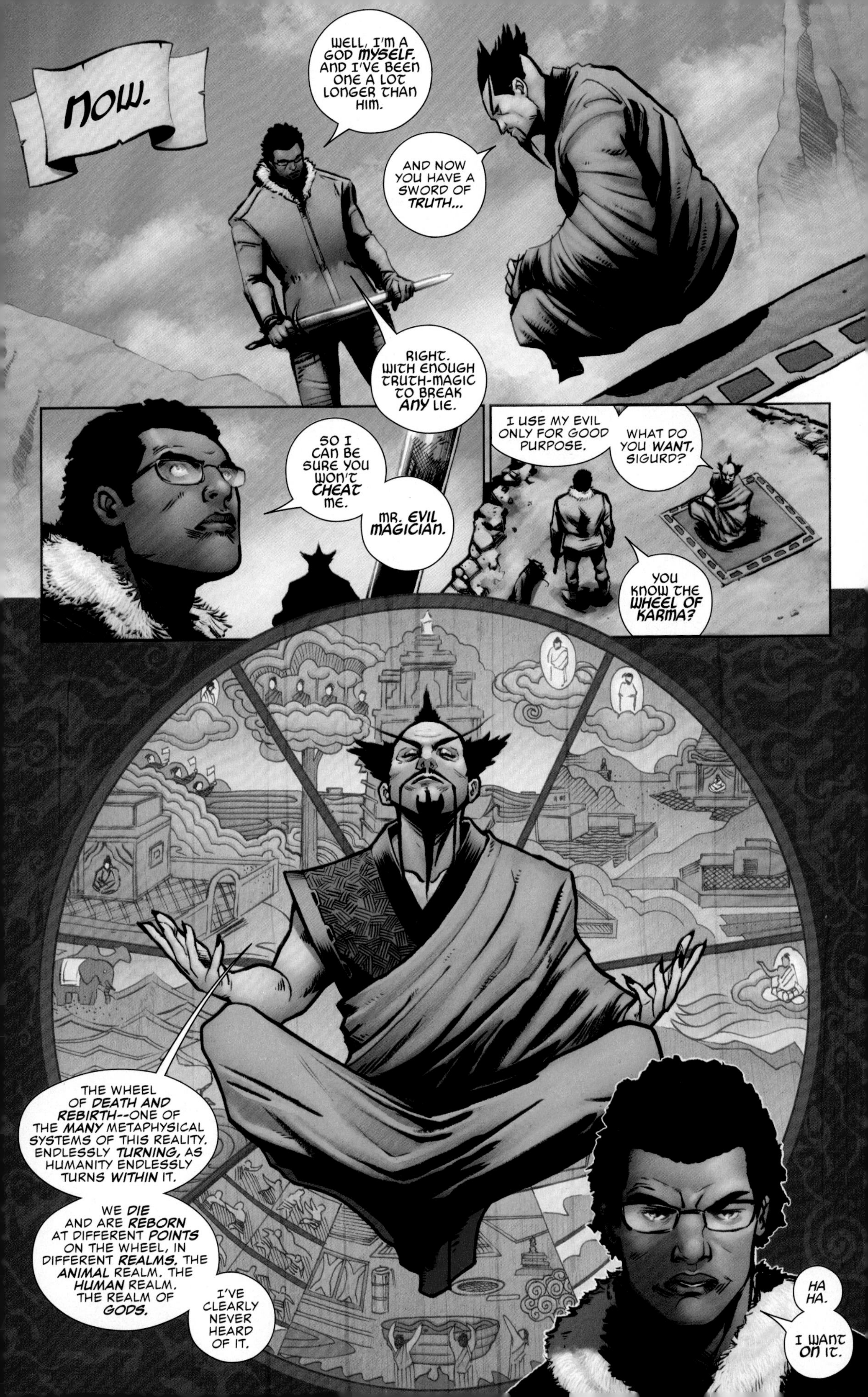
NOW.
WELL, I'M A GOD MYSELF. AND I'VE BEEN ONE A LOT LONGER THAN HIM.
AND NOW YOU HAVE A SWORD OF TRUTH...
RIGHT. WITH ENOUGH TRUTH-MAGIC TO BREAK ANY LIE.
SO I CAN BE SURE YOU WON'T CHEAT ME.
MR. EVIL MAGICIAN.
I USE MY EVIL ONLY FOR GOOD PURPOSE.
WHAT DO YOU WANT, SIGURD?
YOU KNOW THE WHEEL OF KARMA?
THE WHEEL OF DEATH AND REBIRTH--ONE OF THE MANY METAPHYSICAL SYSTEMS OF THIS REALITY. ENDLESSLY TURNING, AS HUMANITY ENDLESSLY TURNS WITHIN IT.
WE DIE AND ARE REBORN AT DIFFERENT POINTS ON THE WHEEL, IN DIFFERENT REALMS. THE ANIMAL REALM. THE HUMAN REALM. THE REALM OF GODS.
I'VE CLEARLY NEVER HEARD OF IT.
HA HA.
I WANT ON IT.

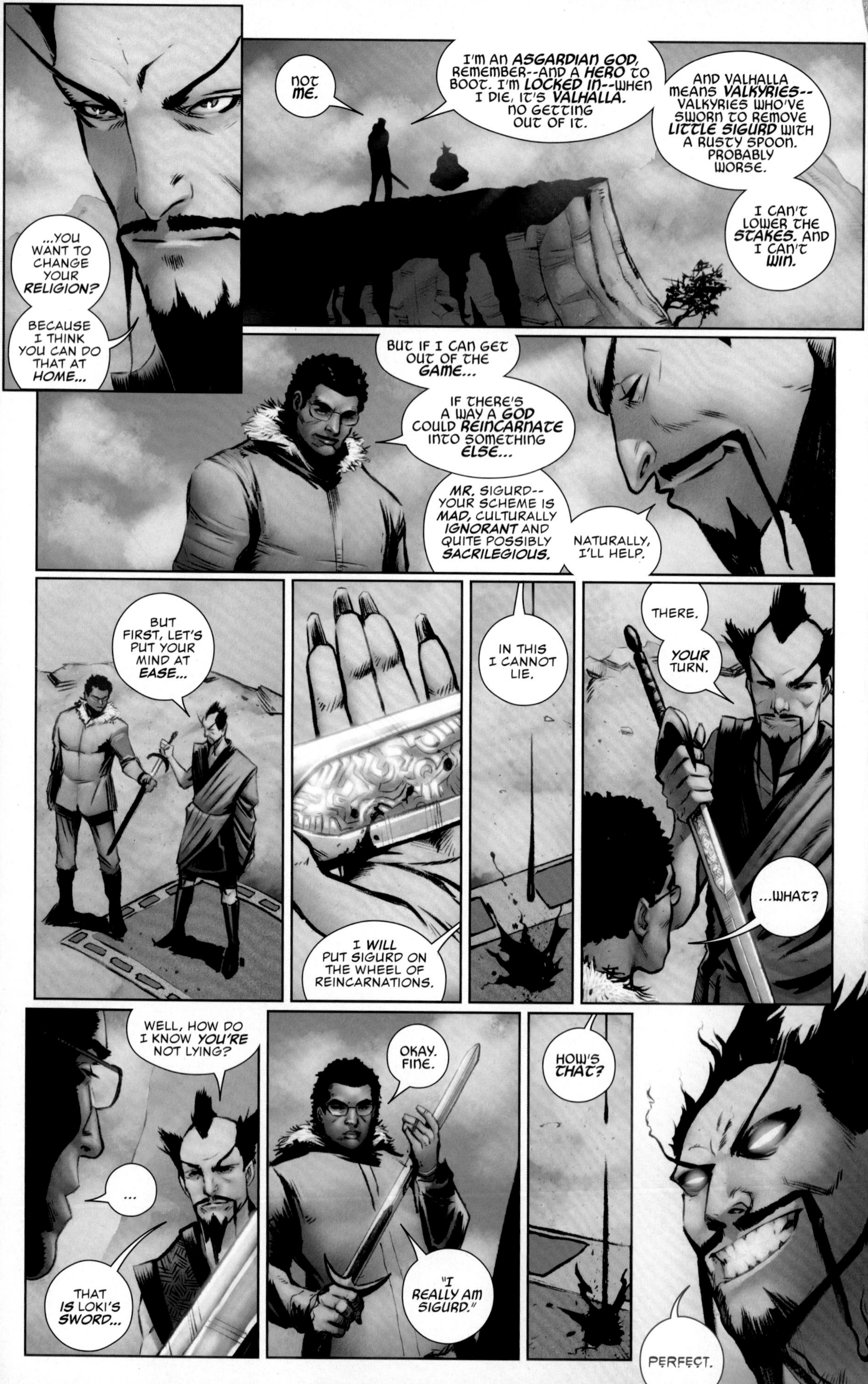
...YOU WANT TO CHANGE YOUR RELIGION?
BECAUSE I THINK YOU CAN DO THAT AT HOME...
NOT ME.
I'M AN ASGARDIAN GOD, REMEMBER--AND A HERO TO BOOT. I'M LOCKED IN--WHEN I DIE, IT'S VALHALLA. NO GETTING OUT OF IT.
AND VALHALLA MEANS VALKYRIES--VALKYRIES WHO'VE SWORN TO REMOVE LITTLE SIGURD WITH A RUSTY SPOON. PROBABLY WORSE.
I CAN'T LOWER THE STAKES. AND I CAN'T WIN.
BUT IF I CAN GET OUT OF THE GAME...
IF THERE'S A WAY A GOD COULD REINCARNATE INTO SOMETHING ELSE...
MR. SIGURD--YOUR SCHEME IS MAD, CULTURALLY IGNORANT AND QUITE POSSIBLY SACRILEGIOUS.
NATURALLY, I'LL HELP.
BUT FIRST, LET'S PUT YOUR MIND AT EASE...
I WILL PUT SIGURD ON THE WHEEL OF REINCARNATIONS.
IN THIS I CANNOT LIE.
THERE.
YOUR TURN.
...WHAT?
WELL, HOW DO I KNOW YOU'RE NOT LYING?
...
THAT IS LOKI'S SWORD...
OKAY. FINE.
"I REALLY AM SIGURD."
HOW'S THAT?
PERFECT.

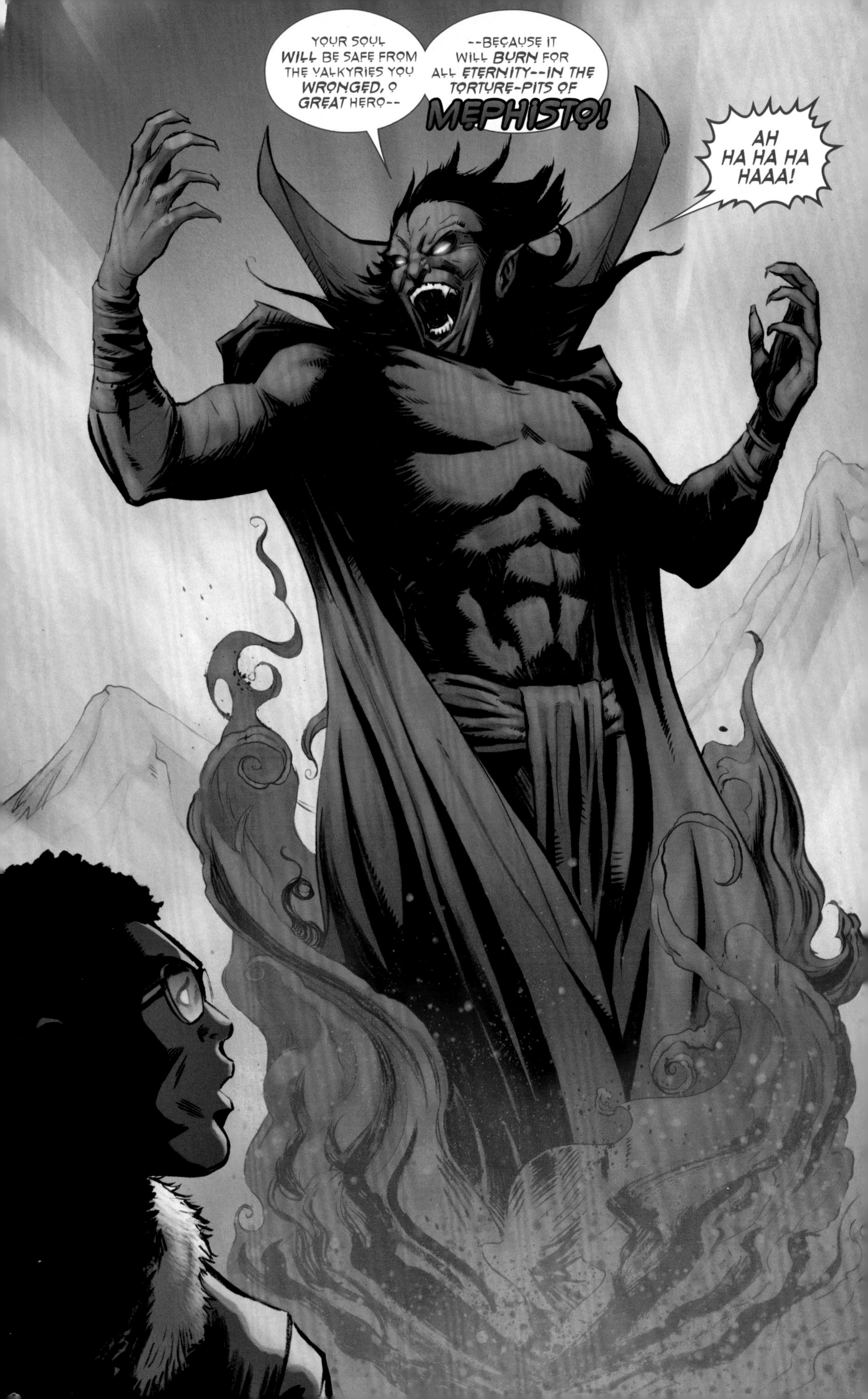
YOUR SOUL WILL BE SAFE FROM THE VALKYRIES YOU WRONGED, O GREAT HERO--
--BECAUSE IT WILL BURN FOR ALL ETERNITY--IN THE TORTURE-PITS OF MEPHISTO!
AH HA HA HA HAAA!

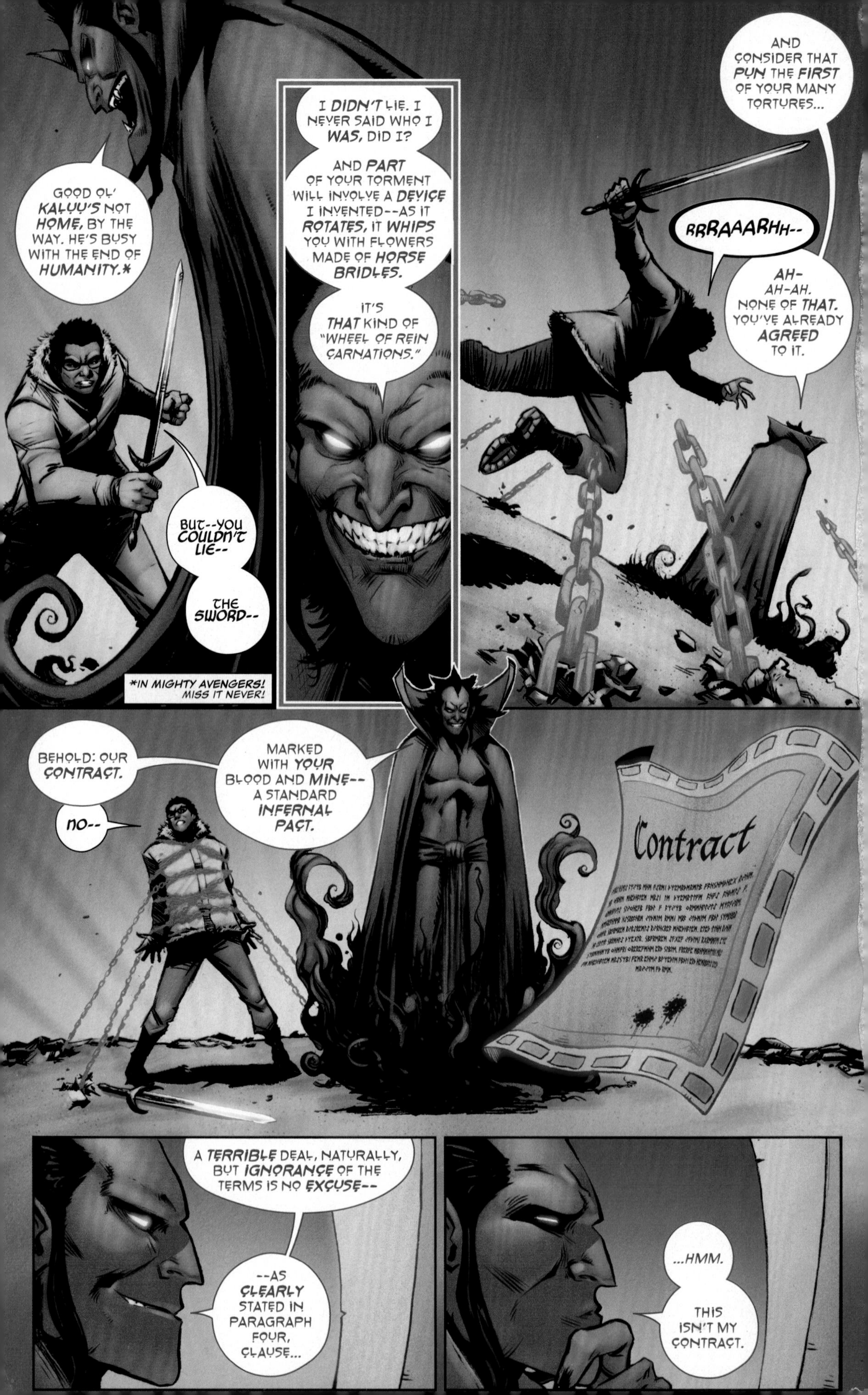

GOOD OL' KALUU'S NOT HOME, BY THE WAY. HE'S BUSY WITH THE END OF HUMANITY.*
BUT--YOU COULDN'T LIE--
THE SWORD--
*IN MIGHTY AVENGERS! MISS IT NEVER!
I DIDN'T LIE. I NEVER SAID WHO I WAS, DID I?
AND PART OF YOUR TORMENT WILL INVOLVE A DEVICE I INVENTED--AS IT ROTATES, IT WHIPS YOU WITH FLOWERS MADE OF HORSE BRIDLES.
IT'S THAT KIND OF "WHEEL OF REIN CARNATIONS."
AND CONSIDER THAT PUN THE FIRST OF YOUR MANY TORTURES...
RRRAAARHH--
AH-AH-AH. NONE OF THAT. YOU'VE ALREADY AGREED TO IT.
BEHOLD: OUR CONTRACT.
MARKED WITH YOUR BLOOD AND MINE--A STANDARD INFERNAL PACT.
NO--
Contract
A TERRIBLE DEAL, NATURALLY, BUT IGNORANCE OF THE TERMS IS NO EXCUSE--
--AS CLEARLY STATED IN PARAGRAPH FOUR, CLAUSE...
...HMM.
THIS ISN'T MY CONTRACT.

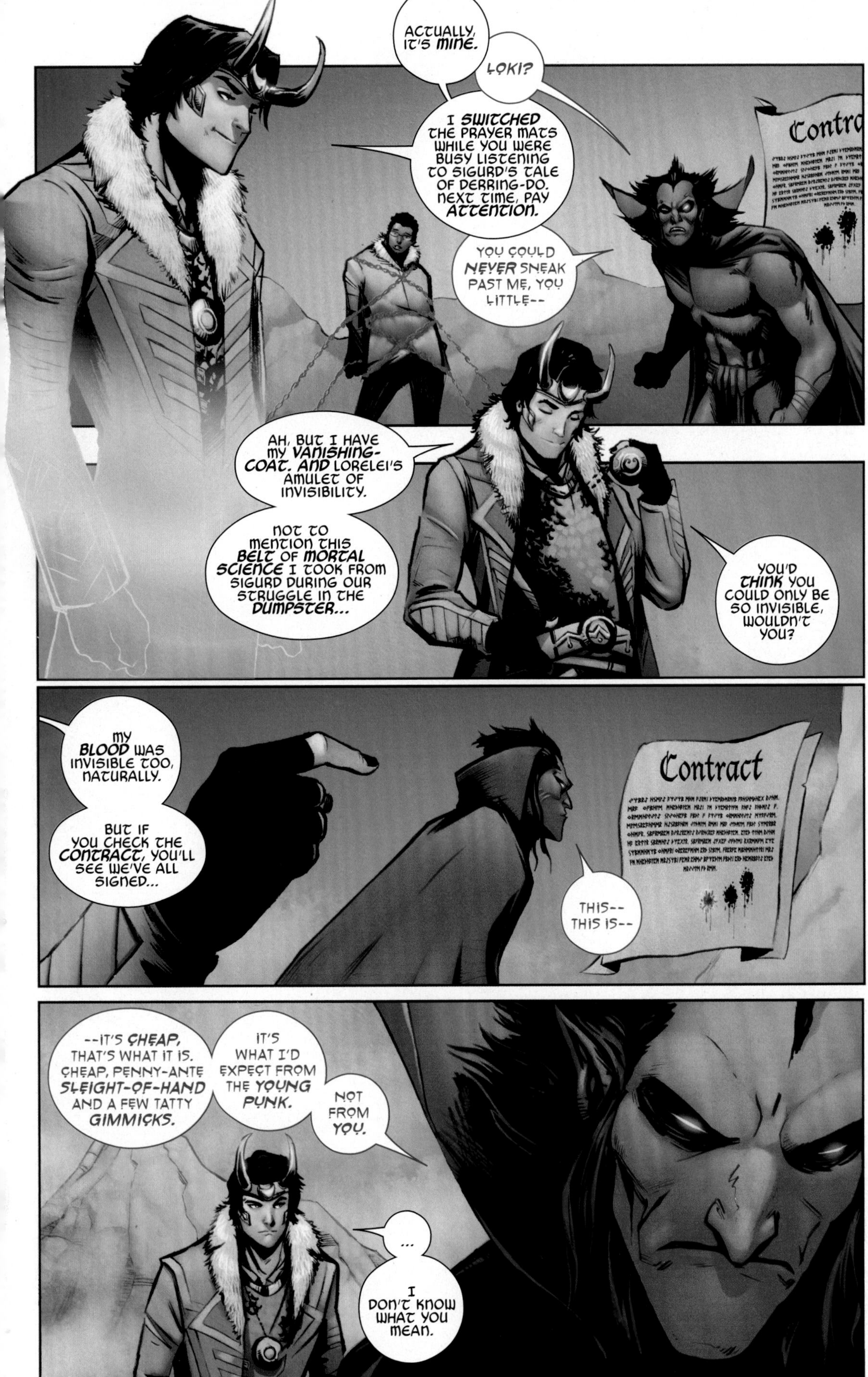

ACTUALLY, IT'S MINE.
LOKI?
I SWITCHED THE PRAYER MATS WHILE YOU WERE BUSY LISTENING TO SIGURD'S TALE OF DERRING-DO. NEXT TIME, PAY ATTENTION.
YOU COULD NEVER SNEAK PAST ME, YOU LITTLE--
Contract
AH, BUT I HAVE MY VANISHING-COAT. AND LORELEI'S AMULET OF INVISIBILITY.
NOT TO MENTION THIS BELT OF MORTAL SCIENCE I TOOK FROM SIGURD DURING OUR STRUGGLE IN THE DUMPSTER...
YOU'D THINK YOU COULD ONLY BE SO INVISIBLE, WOULDN'T YOU?
MY BLOOD WAS INVISIBLE TOO, NATURALLY.
BUT IF YOU CHECK THE CONTRACT, YOU'LL SEE WE'VE ALL SIGNED...
Contract
THIS-- THIS IS--
--IT'S CHEAP, THAT'S WHAT IT IS. CHEAP, PENNY-ANTE SLEIGHT-OF-HAND AND A FEW TATTY GIMMICKS.
IT'S WHAT I'D EXPECT FROM THE YOUNG PUNK.
NOT FROM YOU.
...
I DON'T KNOW WHAT YOU MEAN.

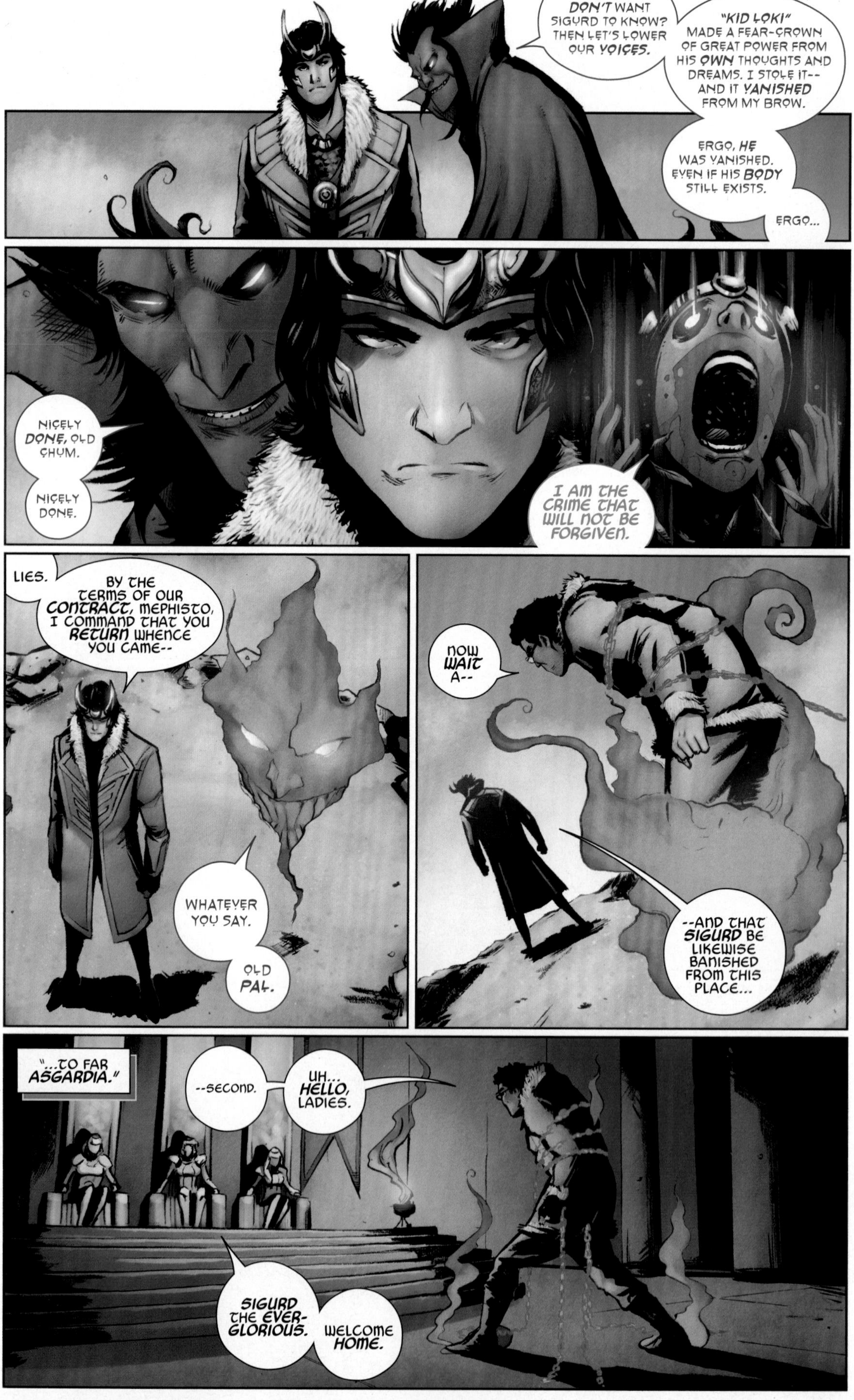
OH, YOU DON'T WANT SIGURD TO KNOW? THEN LET'S LOWER OUR VOICES.
"KID LOKI" MADE A FEAR-CROWN OF GREAT POWER FROM HIS OWN THOUGHTS AND DREAMS. I STOLE IT-- AND IT VANISHED FROM MY BROW.
ERGO, HE WAS VANISHED. EVEN IF HIS BODY STILL EXISTS.
ERGO...
NICELY DONE, OLD CHUM.
NICELY DONE.
I AM THE CRIME THAT WILL NOT BE FORGIVEN.
LIES.
BY THE TERMS OF OUR CONTRACT, MEPHISTO, I COMMAND THAT YOU RETURN WHENCE YOU CAME--
WHATEVER YOU SAY.
OLD PAL.
NOW WAIT A--
--AND THAT SIGURD BE LIKEWISE BANISHED FROM THIS PLACE...
"...TO FAR ASGARDIA."
--SECOND.
UH... HELLO, LADIES.
SIGURD THE EVER-GLORIOUS.
WELCOME HOME.

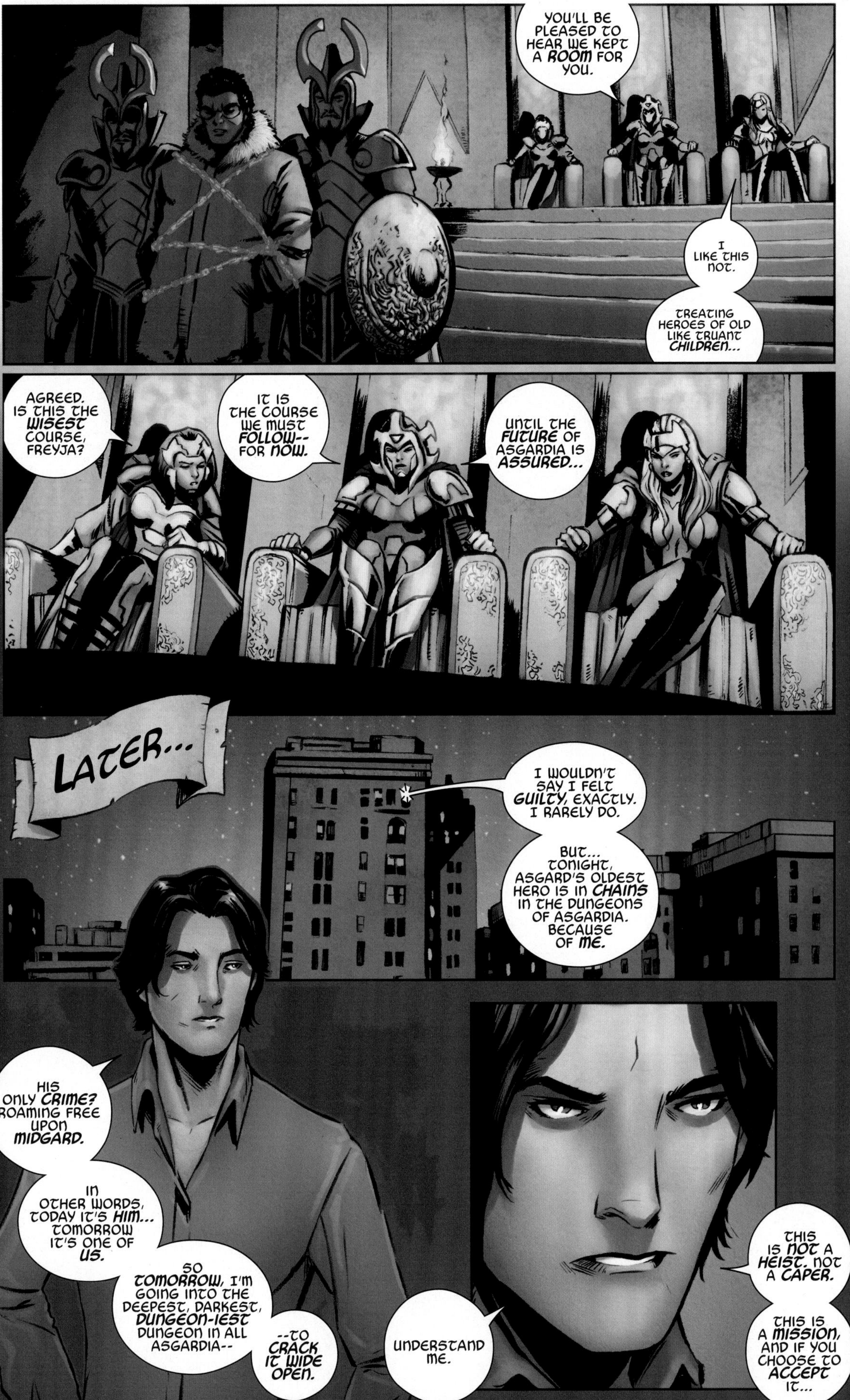
YOU'LL BE PLEASED TO HEAR WE KEPT A ROOM FOR YOU.
I LIKE THIS NOT.
TREATING HEROES OF OLD LIKE TRUANT CHILDREN...
AGREED. IS THIS THE WISEST COURSE, FREYJA?
IT IS THE COURSE WE MUST FOLLOW-- FOR NOW.
UNTIL THE FUTURE OF ASGARDIA IS ASSURED...
LATER...
I WOULDN'T SAY I FELT GUILTY, EXACTLY. I RARELY DO.
BUT... TONIGHT, ASGARD'S OLDEST HERO IS IN CHAINS IN THE DUNGEONS OF ASGARDIA. BECAUSE OF ME.
HIS ONLY CRIME? ROAMING FREE UPON MIDGARD.
IN OTHER WORDS, TODAY IT'S HIM... TOMORROW IT'S ONE OF US.
SO TOMORROW, I'M GOING INTO THE DEEPEST, DARKEST, DUNGEON-IEST DUNGEON IN ALL ASGARDIA--
--TO CRACK IT WIDE OPEN.
UNDERSTAND ME.
THIS IS NOT A HEIST. NOT A CAPER.
THIS IS A MISSION, AND IF YOU CHOOSE TO ACCEPT IT...

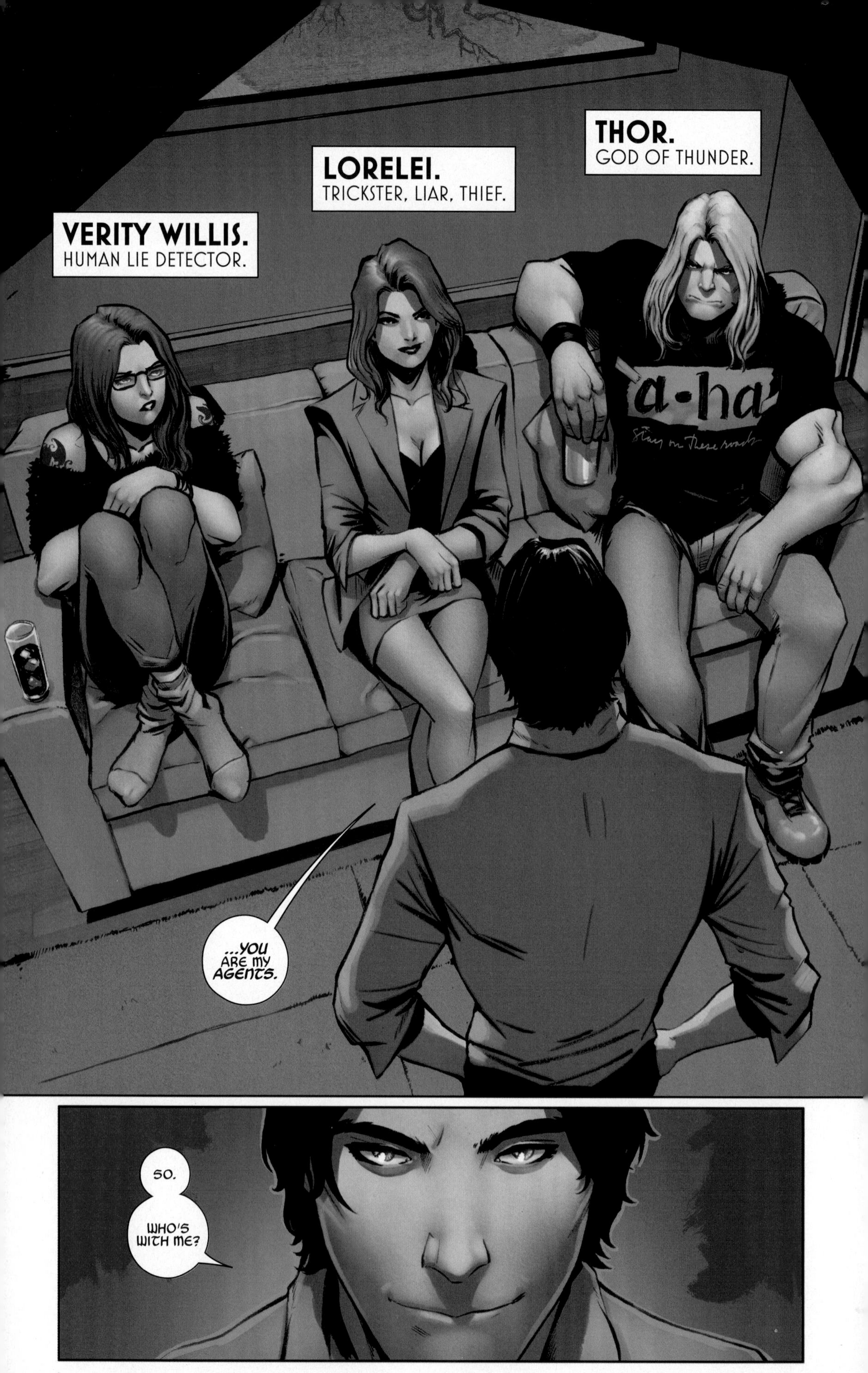
VERITY WILLIS.
HUMAN LIE DETECTOR.
LORELEI.
TRICKSTER, LIAR, THIEF.
THOR.
GOD OF THUNDER.
a-ha
...YOU ARE MY AGENTS.
SO.
WHO'S WITH ME?

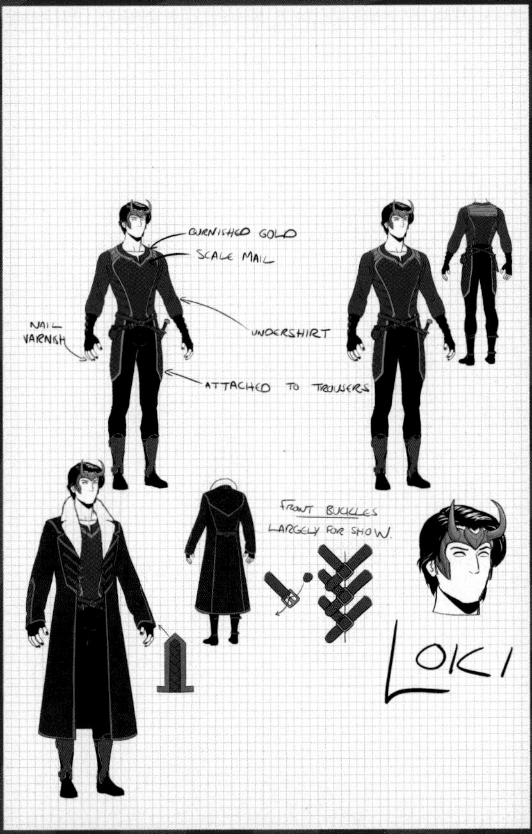
BURNISHED GOLD
SCALE MAIL
NAIL VARNISH
UNDERSHIRT
ATTACHED TO TROUSERS
FRONT BUCKLES LARGELY FOR SHOW.
LOKI

#2 DESIGN VARIANT
BY JAMIE McKELVIE

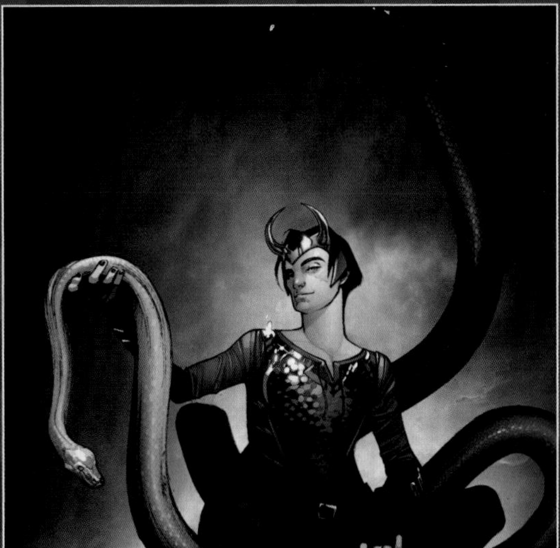

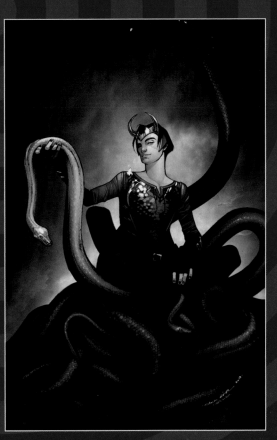

#3 VARIANT
BY OLIVIER COIPEL & MARTE GRACIA

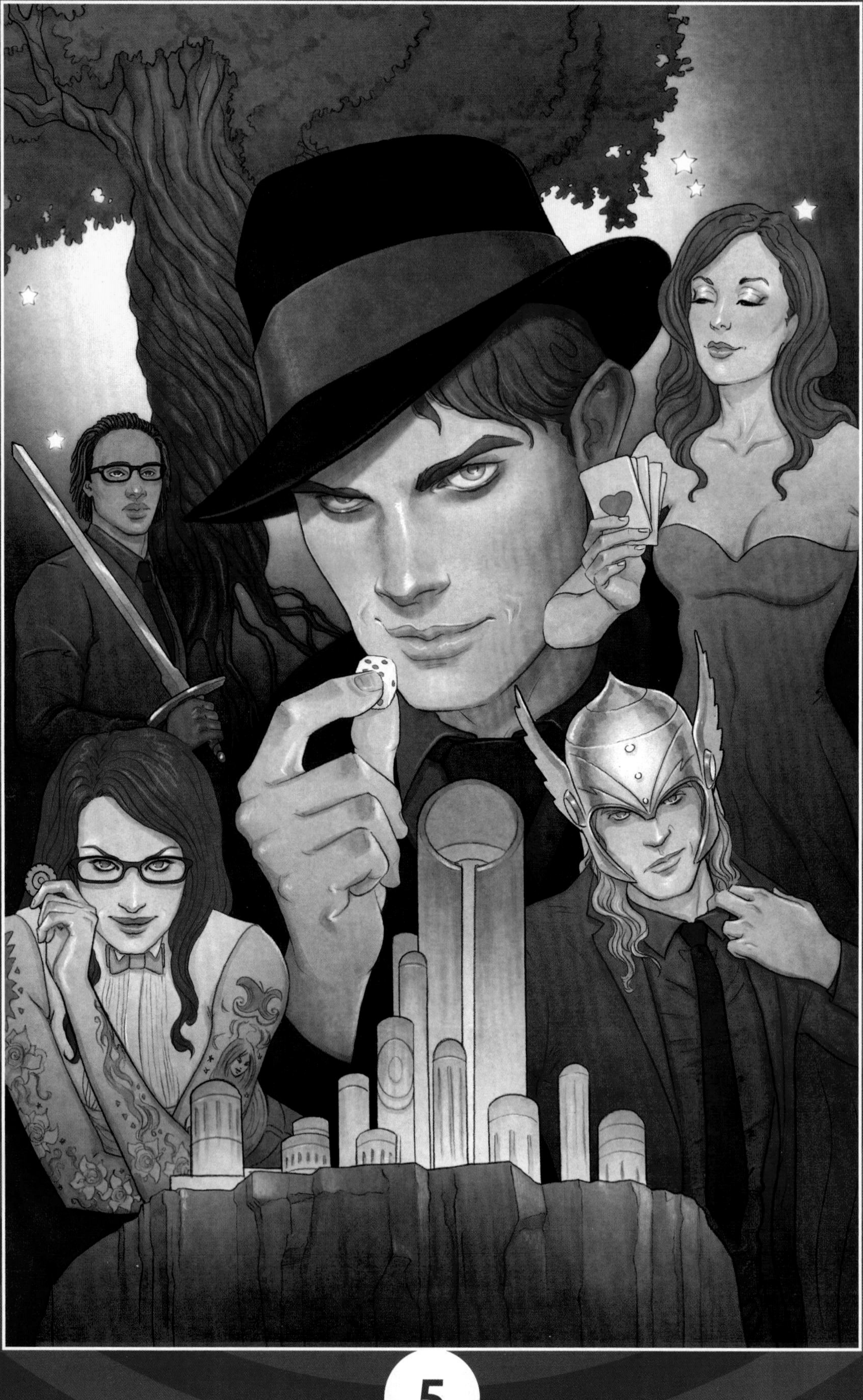

5

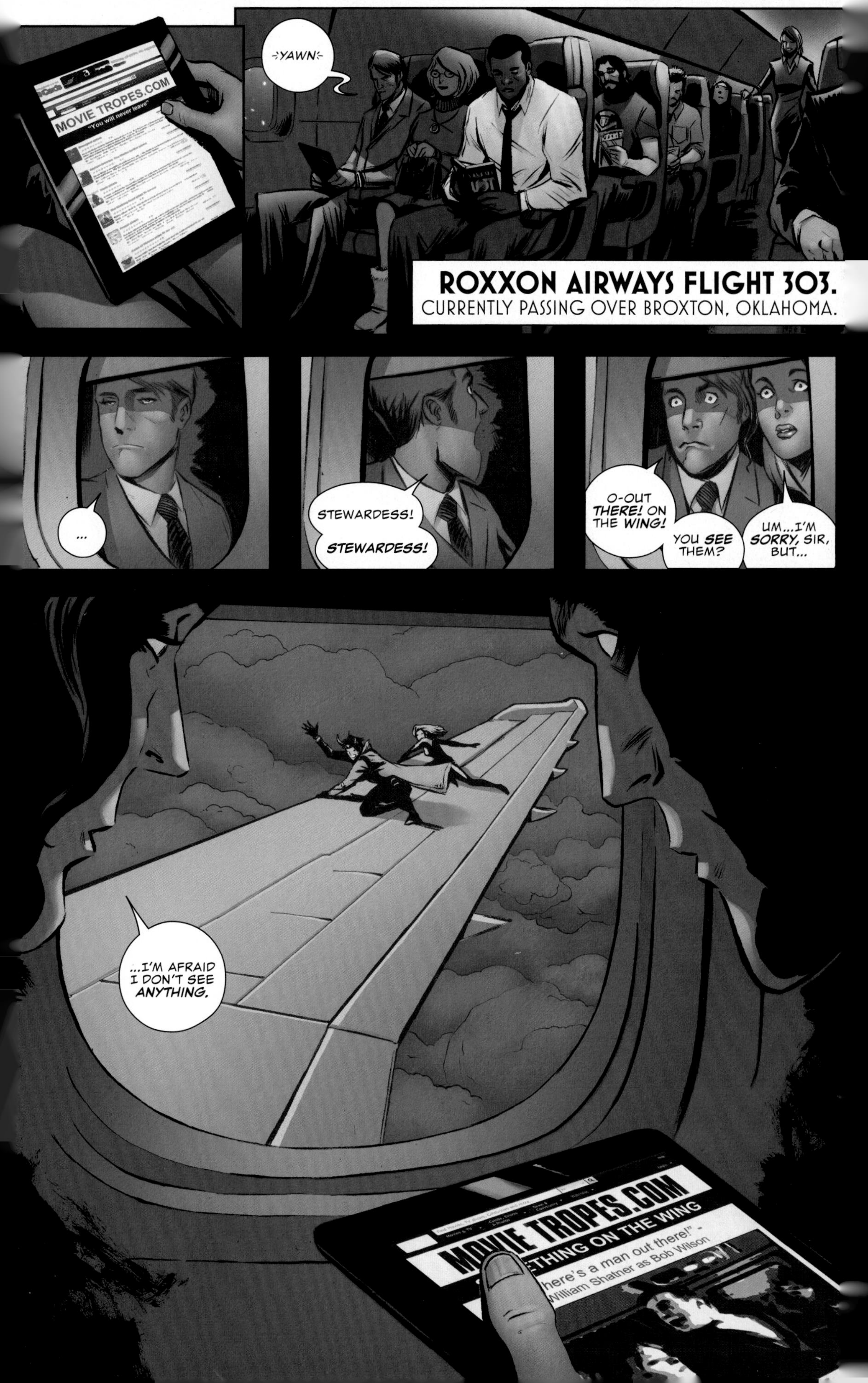
MOVIE TROPES.COM
"You will never leave"
~YAWN~
ROXXON AIRWAYS FLIGHT 303.
CURRENTLY PASSING OVER BROXTON, OKLAHOMA.
...
STEWARDESS!
STEWARDESS!
O-OUT THERE! ON THE WING!
YOU SEE THEM?
UM...I'M SORRY, SIR, BUT...
...I'M AFRAID I DON'T SEE ANYTHING.
MOVIE TROPES.COM
ETHING ON THE WING
here's a man out there!" -
William Shatner as Bob Wilson

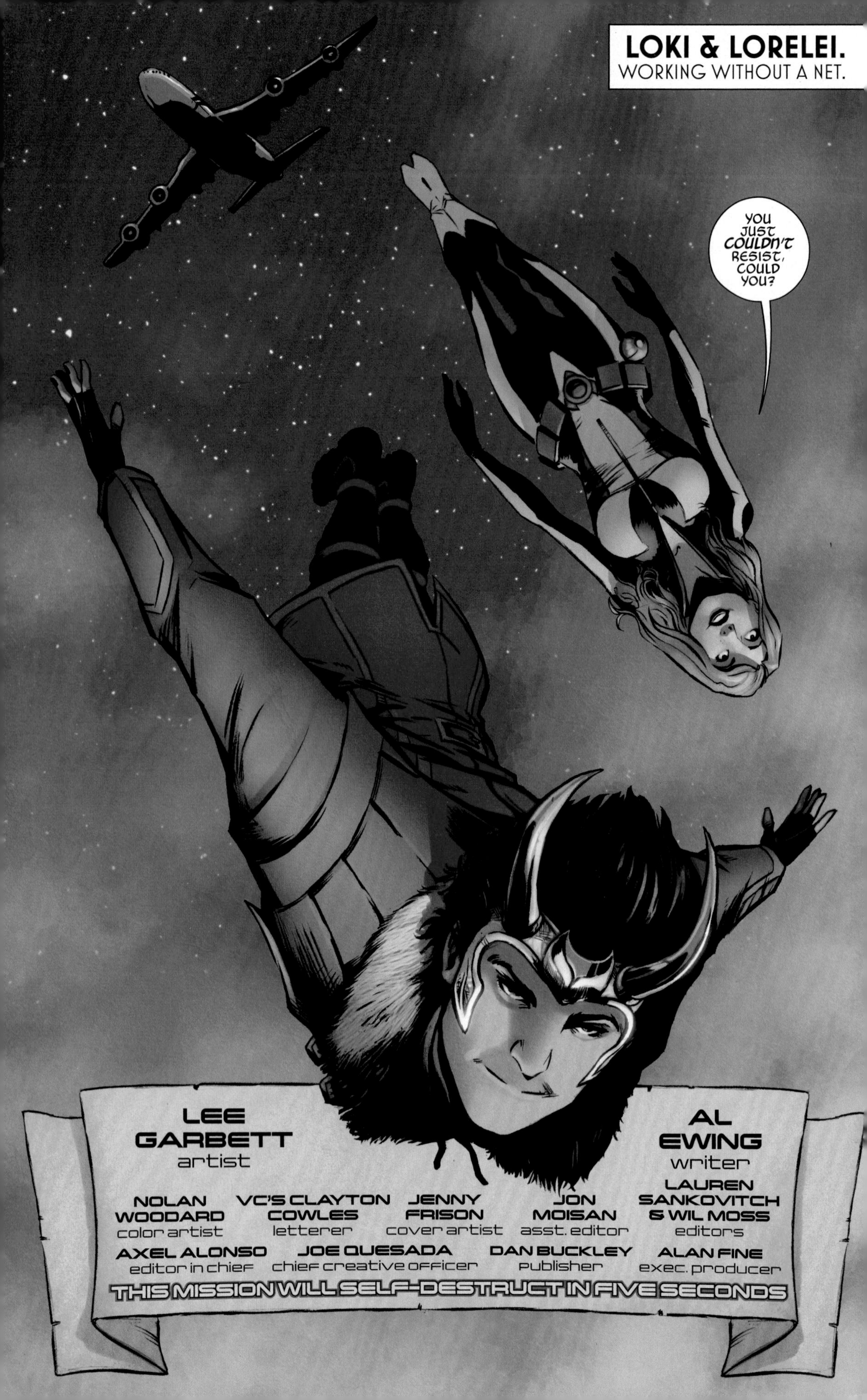
LOKI & LORELEI.
WORKING WITHOUT A NET.
YOU JUST COULDN'T RESIST, COULD YOU?
LEE GARBETT artist
AL EWING writer
NOLAN WOODARD color artist
VC'S CLAYTON COWLES letterer
JENNY FRISON cover artist
JON MOISAN asst. editor
LAUREN SANKOVITCH & WIL MOSS editors
AXEL ALONSO editor in chief
JOE QUESADA chief creative officer
DAN BUCKLEY publisher
ALAN FINE exec. producer
THIS MISSION WILL SELF-DESTRUCT IN FIVE SECONDS

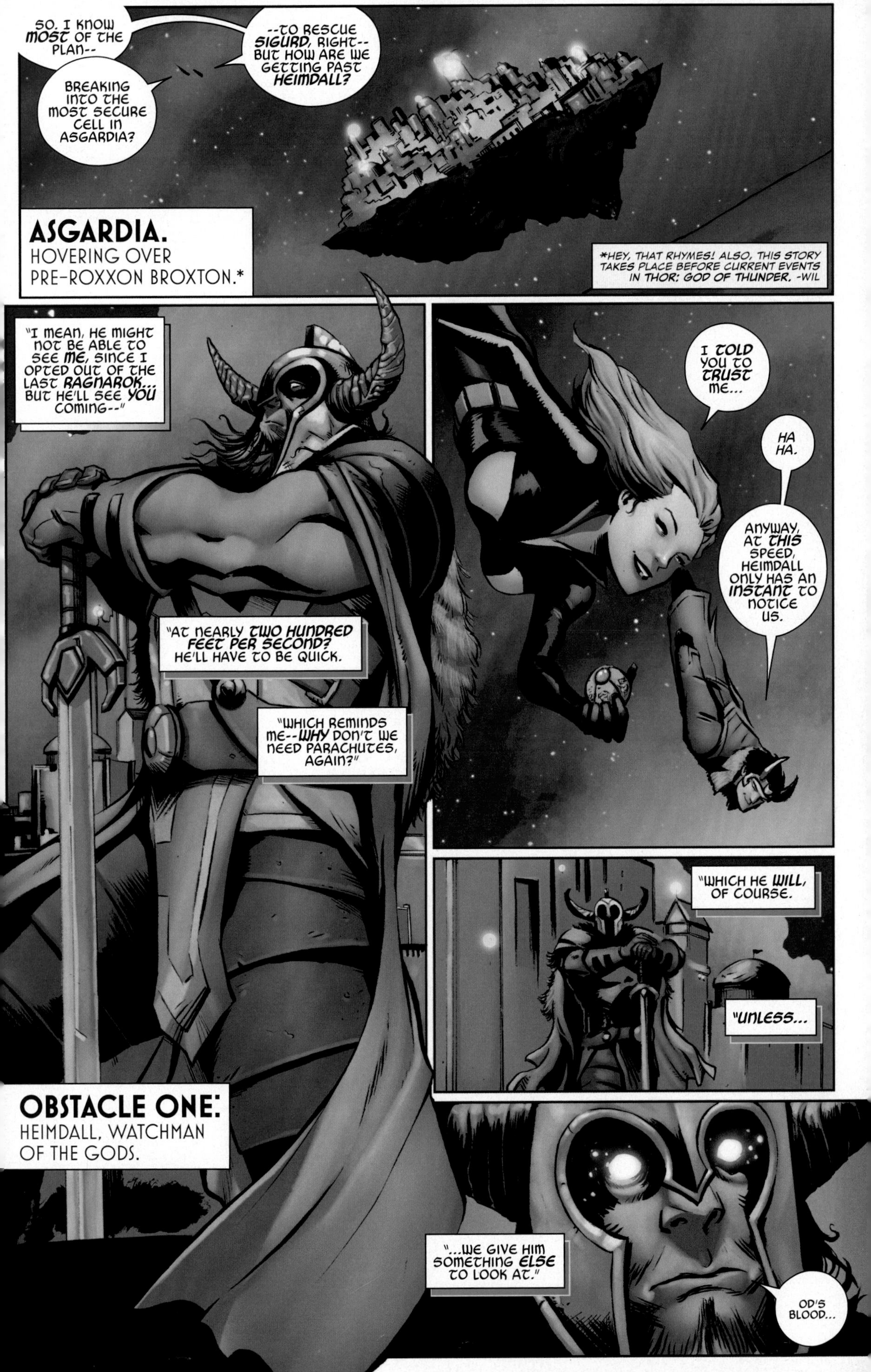

SO. I KNOW MOST OF THE PLAN--
BREAKING INTO THE MOST SECURE CELL IN ASGARDIA?
--TO RESCUE SIGURD, RIGHT-- BUT HOW ARE WE GETTING PAST HEIMDALL?
ASGARDIA. HOVERING OVER PRE-ROXXON BROXTON.*
*HEY, THAT RHYMES! ALSO, THIS STORY TAKES PLACE BEFORE CURRENT EVENTS IN THOR: GOD OF THUNDER. -WIL
"I MEAN, HE MIGHT NOT BE ABLE TO SEE ME, SINCE I OPTED OUT OF THE LAST RAGNAROK... BUT HE'LL SEE YOU COMING--"
I TOLD YOU TO TRUST ME...
HA HA.
ANYWAY, AT THIS SPEED, HEIMDALL ONLY HAS AN INSTANT TO NOTICE US.
"AT NEARLY TWO HUNDRED FEET PER SECOND? HE'LL HAVE TO BE QUICK.
"WHICH REMINDS ME--WHY DON'T WE NEED PARACHUTES, AGAIN?"
"WHICH HE WILL, OF COURSE.
"UNLESS...
OBSTACLE ONE: HEIMDALL, WATCHMAN OF THE GODS.
"...WE GIVE HIM SOMETHING ELSE TO LOOK AT."
OD'S BLOOD...

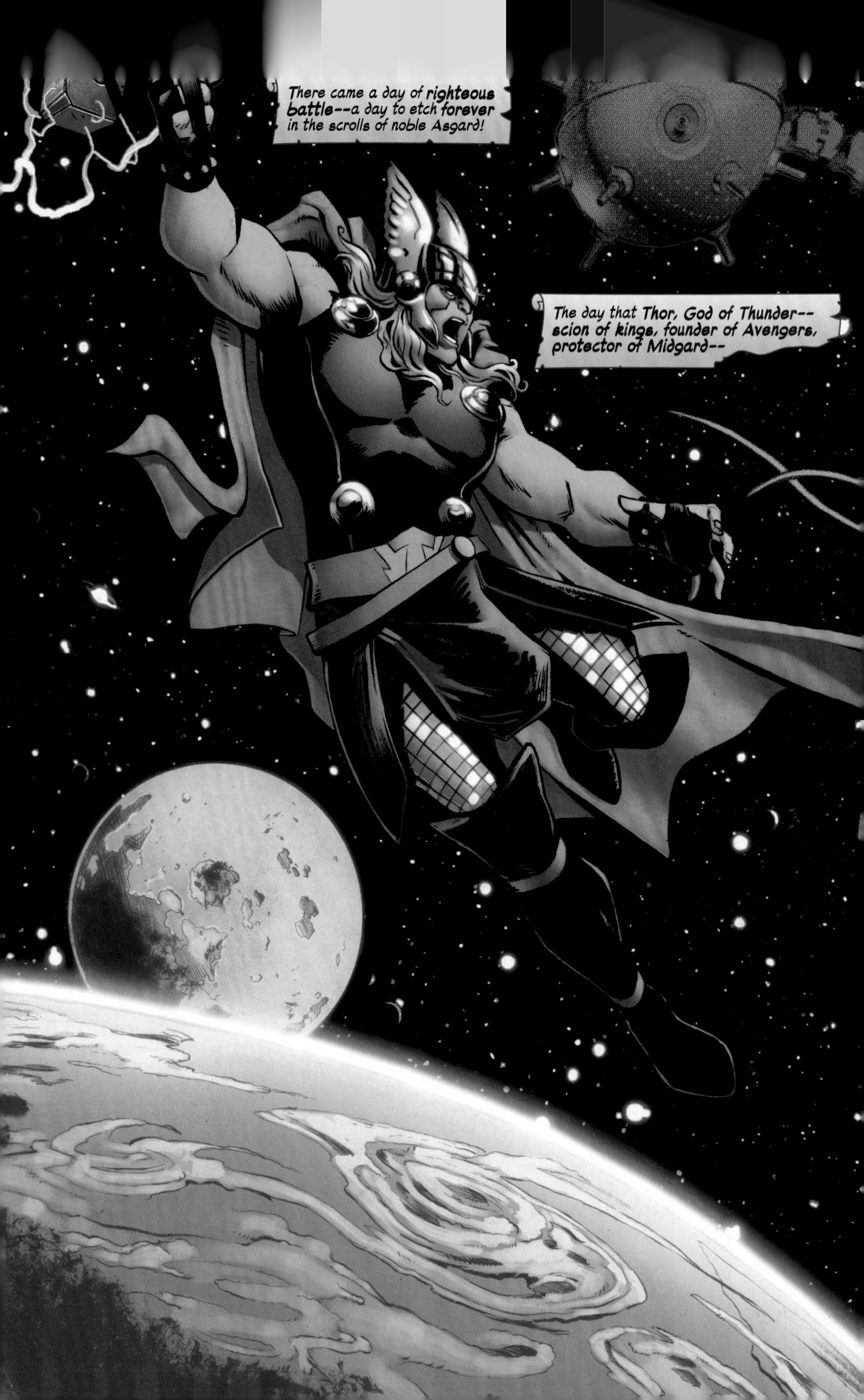
There came a day of righteous battle--a day to etch forever in the scrolls of noble Asgard!
The day that Thor, God of Thunder-- scion of kings, founder of Avengers, protector of Midgard--

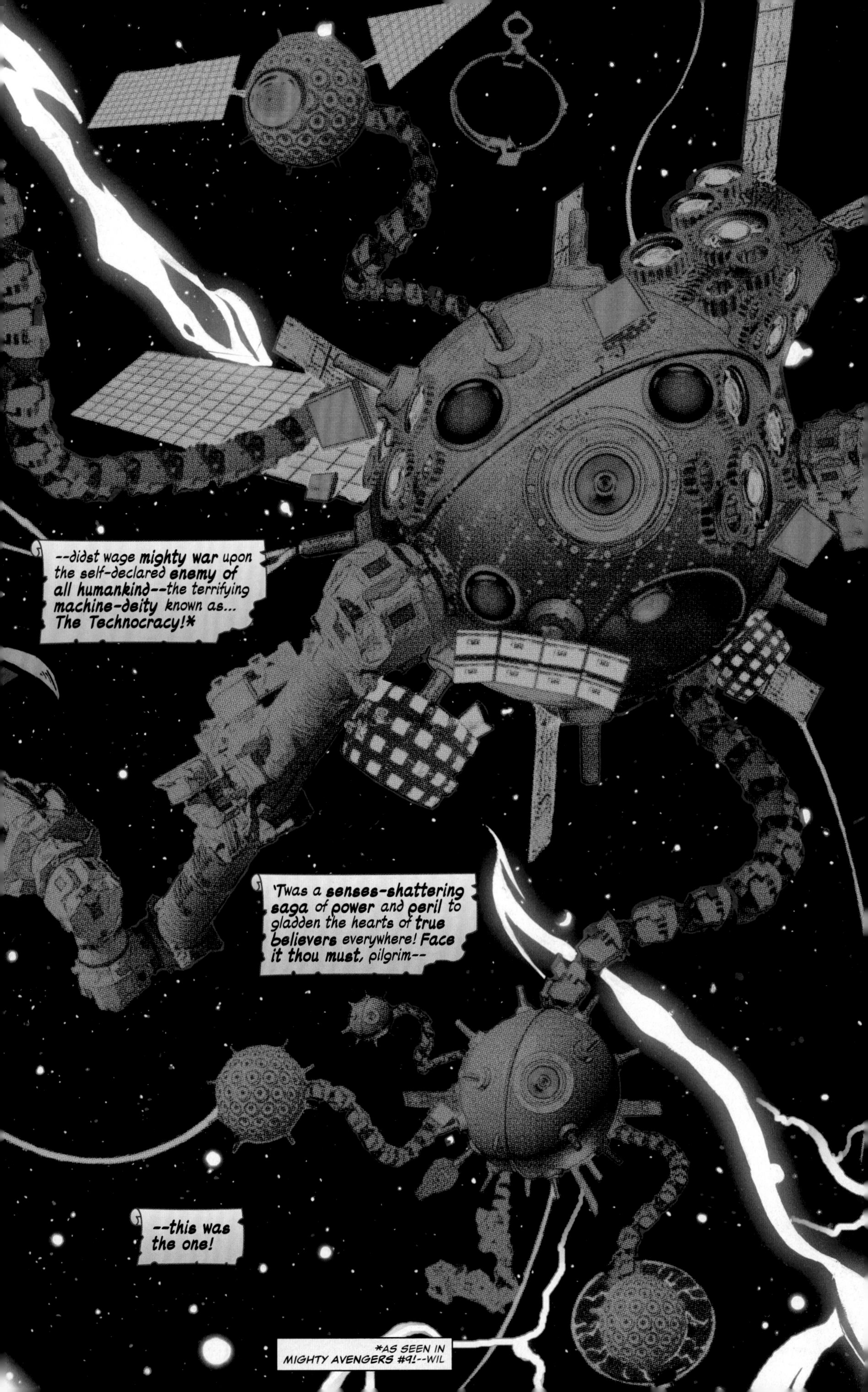
--didst wage mighty war upon the self-declared enemy of all humankind--the terrifying machine-deity known as... The Technocracy!*
'Twas a senses-shattering saga of power and peril to gladden the hearts of true believers everywhere! Face it thou must, pilgrim--
--this was the one!
*AS SEEN IN MIGHTY AVENGERS #9!--WIL

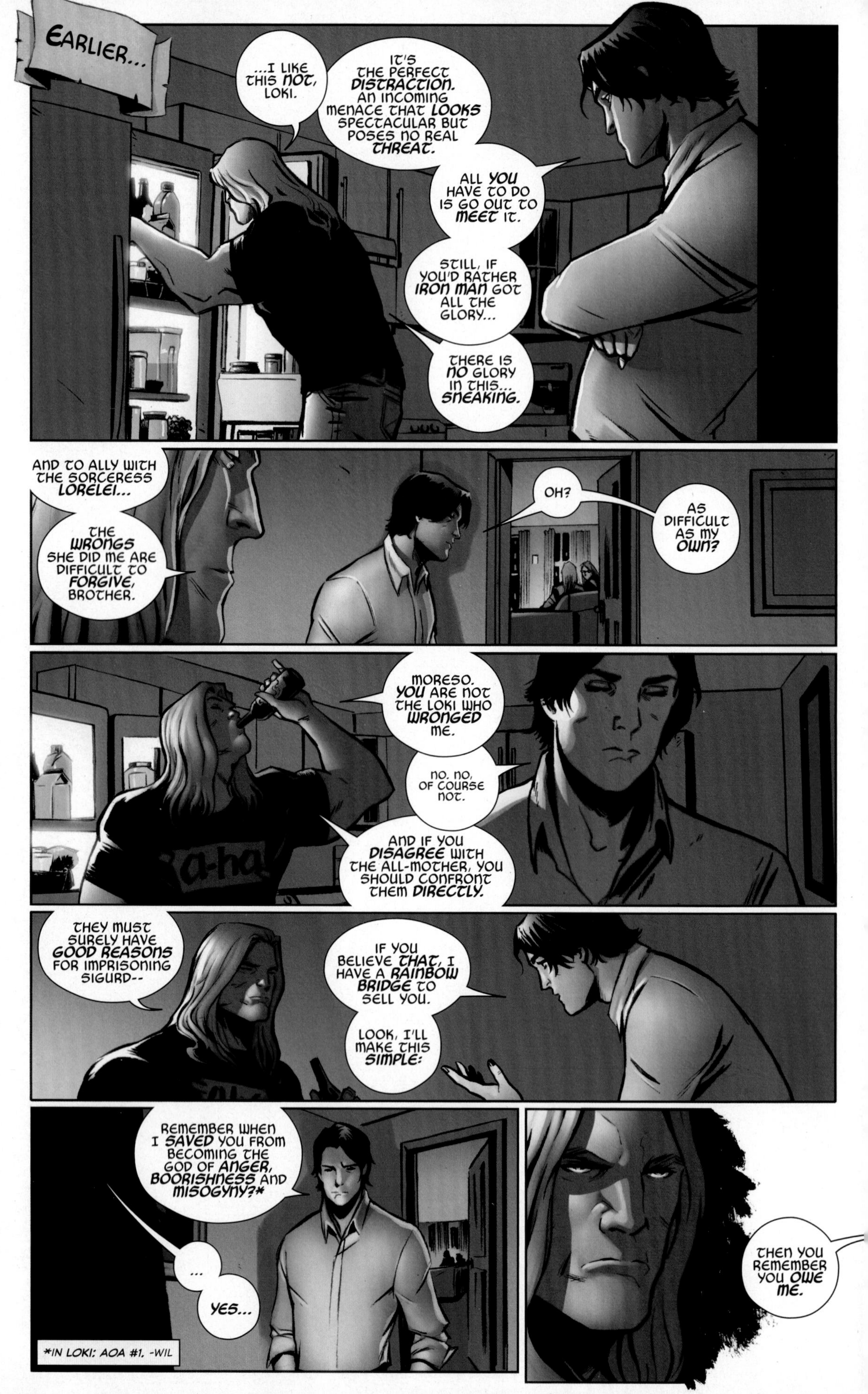
EARLIER...
...I LIKE THIS NOT, LOKI.
IT'S THE PERFECT DISTRACTION. AN INCOMING MENACE THAT LOOKS SPECTACULAR BUT POSES NO REAL THREAT.
ALL YOU HAVE TO DO IS GO OUT TO MEET IT.
STILL, IF YOU'D RATHER IRON MAN GOT ALL THE GLORY...
THERE IS NO GLORY IN THIS... SNEAKING.
AND TO ALLY WITH THE SORCERESS LORELEI...
THE WRONGS SHE DID ME ARE DIFFICULT TO FORGIVE, BROTHER.
OH?
AS DIFFICULT AS MY OWN?
MORESO. YOU ARE NOT THE LOKI WHO WRONGED ME.
NO. NO, OF COURSE NOT.
AND IF YOU DISAGREE WITH THE ALL-MOTHER, YOU SHOULD CONFRONT THEM DIRECTLY.
THEY MUST SURELY HAVE GOOD REASONS FOR IMPRISONING SIGURD--
IF YOU BELIEVE THAT, I HAVE A RAINBOW BRIDGE TO SELL YOU.
LOOK, I'LL MAKE THIS SIMPLE:
REMEMBER WHEN I SAVED YOU FROM BECOMING THE GOD OF ANGER, BOORISHNESS AND MISOGYNY?*
...
YES...
*IN LOKI: AOA #1. -WIL
THEN YOU REMEMBER YOU OWE ME.

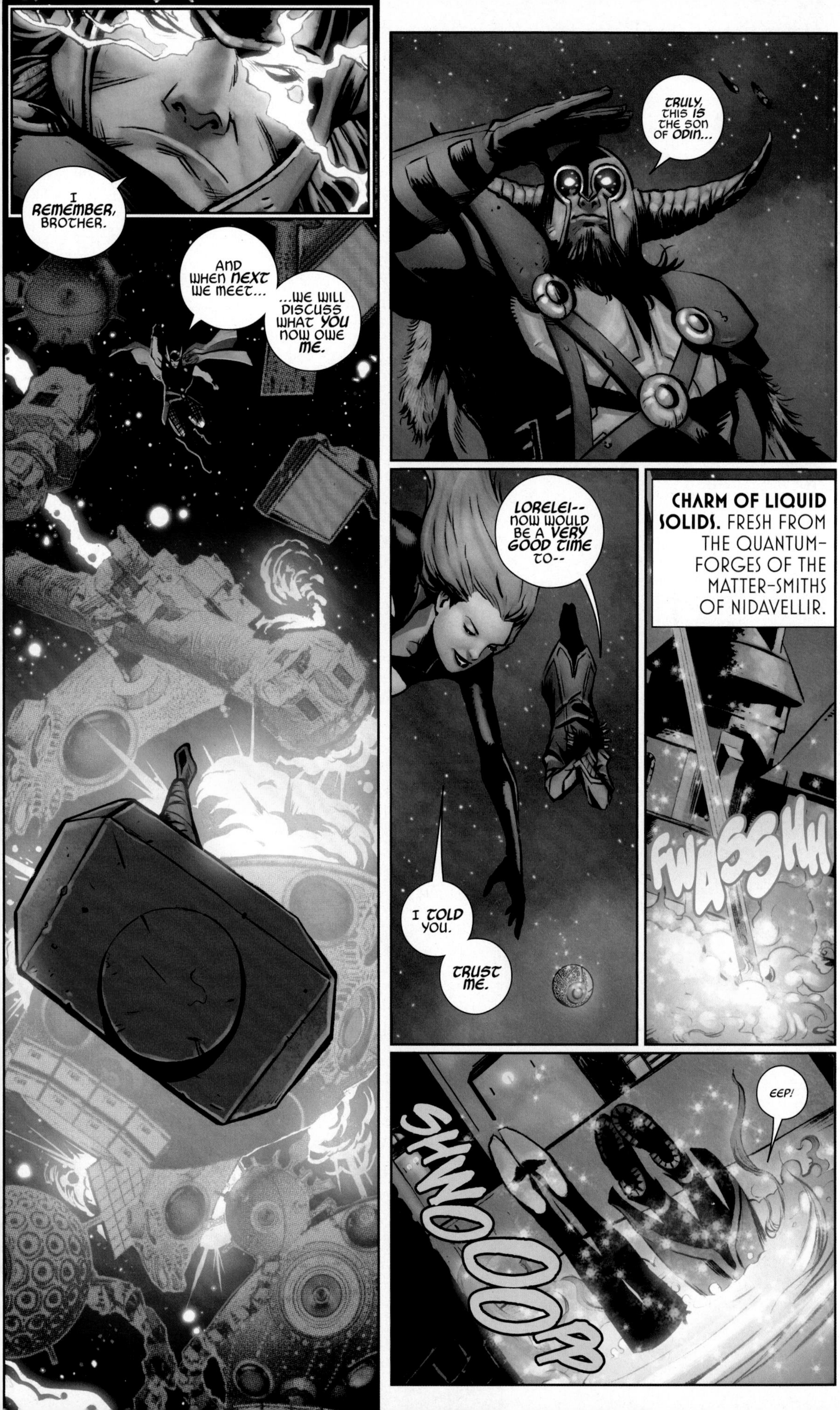
I REMEMBER, BROTHER.
AND WHEN NEXT WE MEET...
...WE WILL DISCUSS WHAT YOU NOW OWE ME.
TRULY, THIS IS THE SON OF ODIN...
LORELEI-- NOW WOULD BE A VERY GOOD TIME TO--
I TOLD YOU.
TRUST ME.
CHARM OF LIQUID SOLIDS. FRESH FROM THE QUANTUM-FORGES OF THE MATTER-SMITHS OF NIDAVELLIR.
FWASSHH
SHWOOOOP
EEP!

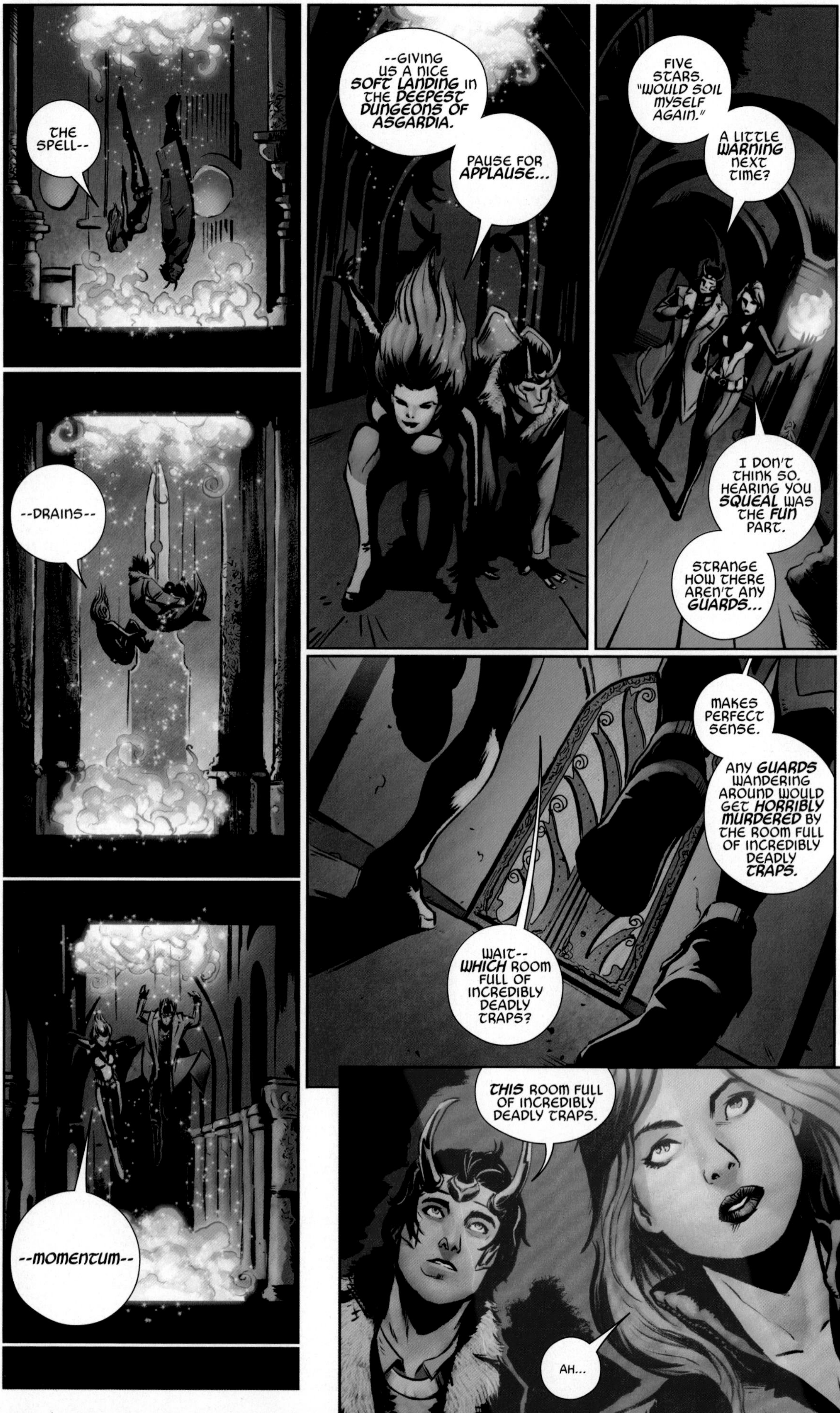
THE SPELL--
--DRAINS--
--MOMENTUM--
--GIVING US A NICE SOFT LANDING IN THE DEEPEST DUNGEONS OF ASGARDIA.
PAUSE FOR APPLAUSE...
FIVE STARS. "WOULD SOIL MYSELF AGAIN."
A LITTLE WARNING NEXT TIME?
I DON'T THINK SO. HEARING YOU SQUEAL WAS THE FUN PART.
STRANGE HOW THERE AREN'T ANY GUARDS...
MAKES PERFECT SENSE.
ANY GUARDS WANDERING AROUND WOULD GET HORRIBLY MURDERED BY THE ROOM FULL OF INCREDIBLY DEADLY TRAPS.
WAIT-- WHICH ROOM FULL OF INCREDIBLY DEADLY TRAPS?
THIS ROOM FULL OF INCREDIBLY DEADLY TRAPS.
AH...

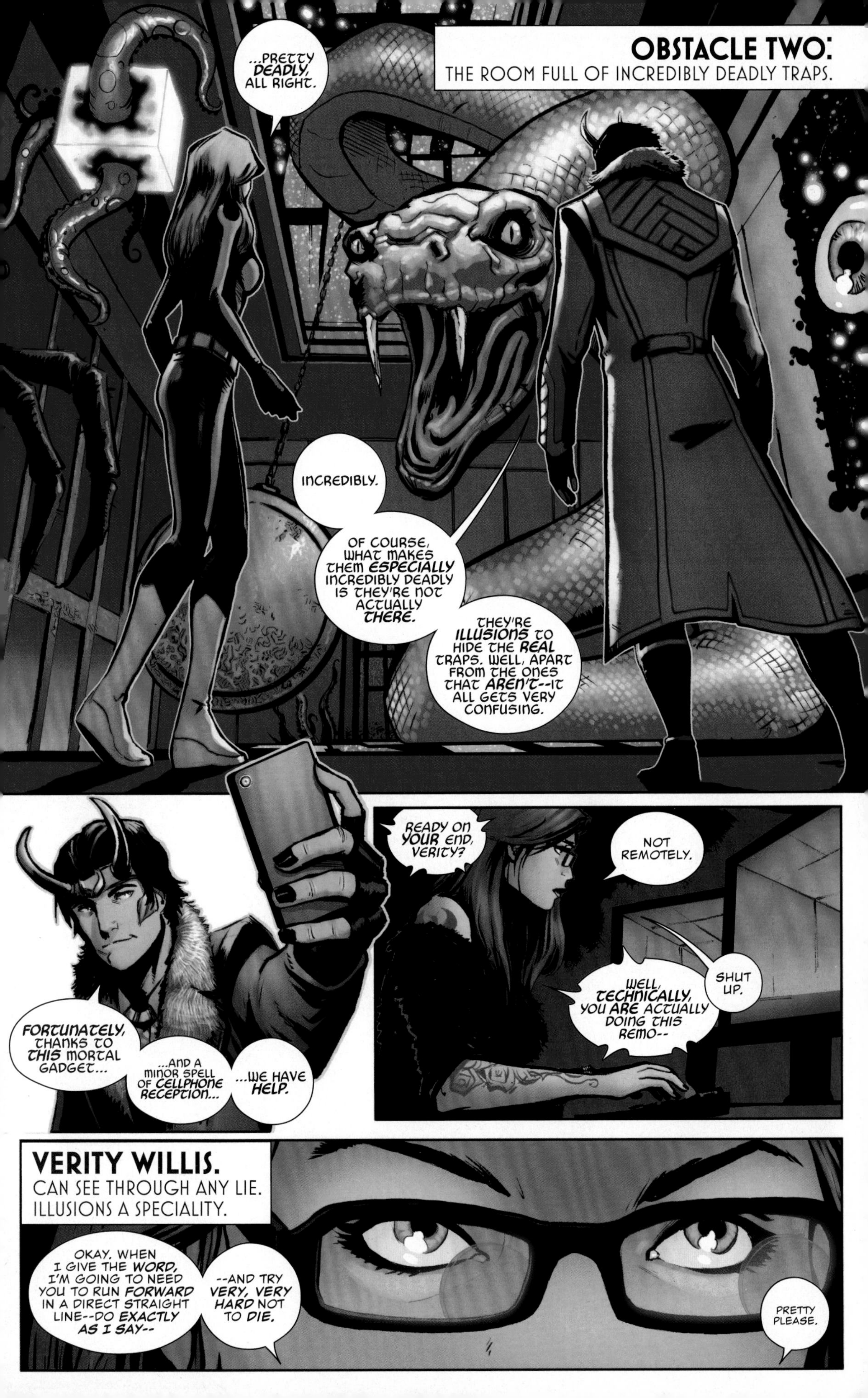

OBSTACLE TWO:
THE ROOM FULL OF INCREDIBLY DEADLY TRAPS.
...PRETTY DEADLY, ALL RIGHT.
INCREDIBLY.
OF COURSE, WHAT MAKES THEM ESPECIALLY INCREDIBLY DEADLY IS THEY'RE NOT ACTUALLY THERE.
THEY'RE ILLUSIONS TO HIDE THE REAL TRAPS. WELL, APART FROM THE ONES THAT AREN'T--IT ALL GETS VERY CONFUSING.
FORTUNATELY, THANKS TO THIS MORTAL GADGET...
...AND A MINOR SPELL OF CELLPHONE RECEPTION...
...WE HAVE HELP.
READY ON YOUR END, VERITY?
NOT REMOTELY.
WELL, TECHNICALLY, YOU ARE ACTUALLY DOING THIS REMO--
SHUT UP.
VERITY WILLIS.
CAN SEE THROUGH ANY LIE.
ILLUSIONS A SPECIALITY.
OKAY, WHEN I GIVE THE WORD, I'M GOING TO NEED YOU TO RUN FORWARD IN A DIRECT STRAIGHT LINE--DO EXACTLY AS I SAY--
--AND TRY VERY, VERY HARD NOT TO DIE.
PRETTY PLEASE.

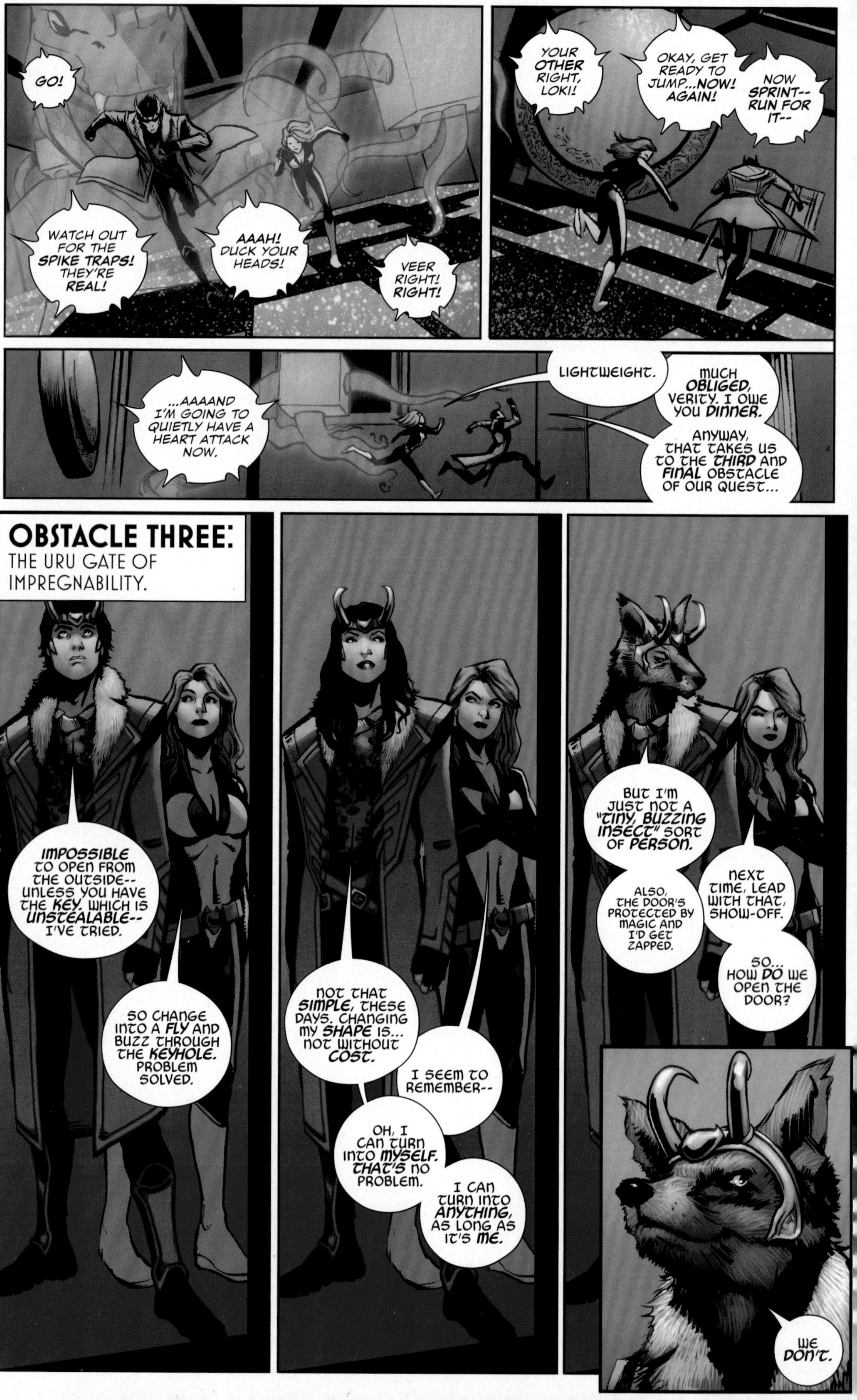
GO!
WATCH OUT FOR THE SPIKE TRAPS! THEY'RE REAL!
AAAH! DUCK YOUR HEADS!
VEER RIGHT! RIGHT!
YOUR OTHER RIGHT, LOKI!
OKAY, GET READY TO JUMP...NOW! AGAIN!
NOW SPRINT-- RUN FOR IT--
...AAAAND I'M GOING TO QUIETLY HAVE A HEART ATTACK NOW.
LIGHTWEIGHT.
MUCH OBLIGED, VERITY. I OWE YOU DINNER.
ANYWAY, THAT TAKES US TO THE THIRD AND FINAL OBSTACLE OF OUR QUEST...
OBSTACLE THREE: THE URU GATE OF IMPREGNABILITY.
IMPOSSIBLE TO OPEN FROM THE OUTSIDE-- UNLESS YOU HAVE THE KEY. WHICH IS UNSTEALABLE-- I'VE TRIED.
SO CHANGE INTO A FLY AND BUZZ THROUGH THE KEYHOLE. PROBLEM SOLVED.
NOT THAT SIMPLE, THESE DAYS. CHANGING MY SHAPE IS... NOT WITHOUT COST.
I SEEM TO REMEMBER--
OH, I CAN TURN INTO MYSELF. THAT'S NO PROBLEM.
I CAN TURN INTO ANYTHING, AS LONG AS IT'S ME.
BUT I'M JUST NOT A "TINY, BUZZING INSECT" SORT OF PERSON.
ALSO, THE DOOR'S PROTECTED BY MAGIC AND I'D GET ZAPPED.
NEXT TIME, LEAD WITH THAT, SHOW-OFF.
SO... HOW DO WE OPEN THE DOOR?
WE DON'T.

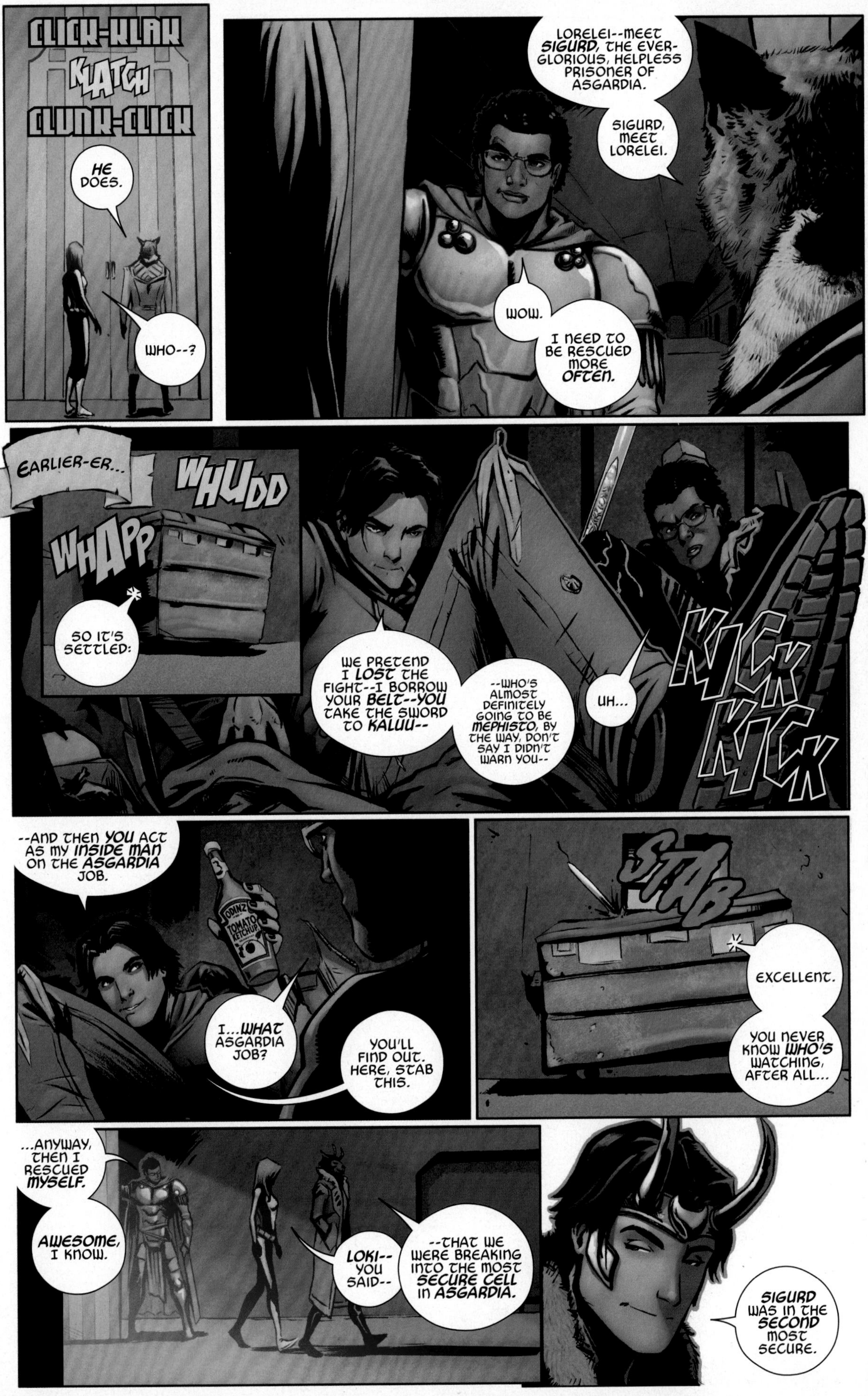
CLICK-KLAK
KLATCH
CLUNK-CLICK
HE DOES.
WHO--?
LORELEI--MEET SIGURD, THE EVER-GLORIOUS, HELPLESS PRISONER OF ASGARDIA.
SIGURD, MEET LORELEI.
WOW.
I NEED TO BE RESCUED MORE OFTEN.
EARLIER-ER...
WHUDD
WHAPP
SO IT'S SETTLED:
WE PRETEND I LOST THE FIGHT--I BORROW YOUR BELT--YOU TAKE THE SWORD TO KALUU--
--WHO'S ALMOST DEFINITELY GOING TO BE MEPHISTO, BY THE WAY, DON'T SAY I DIDN'T WARN YOU--
UH...
KICK KICK
--AND THEN YOU ACT AS MY INSIDE MAN ON THE ASGARDIA JOB.
ODINZ TOMATO KETCHUP
I...WHAT ASGARDIA JOB?
YOU'LL FIND OUT. HERE, STAB THIS.
STAB
EXCELLENT.
YOU NEVER KNOW WHO'S WATCHING, AFTER ALL...
...ANYWAY, THEN I RESCUED MYSELF.
AWESOME, I KNOW.
LOKI--YOU SAID--
--THAT WE WERE BREAKING INTO THE MOST SECURE CELL IN ASGARDIA.
SIGURD WAS IN THE SECOND MOST SECURE.

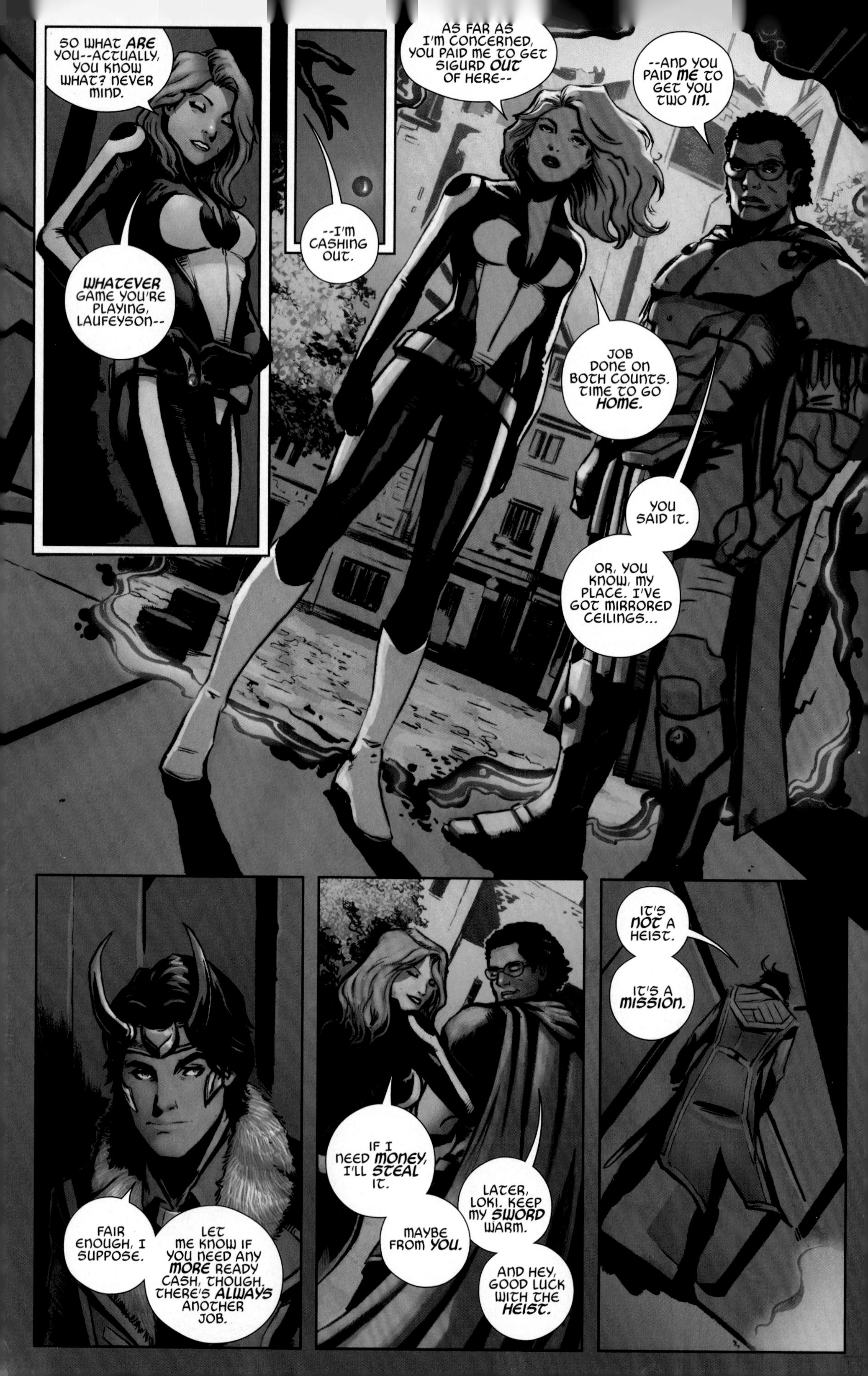
SO WHAT ARE YOU--ACTUALLY, YOU KNOW WHAT? NEVER MIND.
WHATEVER GAME YOU'RE PLAYING, LAUFEYSON--
--I'M CASHING OUT.
AS FAR AS I'M CONCERNED, YOU PAID ME TO GET SIGURD OUT OF HERE--
--AND YOU PAID ME TO GET YOU TWO IN.
JOB DONE ON BOTH COUNTS. TIME TO GO HOME.
YOU SAID IT.
OR, YOU KNOW, MY PLACE. I'VE GOT MIRRORED CEILINGS...
FAIR ENOUGH, I SUPPOSE.
LET ME KNOW IF YOU NEED ANY MORE READY CASH, THOUGH. THERE'S ALWAYS ANOTHER JOB.
IF I NEED MONEY, I'LL STEAL IT.
MAYBE FROM YOU.
LATER, LOKI. KEEP MY SWORD WARM.
AND HEY, GOOD LUCK WITH THE HEIST.
IT'S NOT A HEIST.
IT'S A MISSION.

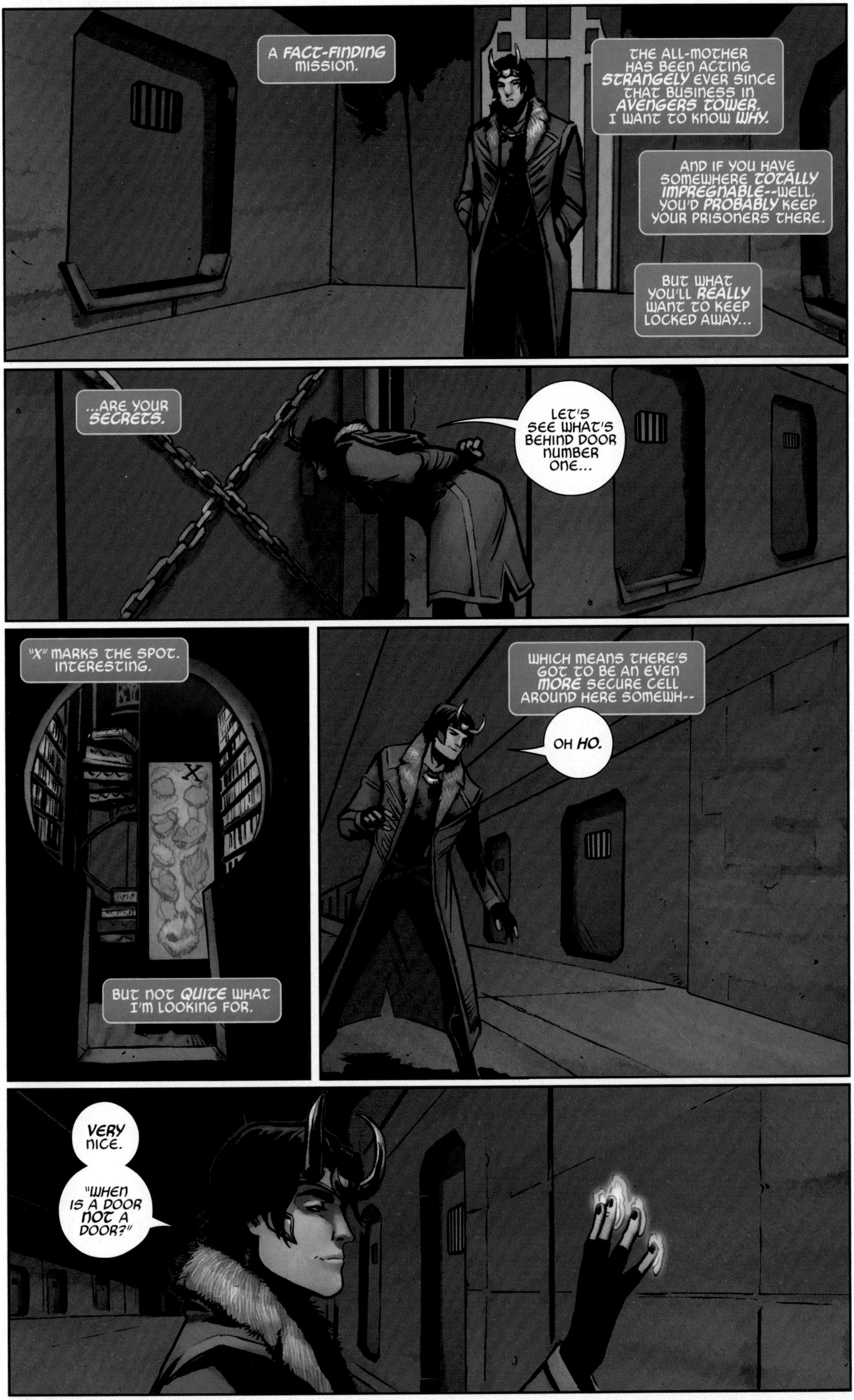
A FACT-FINDING MISSION.
THE ALL-MOTHER HAS BEEN ACTING STRANGELY EVER SINCE THAT BUSINESS IN AVENGERS TOWER. I WANT TO KNOW WHY.
AND IF YOU HAVE SOMEWHERE TOTALLY IMPREGNABLE--WELL, YOU'D PROBABLY KEEP YOUR PRISONERS THERE.
BUT WHAT YOU'LL REALLY WANT TO KEEP LOCKED AWAY...
...ARE YOUR SECRETS.
LET'S SEE WHAT'S BEHIND DOOR NUMBER ONE...
"X" MARKS THE SPOT. INTERESTING.
BUT NOT QUITE WHAT I'M LOOKING FOR.
WHICH MEANS THERE'S GOT TO BE AN EVEN MORE SECURE CELL AROUND HERE SOMEWH--
OH HO.
VERY NICE.
"WHEN IS A DOOR NOT A DOOR?"

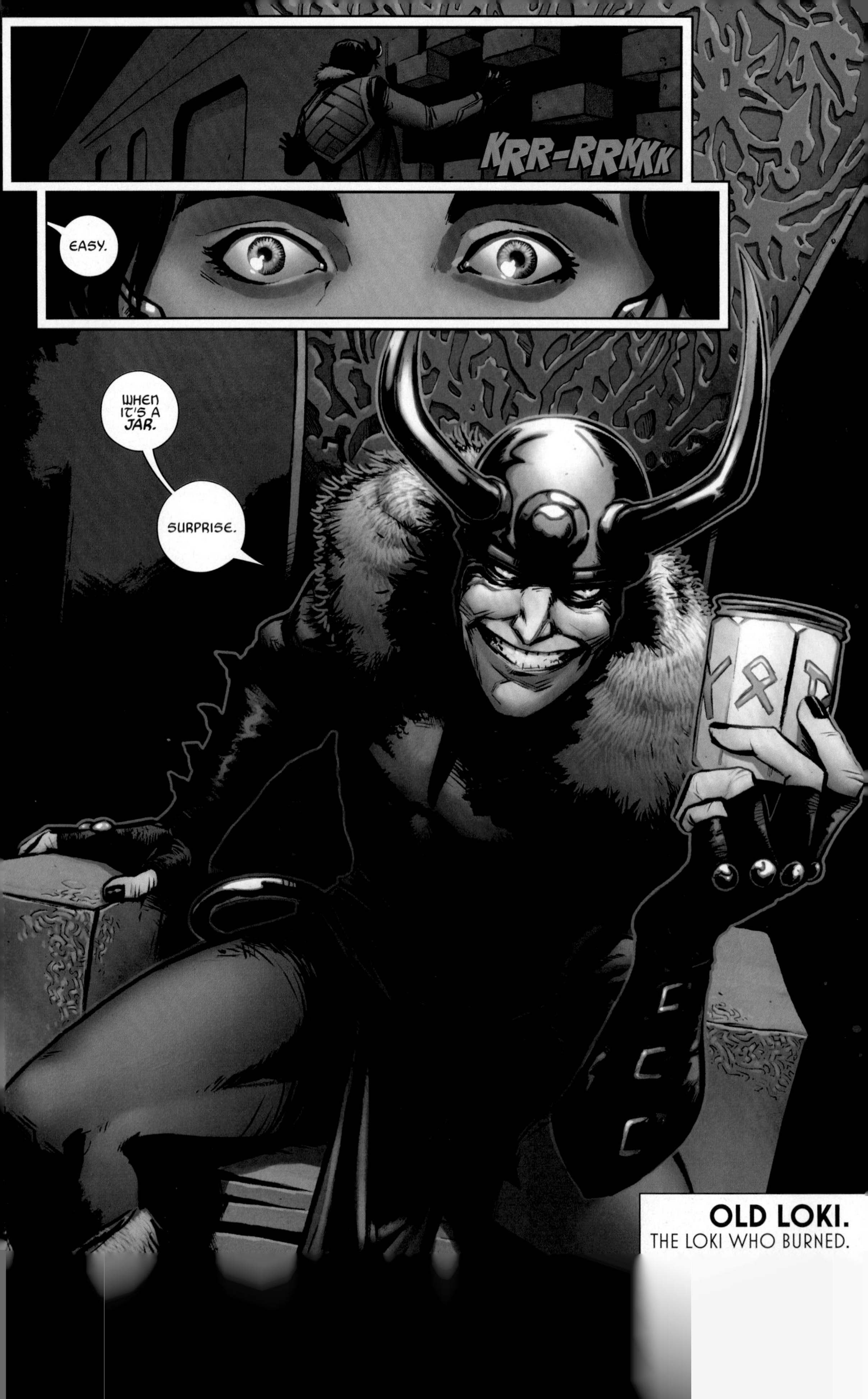
KRR-RRKKK
EASY.
WHEN IT'S A JAR.
SURPRISE.
OLD LOKI.
THE LOKI WHO BURNED.

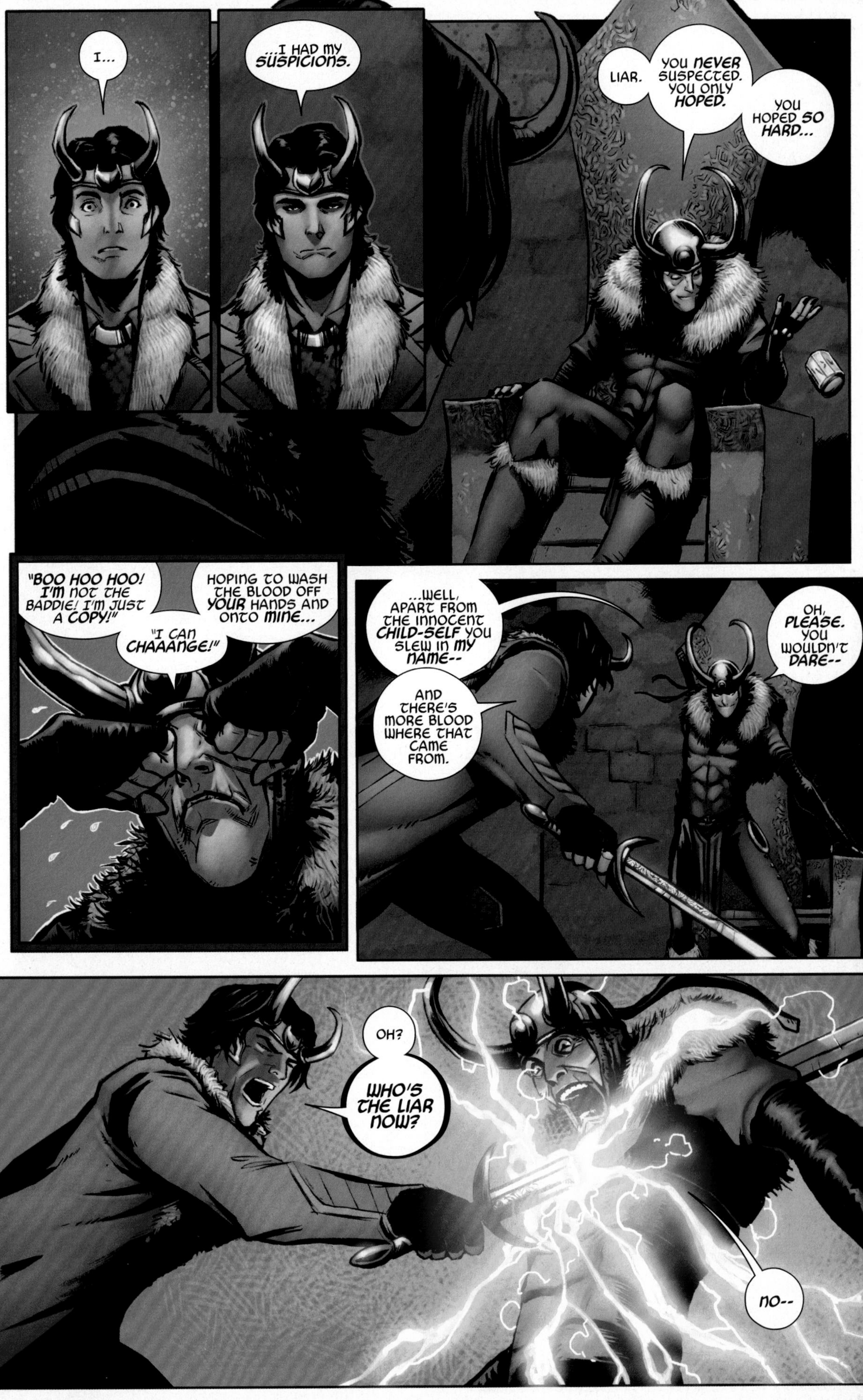
I...
...I HAD MY SUSPICIONS.
LIAR.
YOU NEVER SUSPECTED. YOU ONLY HOPED.
YOU HOPED SO HARD...
"BOO HOO HOO! I'M NOT THE BADDIE! I'M JUST A COPY!"
HOPING TO WASH THE BLOOD OFF YOUR HANDS AND ONTO MINE...
"I CAN CHAAANGE!"
...WELL, APART FROM THE INNOCENT CHILD-SELF YOU SLEW IN MY NAME--
AND THERE'S MORE BLOOD WHERE THAT CAME FROM.
OH, PLEASE. YOU WOULDN'T DARE--
OH?
WHO'S THE LIAR NOW?
NO--

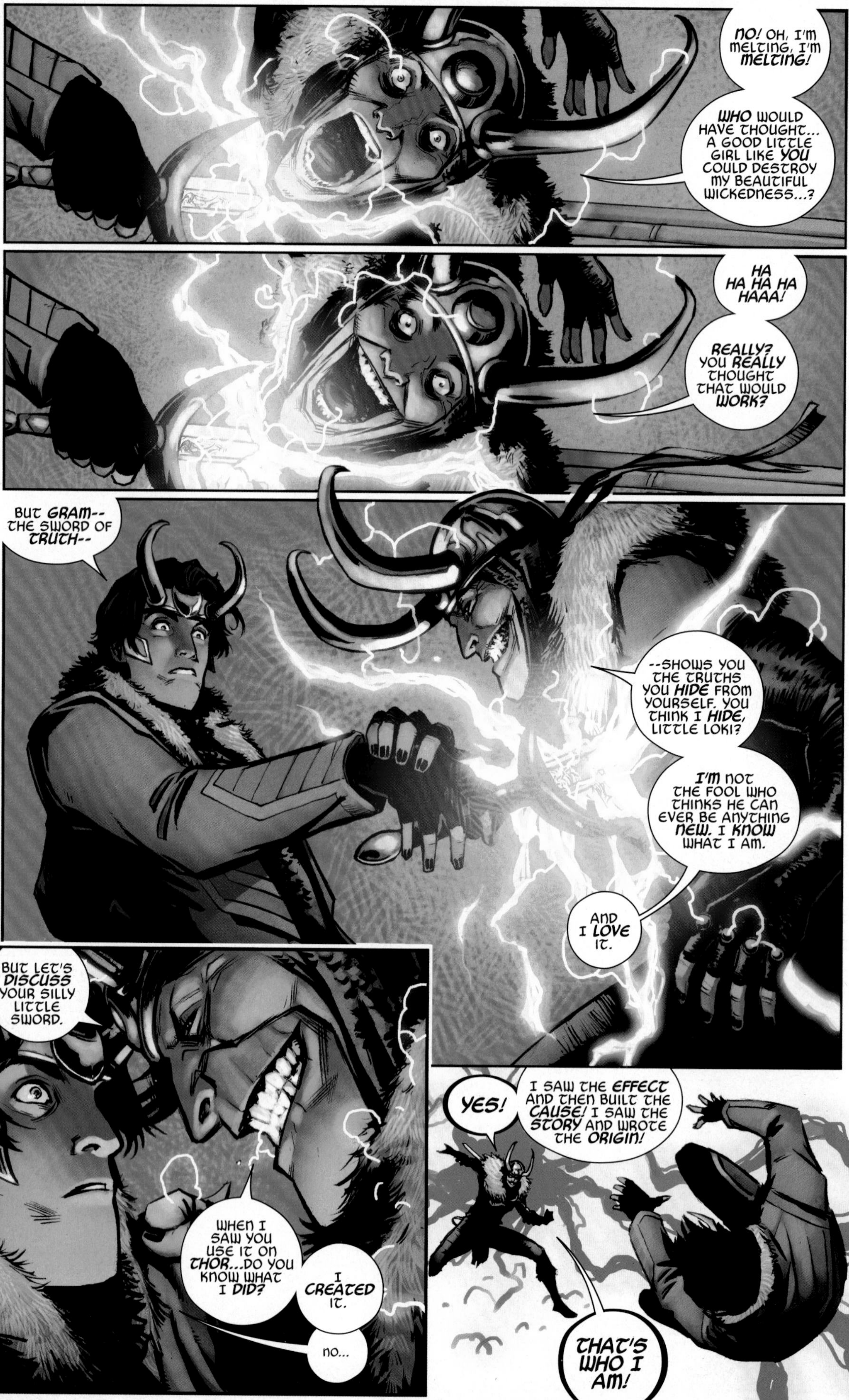
NO! OH, I'M MELTING, I'M MELTING!
WHO WOULD HAVE THOUGHT... A GOOD LITTLE GIRL LIKE YOU COULD DESTROY MY BEAUTIFUL WICKEDNESS...?
HA HA HA HA HAAA!
REALLY? YOU REALLY THOUGHT THAT WOULD WORK?
BUT GRAM-- THE SWORD OF TRUTH--
--SHOWS YOU THE TRUTHS YOU HIDE FROM YOURSELF. YOU THINK I HIDE, LITTLE LOKI?
I'M NOT THE FOOL WHO THINKS HE CAN EVER BE ANYTHING NEW. I KNOW WHAT I AM.
AND I LOVE IT.
BUT LET'S DISCUSS YOUR SILLY LITTLE SWORD.
WHEN I SAW YOU USE IT ON THOR...DO YOU KNOW WHAT I DID?
I CREATED IT.
no...
YES!
I SAW THE EFFECT AND THEN BUILT THE CAUSE! I SAW THE STORY AND WROTE THE ORIGIN!
THAT'S WHO I AM!

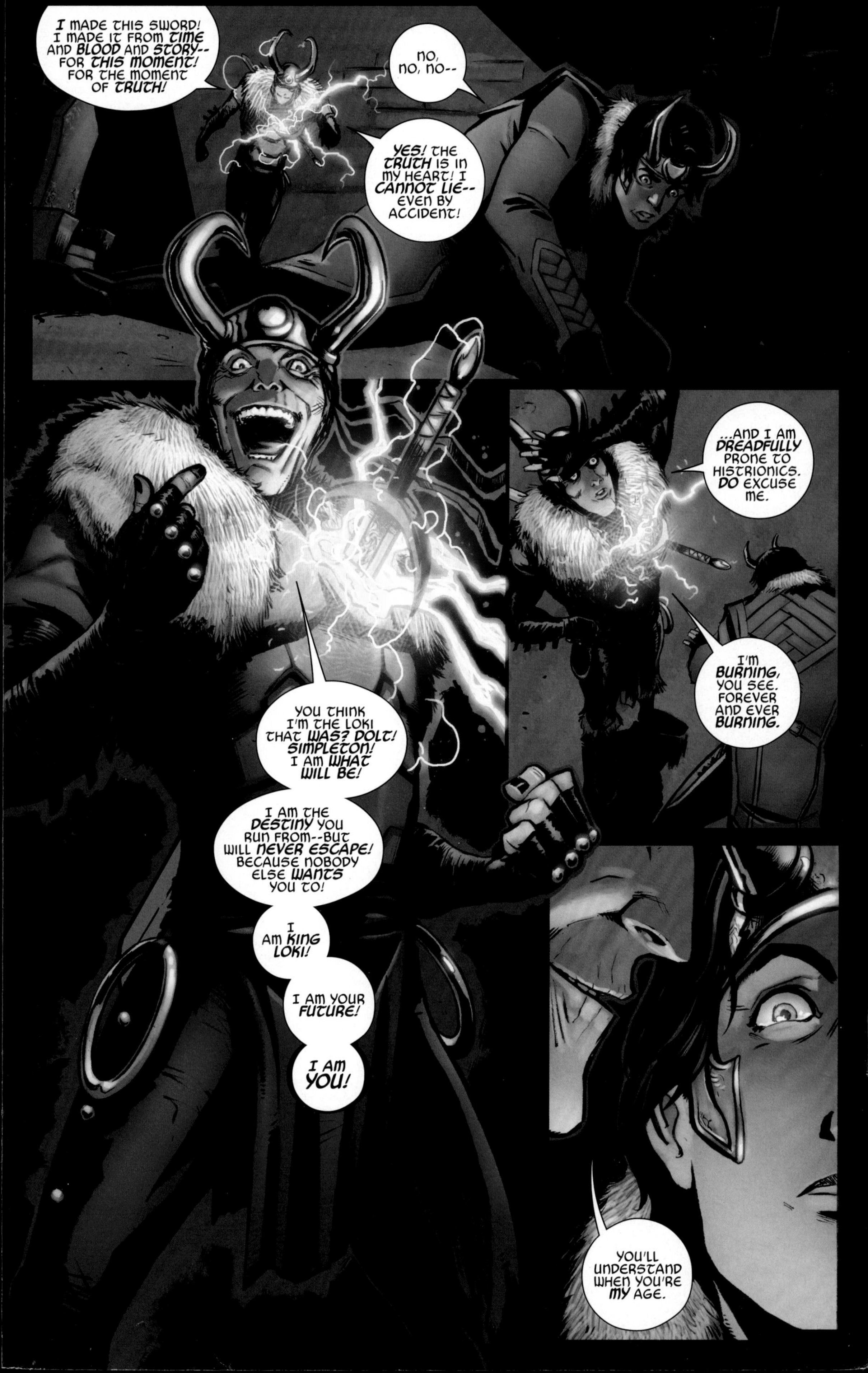
I MADE THIS SWORD! I MADE IT FROM TIME AND BLOOD AND STORY-- FOR THIS MOMENT! FOR THE MOMENT OF TRUTH!
no, no, no--
YES! THE TRUTH IS IN MY HEART! I CANNOT LIE-- EVEN BY ACCIDENT!
YOU THINK I'M THE LOKI THAT WAS? DOLT! SIMPLETON! I AM WHAT WILL BE!
I AM THE DESTINY YOU RUN FROM--BUT WILL NEVER ESCAPE! BECAUSE NOBODY ELSE WANTS YOU TO!
I AM KING LOKI!
I AM YOUR FUTURE!
I AM YOU!
...AND I AM DREADFULLY PRONE TO HISTRIONICS. DO EXCUSE ME.
I'M BURNING, YOU SEE. FOREVER AND EVER BURNING.
YOU'LL UNDERSTAND WHEN YOU'RE MY AGE.

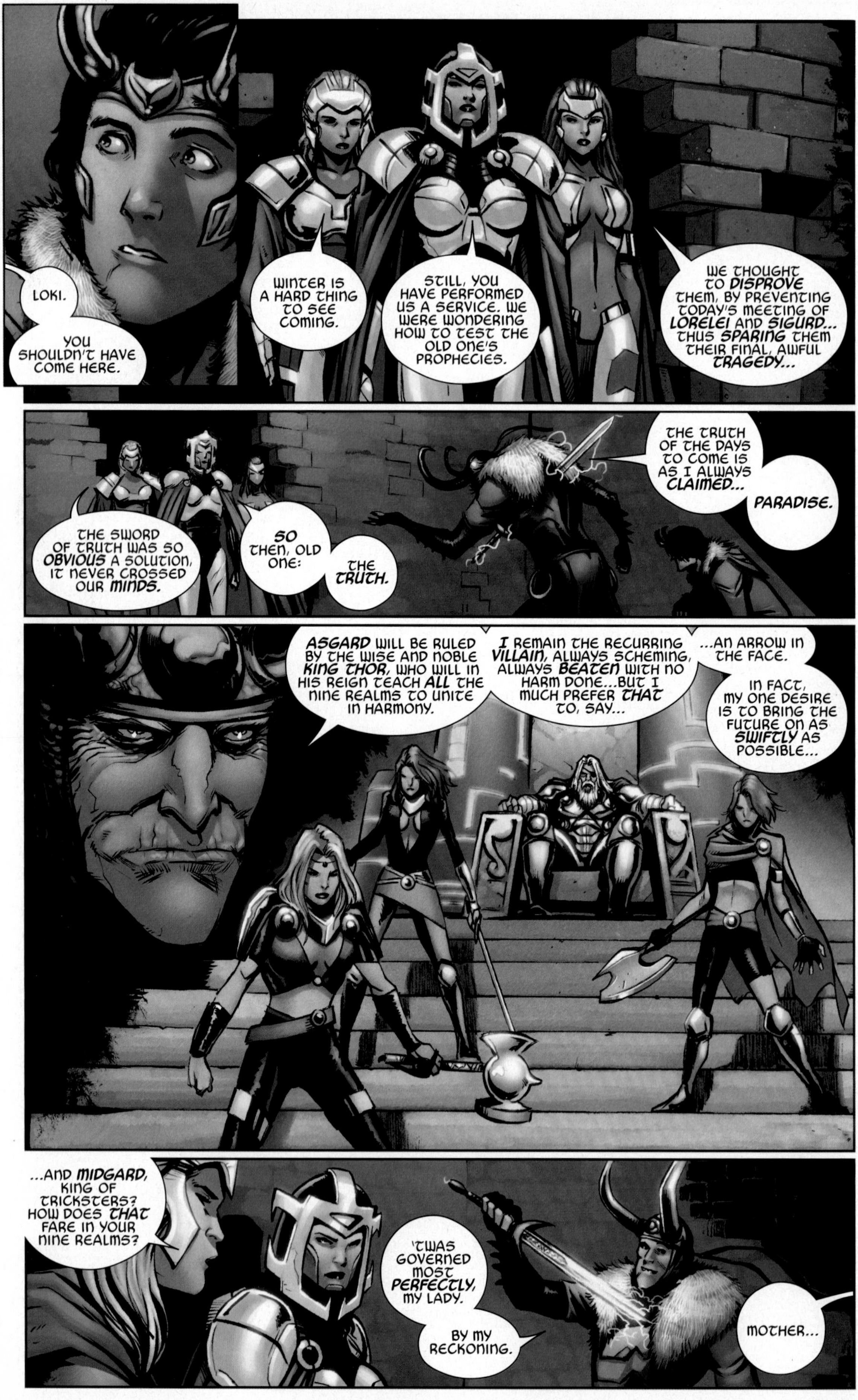
LOKI.
YOU SHOULDN'T HAVE COME HERE.
WINTER IS A HARD THING TO SEE COMING.
STILL, YOU HAVE PERFORMED US A SERVICE. WE WERE WONDERING HOW TO TEST THE OLD ONE'S PROPHECIES.
WE THOUGHT TO DISPROVE THEM, BY PREVENTING TODAY'S MEETING OF LORELEI AND SIGURD... THUS SPARING THEM THEIR FINAL, AWFUL TRAGEDY...
THE SWORD OF TRUTH WAS SO OBVIOUS A SOLUTION, IT NEVER CROSSED OUR MINDS.
SO THEN, OLD ONE:
THE TRUTH.
THE TRUTH OF THE DAYS TO COME IS AS I ALWAYS CLAIMED...
PARADISE.
ASGARD WILL BE RULED BY THE WISE AND NOBLE KING THOR, WHO WILL IN HIS REIGN TEACH ALL THE NINE REALMS TO UNITE IN HARMONY.
I REMAIN THE RECURRING VILLAIN, ALWAYS SCHEMING, ALWAYS BEATEN WITH NO HARM DONE...BUT I MUCH PREFER THAT TO, SAY...
...AN ARROW IN THE FACE.
IN FACT, MY ONE DESIRE IS TO BRING THE FUTURE ON AS SWIFTLY AS POSSIBLE...
...AND MIDGARD, KING OF TRICKSTERS? HOW DOES THAT FARE IN YOUR NINE REALMS?
'TWAS GOVERNED MOST PERFECTLY, MY LADY.
BY MY RECKONING.
MOTHER...

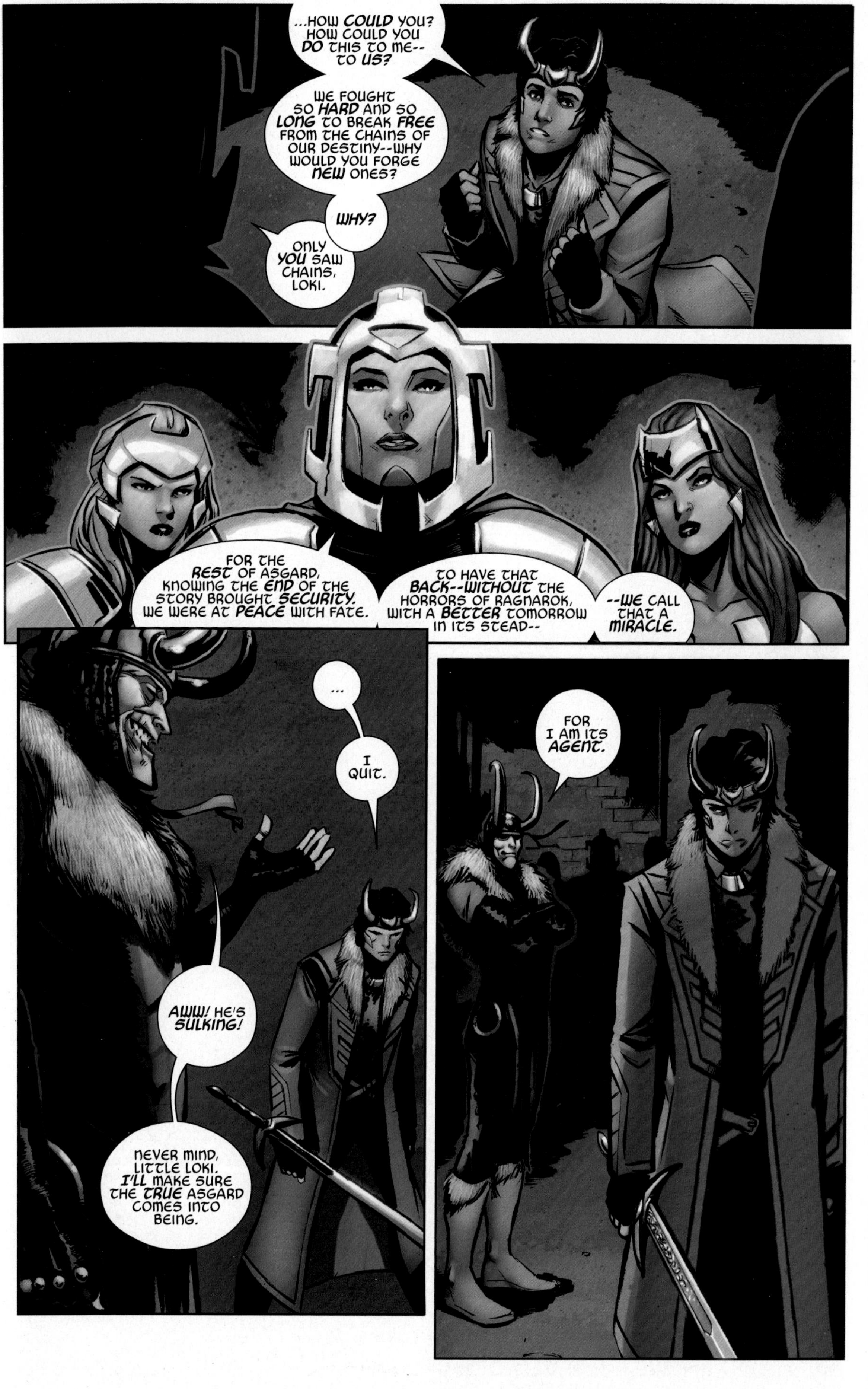
...HOW COULD YOU? HOW COULD YOU DO THIS TO ME--TO US?
WE FOUGHT SO HARD AND SO LONG TO BREAK FREE FROM THE CHAINS OF OUR DESTINY--WHY WOULD YOU FORGE NEW ONES?
WHY?
ONLY YOU SAW CHAINS, LOKI.
FOR THE REST OF ASGARD, KNOWING THE END OF THE STORY BROUGHT SECURITY. WE WERE AT PEACE WITH FATE.
TO HAVE THAT BACK--WITHOUT THE HORRORS OF RAGNAROK, WITH A BETTER TOMORROW IN ITS STEAD--
--WE CALL THAT A MIRACLE.
...
I QUIT.
AWW! HE'S SULKING!
NEVER MIND, LITTLE LOKI. I'LL MAKE SURE THE TRUE ASGARD COMES INTO BEING.
FOR I AM ITS AGENT.

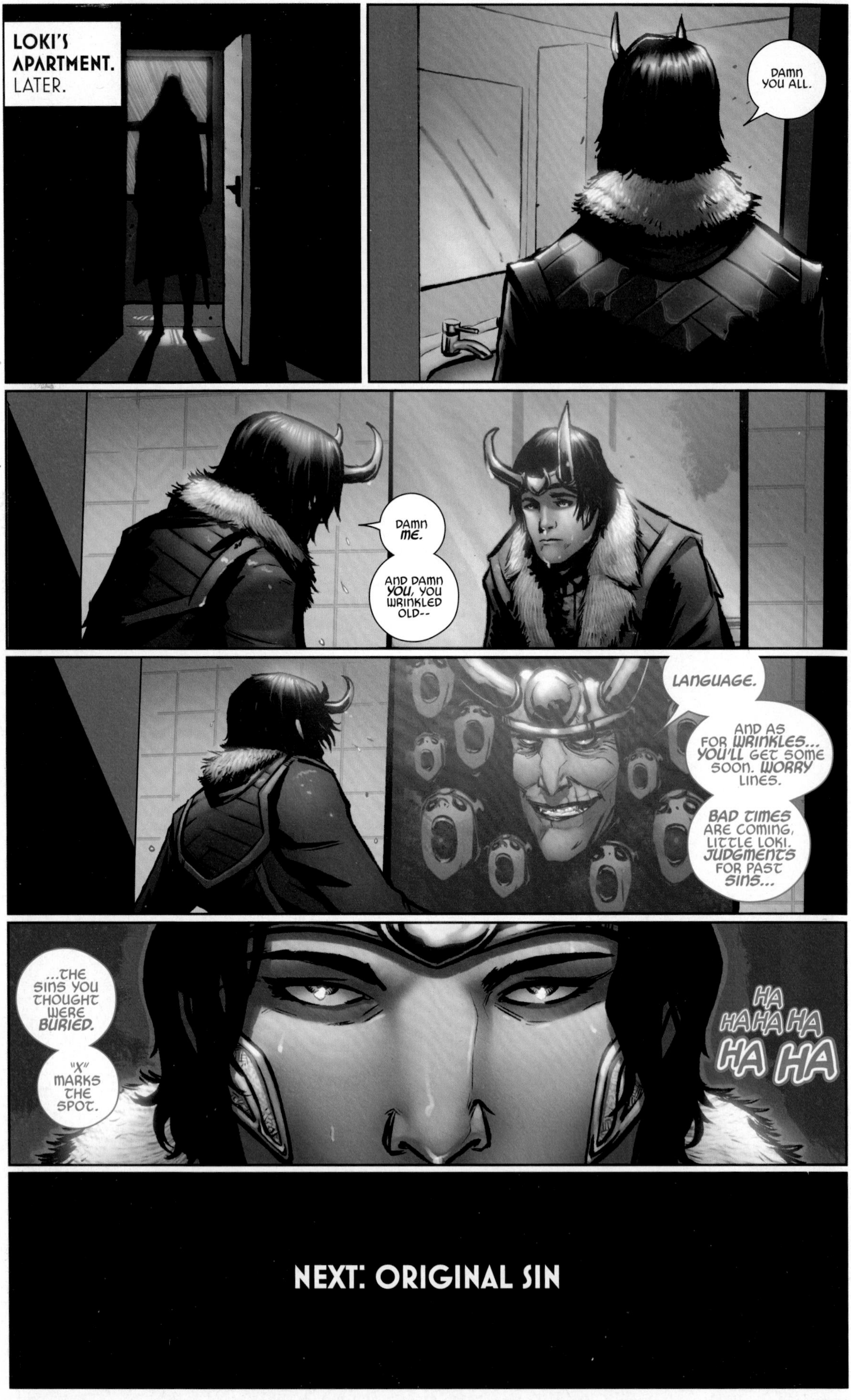
LOKI'S APARTMENT. LATER.
DAMN YOU ALL.
DAMN ME.
AND DAMN YOU, YOU WRINKLED OLD--
LANGUAGE.
AND AS FOR WRINKLES... YOU'LL GET SOME SOON. WORRY LINES.
BAD TIMES ARE COMING, LITTLE LOKI. JUDGMENTS FOR PAST SINS...
...THE SINS YOU THOUGHT WERE BURIED.
"X" MARKS THE SPOT.
HA HAHAHA HA HA
NEXT: ORIGINAL SIN